The Biblical Doctrine
of Infant Baptism

The Biblical Doctrine of Infant Baptism

Sacrament of the Covenant of Grace

Pierre-Charles Marcel

translated by Philip Edgcumbe Hughes

©

James Clarke & Co., Ltd
Cambridge

Published by
James Clarke Co., Ltd
P.O. Box 60
Cambridge
CB1 2NT
England

e-mail: **publishing@jamesclarke.co.uk**
website: **http://www.jamesclarke.co.uk**

ISBN 0 227 17028 8 hardback
ISBN 0 227 17027 X paperback

British Library Cataloguing in Publication Data:
A catalogue record is available from the British Library.

AUTHOR'S FOREWORD

IN preparing my study on Baptism for publication in *La Revue Réformée*, which some close friends and I had founded six months previously, my only thought was to make my modest contribution to the pastors and faithful people of the French Reformed Church in order to offer some enlightenment of mind on the question of the baptism of infants, which in France, as in almost every country, is much in prominence at the present time.

I am extremely honoured, and grateful to God, that this study should have been judged worthy to be translated and presented to English-speaking Christians who find themselves confronted with the same problems. I should like to state that I undertook the preparation of this study (a) in love for the marvellous grace which God has revealed and accorded to us in His Covenant in Jesus Christ, grace which I accept and which I confess ; (b) in respect for Holy Scripture taken in its entirety, and not merely in one of its parts ; (c) in love for my brethren in Christ, whose faith constantly needs to be strengthened so that it may achieve the end which God has assigned it ; (d) in humility before the mysteries of God, which we seek to apprehend by faith, without, however, ever arriving at a result that could be described as final : it was for this reason that the title of the French edition of my work was simply—*Baptism, Sacrament of the Covenant of Grace.*

My desire is that this study should be read and used in the same spirit as that in which I have wished to write it. I should be distressed were certain people to handle it without love as a weapon of battle for reducing the " adversary " to silence. " The wisdom that is from above is pure, peaceable, gentle, and easy to be intreated, full of mercy and good fruits " (James iii. 17).

I express my profound gratitude to the Rev. Philip E. Hughes, who has succeeded in translating me with a rare

5

distinction, and whose vivacity and fluency of style I admire as well as his fidelity. My sincere thanks go, finally, to the publisher of this work who has kindly honoured me with his confidence.

PIERRE CH. MARCEL.

October 30th, 1951.

TRANSLATOR'S FOREWORD

WHEN, soon after its original publication in French, I read M. Pierre Marcel's book on Baptism and found that it had been called into being by circumstances similar to those prevailing at the present time in England, and when, further, I found M. Marcel dealing with the pressing problems of baptism in the Church in a manner that was full, frank, *and scriptural*, I felt certain that it would be of real benefit to English-speaking Christians to be able to read this excellent study for themselves.   Accordingly, with the approval and encouragement of both author and publisher, I undertook the labour of preparing an English translation. In doing so I have endeavoured to provide an accurate reproduction of M. Marcel's thought and expression, but it is only right to point out that in its English garb the work does not correspond in every detail to the original publication : thus, with the willing consent of the author, I have incorporated into the main text most of his long footnotes relating to the modern theological discussion on the subject of baptism ; I have omitted a few sections which are significant in the main only to members of the French Reformed Church ; and in some instances I have supplemented quotations or references given by the inclusion of English sources and definitions. Where Scripture is cited, I have not infrequently given a rendering of the French in order to bring out the emphasis of the author's allusion.   I need only add that M. Marcel has seen and approved the translation as I have prepared it, and I am most grateful to him for his careful co-operation at every stage.

Readers will be interested to have a little information about the author of this work. M. Pierre Marcel is a Pastor of the French Reformed Church, Editor-in-Chief of *La Revue Réformée*, and Vice-President of the Calvinist Society of France.   In addition, he lectures regularly in the Free Faculty of Theology in the University of Paris, and his pen is remarkably active and effective in the production of literature which is of relevance to the theological situation of our own day. As a vigorous and intelligent champion of the Reformed Faith he is following with distinction in the steps of the late Dr. Auguste Lecerf, who was formerly Professor in the Free Faculty of Theology in the University of Paris.

In conclusion, my sincere thanks are due to Mr. W. Kelly, B.A., for his valuable help in the reading of the proofs, and to Mr. A. Douglas Millard for his readiness to commit himself to the publication of this translation even before it had been commenced.

PHILIP E. HUGHES.

CONTENTS

INTRODUCTION

Is the baptism of infants legitimate ? Is it founded on the
Bible ? Ought one to continue to baptize infants, and, if so,
which infants ? These are questions of doctrine and of
discipline which occupy the theological attention of the
Church today, and they confront us with a problem of the
utmost importance. F. Lovsky has depicted the scene of
the " antipedobaptist unrest since the Reformation," [1] and
Pastor Conord, Secretary General of the Reformed Church
of France, has given us a brief survey of the chronology of the
events of the last twenty years.[2] Those who oppose infant
baptism have published studies which have made and still
are making a considerable stir. In the presence of attitudes
which are becoming more and more decisive, and of " the
unrest which today manifests itself in some quarters
concerning the significance of baptism," [3] it was indispensable
that the problem should be studied by the Church herself.
In 1946, at the mandate of the National Synod of Lyons,
the National Council of the Reformed Church constituted
a *Commission on Baptism* charged with the study of the
questions involved.

A large number of believers are interesting themselves
in the question, quite independently of their Church leaders
and counsellors, and rightly so since the affairs of the Church
are their proper affairs. It is self-evident that a question of
this importance cannot be studied by believers as it were
with a blank mind, in view of the fact that each has been
placed before a Bible of a thousand pages. It is a fundamental principle of Reformed theology that the teachers of
the Church ought to think together with the people, and the
people together with the teachers. Who is it that under-

---

[1] *Notes d' Histoire pour contribuer à l'étude du problème baptismal :* Foi
et Vie, Jan. 1950, i.
[2] *Christianisme au xxe siècle,* Feb. 23, 1950, p. 69.
[3] Resolution xxviii of the National Synod of Lyons, 1946.

stands and preaches the Word, if not *the people* of God, whose different functions and specialized offices constitute none the less but one body ? The literature of those who oppose infant baptism has been enriched during these last ten years by important contributions which are easily accessible to all. One may suppose that their authors are satisfied with these works and that they consider that by them the people of the Church have been sufficiently informed of the motives of their convictions.

We declare with regret that the same is not the case with the advocates of infant baptism. " It seems clear that the vast majority of the members of our parishes are attached to the administration of baptism to newly born infants," affirms the Commission.[1] But this does not constitute a proof of the legitimacy of this baptism ! The fact is that the theologians who favour infant baptism have not placed at the disposal of the Church pamphlets or books which permit her to interpret this study seriously, with all the respect owed to the Word of God. The only exceptions are the remarkable *exegetical* work of Professor O. Cullmann[2] and the *dogmatic* response of the Synod of the Reformed Church of the Netherlands which resulted from the consultation with foreign Reformed Churches initiated by the National Synod of Lyons, 1946. These works examine effectively a collection of publications which are extremely brief or are devoted to only one aspect of the question, and of which none, to our knowledge, makes a true appeal to the Reformed position or to the arguments which have been and which remain proper to it. The Reformed Church of France cannot solve the question of baptism in isolation. Her theological reflection ought to be conducted in solidarity with her sister Churches and, together with them, in the fellowship of thought and of faith.

The present study is not addressed merely to theologians, but also to the people in the pews. We shall, therefore, avoid all superfluous theological erudition and also an unduly specialized vocabulary, in order to make it readily

[1] Conclusions of the Commission on Baptism, para. 3.
[2] Oscar Cullmann : *Baptism in the New Testament* (English translation by J. K. S. Reid). S.C.M. Press, 1950.

accessible to the greatest number. Where the sacraments are concerned it is the instruction given to the people which counts most of all. Apart from a certain apparent complexity which might confront those who are not accustomed to studying a theological subject under its principal aspects, we are convinced that every believer of the average spiritual level will be able to read this study and to understand its various parts. It is not beyond their ability. God does not reveal anything of essential importance in Scripture which is beyond the capacity of him to whom He has granted the gift of faith and who makes the effort necessary for obeying the commandment which he has been given, to love God " with all his mind."

DIFFICULTY AND COMPLEXITY OF THE SUBJECT

Certain doctrines are very clearly revealed to us in the Scriptures. No one, however, will disagree that Holy Scripture does not contain a *systematized* doctrine of the sacraments. It speaks, without doubt, of circumcision and the passover, of baptism and the Lord's supper, but in it we never find a general theory of the sacraments of the Old and New Testaments ; no *synthetic* conception of the different sacramental institutions is presented to us. The question of the sacraments is most frequently approached only in conjunction with some other subject which introduces it and which imposes on the author a certain orientation of thought (cf. Rom. vi ; 1 Cor. xii. 17-34). The majority of texts do not speak of *one* sacrament taken by itself, but only of one of its aspects. The texts of Scripture, brief, full of force and weight, are in general partial and only afford tests or definitions that are partial. It seems that in Scripture the sacrament matters more than the concept, or that the concept is expressed or ought to be sought elsewhere in the statement of another fundamental doctrine upon which the sacraments are founded. Without doubt, also, the Hebrew mentality moved with greater ease than our own amongst these questions. The absence of biblical texts, which embrace at a single glance and clearly explain to us the sense, the scope, and the methods of the sacraments, opens the way for a theological work which ought to be conducted in accordance with the methods proper to dogmatics and to the harmonious application of the principle of the *Soli Deo Gloria*.

This declaration ought, from the very beginning, to incite to modesty and humility those who have been called to treat of this question. It will be possible for certain differences to exist between those who agree in recognizing in Holy Scripture the inspired source and standard of all faith, and who confess that nothing must be added to it, nor anything removed from it. Such differences ought to be examined in love : here exclusivism, condemnation without appeal, sectarianism, are banned.[1] Some difficulties result from our sources of information, but others arise through our own fault, from our own nature, while others again are connected with the extreme complexity of the subject.

A priori considerations often play a large part in any development affecting the sacraments. They do not belong to the virgin spirits, the fresh hearts, who inquire into this problem, but to men who have a mentality which is largely indebted to *a priori* philosophical notions and who instinctively mark what they touch with the stamp of this mentality. It is because of *a priori* ideas, associated in the first place with human philosophies, that the same texts cited on one side and on the other are interpreted in a different sense and according to the viewpoint from which they are being considered. These *a priori* notions explain the differences of interpretation, the wilful rejection of one text, and even the " inadvertent oversight " of others, however essential they may be. The recent debate opened in the bosom of the Reformed Churches confirms once again this remark. These *a priori* considerations provide the explanation why, in the course of history, this debate is always resumed on the same terms, without any notable progress being recorded ; each one stands by the positions which, through their continuance, have become the *historic* positions. The problems remain enclosed within the same limits.

Much integrity and clarity of thought are required if the

---

[1] It is obvious that those who treat the Word of God as they please can in this matter, as in others, be led to conclusions which ought to be strongly denounced. This " modesty " of which we speak will not cause us to make light of fundamental biblical themes.

sacraments are to be treated objectively. It is a simple
question of scientific honesty to indicate one's philosophical
presuppositions, to avow them plainly, after having made a
critical examination of the "immediate" data of one's
method of working. When an *individualist* exegete has
explicitly avowed that he is individualist, he will have done
much to elucidate and simplify the debate. It will be easier
to make the distinction between that which comes from
man (the commentary on the texts) and that which can
truly be imputed to Scripture (the truly scriptural sense
to which it behoves us to strive to attain).

It is incontestable, and a point of capital importance,
that the question of the sacraments cannot, in theology,
be treated in isolation, as certain writers seem to wish.[1]
The task of exegetes is, indeed, to attempt to circumscribe
the problems and, in accordance with the plan of the
exegesis, to define in the best manner possible the sense
and the scope of such or such a sacrament. But the exegetes
themselves find it impossible to remain on the exact terrain
of the exegesis of texts. In studying the sacrament of
baptism, as *baptism* or as *sacrament*, they voluntarily commit
themselves to constructions which exceed to a considerable
extent the strict sense of the texts under consideration.
Discerning that the question of sacraments is a point of
convergence of numerous doctrines, they have recourse to
innumerable interconnected notions which it is important
to have disentangled from elsewhere, and to associations of
ideas—often quite legitimate—and they construct systems
of doctrine.

Whether they wish it or not, numerous exegetes transform
themselves into New Testament dogmaticians. To integrate,
without further reference, the fruit of their studies in a
dogmatic debate on baptism is to throw it into confusion.
Dogmatics cannot be either New or Old Testament dogmatics : it must be *biblical* dogmatics, that is to say, it must
take into account the whole of revelation. We are in agreement with O. Cullmann when he says that " all discussions
about Baptism should begin with this question, viz. with
the theological definition of the essence and meaning of

[1] Cf. F.-J. Leenhardt, *Le Baptême chrétien*, pp. 69-70.

Baptism "[1]; and again : " The question must be put from
another standpoint than that of evidence. The position is
that it can be decided only on the ground of New Testament
doctrine : Is infant Baptism compatible with the New
Testament conception of the essence and meaning of
Baptism ? "[2]

Karl Barth, in his pamphlet,[3] does not quote a single text
of the Old Testament, with the exception of Isaiah lv. 10 f.,
which, however, has reference to the efficacy of the Word of
God. This is undoubtedly a fact unique in a study of baptism,
producing a collection of serious consequences and an
impressive number of categorical judgments. On this
particular question, on the sacraments or every other
question which has anything to do with baptism, the Old
Testament counts for nothing, it does not even exist ! On
this question there is an absolute cleavage between the Old
and the New Testaments, nay, even a drastic opposition—
as witness Barth's judgment regarding circumcision and the
cancellation of the principle " from generation to generation "
in the covenant of grace : we shall return to this point. On
this question the Bible is cut into two. Karl Barth wishes
to base the study of baptism on the New Testament point
of view alone.[4] We might contest the *limited* choice of New
Testament texts which he makes and the perspective in
which he interprets them.[5] But we put the question : Is
such a method of " dogmatic reflection " valid ? Where does
it find its justification ? Is it there in *regular* dogmatics ?
Or perhaps, has not Barth, in contrast to his *regular* dogmatics, voluntarily given us in his pamphlet an example of
irregular dogmatics, in order to disturb the Church and
oblige her to rethink critically her dogmatics ?[6]

The dogmatician as well will seek to elaborate a general
conception of the sacraments to assist in the assembling

[1] *Op. cit.* (English translation by J. K. S. Reid), p. 24.

[2] *Ibid.*, p. 26.

[3] *The Teaching of the Church Regarding Baptism* (English translation by
Ernest A. Payne), p. 42 ; S.C.M. Press, 1948.

[4] Cf. *Op cit.*, pp. 43, 44.

[5] O. Cullmann considers that Karl Barth's interpretation " is not true
to the New Testament in its essential conclusions." *Op. cit.*, p. 27.

[6] The Conclusions of the French Commission on Baptism, II, Preamble,
also, in this point, reduce " Scripture " to the New Testament.

of the indications which he finds in Scripture. The work of the exegetes will occupy his attention. But, in taking notice of the meagre sources which are strictly sacramental that Scripture places at his disposal, the dogmatician will inquire whether it is not the case that Scripture is so discreet regarding sacraments taken in themselves for the reason that they have not in reality the importance which one has formerly wished to accord to them, or quite simply for the reason that they have reference to other ideas and to other spiritual realities expressly revealed, of which, under another form, they are only the secondary expression. We shall endeavour to show that such is in fact the case with sacraments : they have reference to preaching, to Jesus Christ, to the covenant of grace, regarding which we have abundant instruction.

The celebrated dogmatician H. Bavinck has well remarked[1] that the doctrine of the sacraments has always been the shibboleth, the touchstone, of every dogmatic system. It is there that the principles from which one sets off in the Church and theology, in questions of faith and of life, find their practical and concrete issue. The doctrines of the affinities of God and the world, of creation and regeneration, of Christ's divine and human natures, of the modes of action of the Holy Spirit, of sin and of grace, of spirit and of matter, are all more or less present and implicit in the doctrine of the sacraments. The diverse roads of theology converge, whether one wishes it or not, sooner or later, consciously or unconsciously, in the highway of the sacraments. It is necessary to take this into account.

It is an illusion to wish to treat of this or that sacrament *in abstracto* or taken by itself. Every divergence of view in the manner of conceiving the sacraments finds its origin in other doctrines envisaged in a different manner. Going to the root of the matter, when parties confront each other they have the impression that they do not understand each other, and that too in the interpretation of what at first sight are the most simple of texts, because, at root, they do not understand each other any more in connection with many other antecedent questions. Failing a return to the true

[1] *Gereformeerde Dogmatiek*, IV, p. 221.

B

sources, the sound of the discussion rises and quickly takes a most disagreeable turn : recent publications and articles afford proof of this.

A further requirement for an intelligible treatment of the sacraments is therefore the possession of a general view of theology, a perspective and panoramic view of the whole content of revelation, lacking which one will condemn oneself to the inability of ever dealing with more than a portion of the question and to a relapse into internal contradictions which cannot be resolved. On the one hand, whatever affirmation one makes respecting baptism must not come into conflict with the plainest themes of Scripture ; on the other hand, it is not only a duty, but a scientific necessity, to make common cause with those truths which are clearly revealed and which have such close connections with the sacraments. To take this into account will permit the resolution of questions which otherwise would remain dependent on man's subjective opinion. The dogmatics of baptism must be a " regular " dogmatics. Advocates or opponents of infant baptism have too frequently, for want of general perspectives, done disservice to the cause which they have claimed to defend. The idea which one can obtain of the palm of the hand depends also on the knowledge which one has of the wrist and the arm which bear it, and of the five fingers which it holds together and whose movements it co-ordinates. To speak of the palm by itself would be to speak very inadequately of it. A study of baptism which is too specialized will always be a bad study.

METHOD

It is beyond dispute that a great many theologians and Protestant pastors have maintained and practised, and do maintain and practise, the baptism of infants without preserving (for the reason that they have renounced or *forgotten* it—a fact more frequent than one might think) the theology which was and which remains at the foundation of the justification and of the possibility of the baptism of *certain* infants, namely, those of believers. That does not necessarily mean that they no longer had or have *any* reason for baptizing infants. Those who keep in close contact with

Holy Scripture taken in its totality often have powerful internal motives which are founded on the knowledge and the experience of the Word, but, failing a theological explanation, these motives take a subjective and sentimental turn which those who oppose infant baptism violently take to task—and justly so ! Many are those who feel and know that those who oppose infant baptism are wrong but find themselves unable to prove theologically why or how they are wrong.[1]

At this present moment the cause of pedobaptism is *theologically* lost, and its advocates, deprived of *theological* arguments, attempt to find a precarious refuge in facts and notions which cannot afford the least bit of genuine justification, such as the testimony of history, the tradition of the ancient Church or Reformed tradition, inscriptions, mosaics, sculptures, pieces of money, citations from the fathers, and so on—what have they not tried to seize upon !

O the inconsistency of Protestants who wish to found baptism upon tradition or upon " the authority " of the Reformers ![2] As though for us who are Reformed tradition could have any value *in itself* and did not need, when it exists, to be ceaselessly at each instant, *even today*, biblically justified and confronted with the Word of God as fundamental and formative ! The testimony of tradition can have some value for Reformed Christians, but *only after* the biblical foundations have been brought into prominence. In a question of this importance a tradition merely " ecclesiastical " or merely " Reformed " establishes and justifies *nothing*. " It would be a very poor and miserable refuge," says Calvin,[3] " if, in defending the baptism of little children, we were obliged to have recourse to the bare and simple authority of the Church ; but it will become plain that this is by no means the case."

[1] Assuming that it is possible to prove an article of faith. This proof can only be effective in the case where it is addressed to someone who is disposed in advance to believe the Word of God and, when it has been admitted, who finds in its proper truth his internal force of conviction. The application of such proof leads one right back to the question of the efficacy of the Word of God and of preaching.

[2] " Several amongst us invoke the authority of the Reformers " : Conclusions of the French Commission on Baptism, II, para. 1.

[3] *Instt.* IV. viii. 16.

Still less do we need to lean on the traditions of the second and third centuries, however firmly established they may be, for it could well be that *in that age* infants were baptized for motives other than those to which Reformed theologians can or ought to give pre-eminence, motives otherwise identical with those invoked at *the same moment* for *delaying* baptism until the adult stage or until the hour of death. On this point those who oppose infant baptism ought to revise their method. No more have they, if they are Protestants, any right to lean on tradition. And if their conception of baptism is not that which prevailed in the second and third centuries, the *historical* proofs which they claim to adduce concerning the baptism of adults and the theological reason for these adult baptisms such as were practised are not valid *for them*. From the theological point of view this method is doubly vicious.

Nor is it necessary for us to scrutinize feverishly the patristic texts in order there to seek and discover, or to insert, by means of complicated commentaries, traces of the baptism of infants ; and we ought not to venture on to this terrain because it is completely unnecessary for us to engage in such researches. It is for this reason that studies of a certain type, like that of Ph.-H. Menoud,[1] *when* they are understood as though the author had wished to establish and justify infant baptism historically, justly arouse opposition which is more lively and, in our opinion, in principle more pertinent.[2]

By all means let historical texts, inscriptions, mosaics, sculptures, coins, and whatever else you will, produce their testimony ! But if we are *Reformed*, that is to say, established on the Word of God, this testimony is in no way essential for us. It is even *forbidden* for us to make common cause with them *before* we have completed our task as men of the Bible and dogmaticians.

For certain advocates of infant baptism the sky has seemed

[1] *Le Baptême des enfants dans l'Eglise ancienne*, Verbum Caro, Feb. 1948, pp. 15-26.

[2] Cf. F. Lovsky, *Notes d'histoire pour contribuer à l'étude du problème baptismal*, Foi et Vie, March 1950, pp. 109-138. But historical conclusions are of no more service to those who contradict us for establishing their thesis theologically !

suddenly to have become clear ! The works of Professor
J. Jeremias confirm the baptism, from the commencement
of the Christian era, and for some exponents even earlier,
of proselytes coming over to Judaism and of their minor
children.[1] J. J. von Allmen considers that the importance
of this pamphlet is " decisive." [2] Certainly, the conclusions
of Jeremias are of the greatest interest and in certain respects
of capital importance. But let us beware lest we rejoice
unduly !—and this for three reasons. Firstly, as good
Reformed Christians it is impossible for us to found infant
baptism on extra-canonical texts, no matter how compelling
their authority may be. In the *Christian Reformed* Church
the baptism of infants must be established and justified
biblically. Secondly, the fact is that those who oppose infant
baptism are in no way disconcerted by the new facts which
have come to their knowledge. Some of them criticize the
date of the texts and move them on to the commencement
of the second century, which leads us back to the problem
of the utilization of tradition [3] ; others contest the sense,
the scope, and the validity of the texts, and, from the
methodological viewpoint, we affirm that they are right.[4]
Thirdly, it would, in fact, be catastrophic if theological and
dogmatic reflection were to be brought to an end because it is
considered that historical proof is sufficient. Rather the
contrary ! *Historical* proof should imperiously demand
theological and *dogmatic* justification and should compel
exegetes and dogmaticians to get to work.

These new facts will not change by a single jot the
arguments or the method of discussion of those who disagree
with us ; no more will they afford us a new weapon with

[1] Joachim Jeremias : *Hat die Urkirche die Kindertaufe geübt ?* 2nd edn.,
1949.
[2] J. J. von Allmen : *L'Eglise primitive et le baptême des enfants*, Verbum
Caro, No. 13, pp. 43-47.
[3] Cf. A. Benoît : *Le Problème du pédobaptisme*, Revue d'Histoire et de
Philosophie religieuses, 1948-1949, No. 2, p. 135.
[4] F.-J. Leenhardt, *Le Baptême des enfants et le Nouveau Testament*,
Foi et Vie, Jan. 1949, p. 90 : " I find no reason at all for thinking that that
which passed for Judaism, in so far as a rite of purification is concerned,
should have a value which is normative, or even only significant, in so far
as Christian baptism is concerned. Besides, there is not the least justification for deriving this connection from the realm of pure conjecture."

which to oppose them. Unless we are bemused by trouble-some illusions or false hopes, we ought from now on to be persuaded of this.

But if we delay to place the question of infant baptism in its true *biblical* and *theological* setting, our adversaries will attack us with perfect justification, as they have begun to do, by accusing us of being able to defend infant baptism only with *a bad conscience*[1] on grounds that we ourselves recognize as " far from certain," by " a method of argument which is as little worthy of faith as our exegetical founda-tions are unsatisfactory," and without which we could never pretend to be " certain of our case," etc. . . .

Let us admit that the vigour and the persistence of these attacks has succeeded in giving a " bad conscience " to certain pedobaptists who find themselves *temporarily* unable to justify their point of view theologically. So far from reproaching those who disagree with us because of this, we ought to thank them for it. To point out the weaknesses of his armour to one who is engaged in battle is always to render him a great service. It is as though one were crying to us : " It is high time for you to awake out of sleep ! " (Rom. xiii. 11). Let us hearken to this brotherly call ! Would, then, that the sleepers would rouse themselves, whatever has been the cause of their languor, and that they would devote time to the repairing of theology ! " If history proves that pedobaptism is not an invention of precatholicism," says J. J. von Allmen,[2] " but that it was admitted without discussion and without uneasiness by the canonical age, it follows that then they had a *doctrine* of baptism within the context of which pedobaptism was neither discordant nor ill-fitting, nor a facile and deplorable means of ensuring the recruitment of the Church, nor a distortion of the new covenant between God and His people."

In all good Christian conscience, in all good theological conscience (this conscience also has its value !), *we believe*

---

[1] This is the gravest accusation which could be formulated against Christian brothers, and it is necessary to pay heed to it ! It would be less humiliating if they treated us simply as imbeciles. Cf., for example, Karl Barth, *op. cit.*, p. 49 ; F.-J. Leenhardt, *op. cit.*, pp. 66, 67. We shall have occasion to return to these animadversions.

[2] *Op. cit.*, p. 47.

*that this doctrine existed and exists, that it is biblical, Christian,
and Reformed.* We shall endeavour to delineate it, for we
are not unmindful of sound doctrine, and to show to all who
are willing to study our arguments really seriously that we
do not belong to the class of people who find themselves
under the obligation of " snatching at rags of texts in order
to make weapons of them." [1]

The method of the present exposition is therefore dogmatic.
It leans upon the works of *Reformed* exegesis and effects a
synthesis in accordance with the standards which characterize
its discipline. That is to say, it is not bound either in order or in
methods to the critical exegesis. The last word of an exegetical
study on baptism, namely, that it is a *seal* of grace, can legitimately become one of the first words of a dogmatic study.[2]

We regard Holy Scripture as a whole. We study it in
accordance with the classical principle of the analogy of faith.
We believe that if the Word of God is self-consistent it will
show that the *Soli Deo Gloria* is also the spirit that inspires the
whole doctrine of the sacraments. From the philosophical
viewpoint we are neither individualists nor subjectivists,
and this for no *a priori* reason, but because we have not
succeeded in discovering in Scripture the least trace of the
modern individualist and subjectivist ideas. On the contrary,
Scripture *compels* us to be most attentive on the one hand
to the objectivity of the Word, of the promises and acts of
God, and on the other hand to the realities of spiritual
solidarity—realities which we experience *objectively*, realities
which proclaim the revealed intentions of God—which never
cease to throw into relief the unity of the family, of the nation
of Israel, of the Church visible or invisible, and of the
intimate communion which unites objectively those whom
God calls, and not only those whom He elects, to the body of
Christ. We shall adduce scriptural proofs of these facts.

But the pressure of philosophy and of individualistic
conceptions upon the mentality of the children of this age
is such that we are not, however, certain that we are free from
all individualism. Without doubt traces will still be found in

---

[1] This reproach has been actually formulated by F.-H. Leenhardt.
op. cit., p. 67.
[2] F. -J. Leenhardt : *Le baptême chrétien*, p. 65, last line.

the course of this exposition, one or other part of which could have been presented in a yet more biblical sense. We should be grateful if clear-sighted spirits would point them out to us. We have explained above the character of general simplicity which we desire to give to this exposition.

PLAN

What will be our plan of study ?

First.—We shall start off from the biblical affirmations of the New Testament relative to the sacraments, and we shall establish their relation to the Word.

Second.—We shall declare that the sacraments have reference to Jesus Christ Who is their central content.

Third.—Christ being the Executor, the Mediator, of the promise of redemption by His sacrifice, we shall turn to the reason for His coming, which is the covenant of grace, the actualization in history of God's eternal decree that He should be the Saviour of sinful man.

Fourth.—We shall declare that the covenant of grace is unique, as much within the Old Testament as within the New, and that the sacraments are all the sacraments of the covenant. Though starting from the New Testament, our study will have become biblical.

Fifth.—Having traversed (in accordance with a method of investigation which we believe to be rigorous, scientific, and conformed to a " normal " dogmatic exposition) the road : sacraments, Jesus Christ, the Promise, the covenant of grace, we shall return from this summit and, traversing the inverse route, we shall study the consequences of the covenant for those to whom it is in the first place addressed, then in the doctrine of the Church, then the sense, the scope, the practical application and the validity of the sacraments, in particular of baptism, and of the preaching of the promise and its efficacy.

Sixth.—We shall specify what is the doctrine of baptism as founded upon the covenant of grace, and we shall justify theologically the baptism of the infants of the covenant.

Seventh.—Finally, we shall reply to some objections.

FIRST PART

GENERAL STUDY OF
THE SACRAMENTS

I

THE MEANING OF THE TERM

THE ecclesiastical significance of the term "sacrament" has been very variable during the course of the Church's history and has been influenced by a diversity of circumstances.

Etymologically and in its proper sense this word has reference to something sacred or consecrated, and in consequence to that which possesses a significance which is sacred, secret, or related to a "mystery." It was used in this sense to designate religious rites and ceremonies. In its religious sense the word "sacrament" is allied to the Greek word *mysterion*, which signifies a secret, a mystery, into the knowledge of which a man has to be initiated. It is for this reason that in the Vulgate *sacramentum* is used to translate the word *mysterion*, in particular in Eph. i. 9, iii. 2 f., 9, 32 ; Col. i. 26 f. ; 1 Tim. iii. 16 ; Rev. i. 20, xvii. 7. In a wide sense, then, the word was used to designate any sign which possessed a hidden meaning. Religious rites and ceremonies, the sign of the cross, anointing with oil, preaching, confirmation, prayer, aid to the sick, the mystical or allegorical explanation of Scripture, etc., were equally called sacraments.[1] The meaning of the word was, up to the Middle Ages, so vague that Abelard counted but five sacraments, while Hugo of St. Victor enumerated thirty of them !

It is self-evident that the primary religious significance of the word is too comprehensive and its use too free for it to be

---

[1] " But it would take too long to discuss suitably the variety of signs which are called sacraments because they have to do with divine things."
—Augustine, Letter 138, Benedictine edit., Paris, 1836 ff., Vol. vii, p. 615. " Things are called sacraments, brethren, because in them one thing is seen and another is understood. What is seen has a corporeal appearance, but what is understood has a spiritual fruit."—Augustine, Sermon 252, *ibid.*, Vol. v., p. 1614. " Preaching, blessing and confirming, giving communion, visiting the sick, and praying, are sacraments of God."—Jerome, *Loc. Theol.*, XIX. i. 6, 9.

possible for theologians to employ it without risk of confusion. For this reason theologians early relinquished the field of etymology and philology and endeavoured to assign to the word definitions which were more or less exact according to the teaching of the New Testament on the subject. Two definitions in particular held the attention before the Reformation : that of Augustine—*accedit verbum ad elementum, et fit sacramentum,* " The Word is added to the element and it becomes a sacrament " [1] ; and that of Peter Lombard (*d.* 1164) given in his book of *Sentences* [2]—*sacramentum est sacrae rei signum,* " a sacrament is the sign of a sacred thing," which is specified in the formula which has become famous—*sacramentum est invisibilis gratiae visibilis forma,* " a sacrament is the visible form or expression of an invisible grace."

These definitions, however, have seemed and still seem too unprecise and vague to Reformed theologians. They are inadequate for expressing the meaning and the scope of the sacraments which are common to *all* believers, namely, baptism and the Lord's supper, nor are they adequate for defining the sacraments which were in common usage in the Old Testament. It was necessary to choose between two alternatives : either to change the word or to delimit the matter by giving the same word a more adequate meaning.

During and immediately after the period of the Reformation there were some who tried to exchange for the word that of *signs* or *seals* or *mysteries.* Today, again, there are some who would not hesitate to alter the term for another which would be really better. But the force of usage is such that it would be difficult to find a word which offers, without any other inconveniences, the same advantages as that which has been hallowed by custom. While they drew the attention of believers to the fact that the word *sacrament* was not employed in its original sense, Luther and Calvin considered, and together with them the Churches of the Reformation, that it is usage which ultimately determines the significance of a word much more than its etymology. Words are of little consequence, provided the thing itself is preserved.

---

[1] *Tract.* lxxx. 3 on John xv. 1-3.   [2] *Lib.* iv, dist. 1, B.

The only sure and satisfactory method of arriving at the
most precise idea possible of the meaning of the word is to
refer to the ceremonies which, by general consent, are
recognized as being sacraments, and, by analyzing them, to
define their essential and characteristic elements.[1]
There is unanimity in acknowledging that in the New
Testament economy baptism and the Lord's supper are
sacraments.[2] An exegetical study leads to the following
essential conclusions :

1. Baptism in its Christian form and the Lord's supper are
ceremonies instituted by Christ (cf. Mt. xxviii. 19 ; Mk. xvi.
16 ; Mt. xxvi. 26-29 ; Mk. xiv. 22-25 ; Lk. xxii. 14-20 ;
1 Cor. xi. 23-29).

2. Their usage is perpetual, that is to say, it ought to be
maintained until the return of Christ. Then they will be of
no further use because the promises, being fulfilled, will no
longer require to be preached, represented, or sealed (1 Cor.
xi. 26).

3. Both of them are *signs*. Baptism represents, figures, and
signifies purification ; the Lord's supper represents, figures,
and signifies spiritual nourishment. The sacraments are
extraordinary external signs which, commencing from
sensible things, according to a predertermined analogy, are
designed by God to display and explain to us, by making
them more clear, those benefits which are invisible and
eternal.

4. Sacraments are not only signs, but also *seals* which serve
to confirm and strengthen faith. It is the recognition of the
worth of this biblical affirmation which gives the Reformed
doctrine of the sacraments both its original character and,
at the same time, its grand precision.

[1] By this method we believe we shall avoid the reproach voiced by
Th. Preiss against the classical notion of a sacrament when he says
" that a general concept of a sacrament will always have a strong likelihood
of being any kind of article introduced from philosophy."—*Le Baptême
des enfants*, Verbum Caro, Aug. 1947, p. 114.
[2] Thus all other ceremonies of divine or human institution in which
these characteristics are not found will be excluded from the category of
sacraments.

Seals are distinct from signs in that they not only remind us of invisible things, but also authenticate these things to our religious consciousness by making them more certain and sure to us. During our daily practical life we constantly make use of seals, tokens for combating fraud, falsehood, and counterfeits. It is, in fact, necessary to distinguish the true from the false, what is authentic from what is not, the original from the counterfeit. A trade mark serves to authenticate and guarantee the source and quality of a product. Hall-marks declare the standard of alloy, the exact value, and the nationality of gold or silver articles. On weights and measures they testify to the accuracy of the inscription by reference to the scientifically determined original which they represent. Stamps, seals, and signatures guarantee the perfect authenticity of an important document —and so on. Scripture attests the usage of seals when there is concern to prove that something is really authentic and when it is of importance to guarantee it against all falsification.[1] Men, therefore, take great trouble to guarantee the authenticity of their actions, their thoughts, their products, and to preserve them to the greatest possible degree from all profanation.

It is a fact of capital importance that Scripture teaches us that God does the same thing with regard to His works, His Son, the Church, and those who are dear to Him ; He seals them with His seal in order to guarantee the authenticity, whether it be of persons or of things, and also with a view to their being preserved from all profanation.

The living God possesses His seal (Rev. vii. 2). He places a seal upon the Book of Judgment of such a kind that no one except the pure and spotless Lamb is able to open and read it (Rev. vi. 1, etc.). He seals the entrance of the abyss into which Satan is cast, so that he is no longer able to deceive the nations (Rev. xx. 3).

God does the same thing with people who are dear to Him.

---

[1] Scripture informs us that seals were placed on the letters of princes (1 Ki. xxi. 8 ; Neh. ix. 38 ; Esth. iii. 12) or of other persons (Jer. xxxii. 10), on laws which had been promulgated (Isa. viii. 16), or on important books (Dan. xii. 4 ; Rev. xxii. 10). In order to safeguard them from all interference the den of lions of Daniel (Dan. vi. 18) and Christ's tomb (Mt. xxvii. 66 ff.) were sealed.

By means of numerous signs He marks the Messiah with His seal so that no one may doubt that it is He who gives the food which endures unto everlasting life (Jn. vi. 27). He seals all believers with the Holy Spirit in order that as heirs they may be kept for the coming day of redemption (2 Cor. i. 22; Eph. i. 13; iv. 30). In blessing the work of the Apostle Paul, God gives him a seal which confirms his apostleship : " You are the seal of my apostleship in the Lord," says Paul to the Corinthians (1 Cor. ix. 2). God places His seal on the building of the Church for the purpose of assuring and guaranteeing that it is His personal property (2 Tim. ii. 19).

Holy Scripture teaches that in a similar manner the sacraments are seals. It was thus that Abraham received a seal in the sign of circumcision (Rom. iv. 11), that is to say, a confirmation, a ratification, a guarantee of the righteousness which he had obtained through faith. Eph. i. 13 and iv. 30, which in the opinion of the exegetes have reference to baptism, show that baptism is also described as a seal.[1]

Sacraments therefore are not only signs, *but also seals* which are affixed to the Word, in order that this Word may be apparent to us in all its veracity, in all its trustworthiness, and in all its certainty—apparent to *us* : for it goes without saying that, taken in itself, *the Word* of God, inasmuch as it is the Word *of God*, is sufficiently sure, true, and veracious for it not to require any confirmation. It is to our conscience, our heart, our spirit, that God confirms His Word by the *seal* which the sacrament impresses on it for authenticating it and preserving it from all doubt and profanation. The sacraments do not help God ; they help us.

Karl Barth[2] is in full agreement on this point. F.-J. Leenhardt is not. For the latter, the sacraments are not seals. This proceeds quite plainly from the fact that (a) if we have read him accurately, the word " seal " is used only once in the development of his thought,[3] and, as though by

---

[1] O. Cullmann, *op. cit.*, pp. 45 f., 57. It seems that it is impossible for F.-J. Leenhardt to deny this fact after having given his exposition of the relationship between baptism and the Holy Spirit, although he refuses here, as far as the terms are concerned, to see anything other than a play on words.

[2] *Op. cit.*, p. 29.   [3] *Op. cit.*, p. 65.

accident, in the last line of his exposition ; (*b*) this notion
is explicitly remote from the definition of a sacrament
adopted by Leenhardt [1]—" It is sufficient to say that the
sacrament is the visible sign of an invisible grace, as the
Reformed tradition repeatedly says " ;   (*c*) he directly
denies it : " No one will find the least demonstrative value
in the fact invoked by O. Cullmann that Paul calls circumcision a seal and that he employs the verb ' to seal ' in
alluding to baptism " (Rom. iv. 11 ; Eph. i. 13, iv. 30).
But the fact invoked by Cullmann has long since been
regarded and still is today regarded by the whole Reformed
school as classical. To our mind such an exegesis is perfectly
regular and is invested with an evident demonstrative value.
The Apostle's language is of sufficient precision for the same
root, employed in the form either of a verb or of a substantive,
to be able to have the same meaning in two distinct passages.
Leenhardt seems to us to be unwilling for his thought to be
confined within the limits of precise language. We must
confess that, in this matter, we have had some difficulty in
apprehending Leenhardt's thought exactly. For this we
may be partly to blame, but it should be stated that the task
is not made easier by the frequently unprecise vocabulary
of the author.

As for the definition of a sacrament adopted by Leenhardt
—" the visible sign of an invisible grace " [2]—we are obliged
to contest the assertion that it is the " traditional formula "
of the " Reformed tradition." [3]   Giving the words their
meaning, this is exactly Peter Lombard's definition of a
sacrament, and if it has found a place in Protestantism it is
not, however, in *Reformed* but in *modernist* tradition, whether
it be the modernism of the sixteenth century or that of
today. Leenhardt's definition is not that of any of our
confessions of faith, nor of any *Reformed* dogmatics or
exegesis. It is no use insisting on the importance of the
consequences which result from the laying down of such a
definition at the commencement of his treatise. The author
himself indicates its gravity : " The interpretation of all
the New Testament teaching on baptism is responsible for a
certain notion of a sacrament. Besides, and by way of

[1] *Op. cit.*, p. 64.   [2] *Ibid.*, pp. 11-14, 64, 65, 78.   [3] *Ibid.*, p. 65.

consequence, the ecclesiastical doctrine of baptism will similarly depend on the positions taken up from the beginning on this question." [1] That is obvious, and it provides the reason why we cannot agree with Leenhardt on several of his subsequent conclusions. Here the point of departure is *decisive*. Is the method in which the significance of a sacrament has been sought,[2] without any comparison with the sacraments, legitimate ? Leenhardt puts the question [3] : " What position conformable to the Reformed tradition itself could have been adopted apart from that which we, Karl Barth and I, have adopted ? " To this we can only reply : *the position of the Reformed tradition itself*, which you are trying to depict. Apart from this, we are far from concluding that, on this point, the positions of Leenhardt and Karl Barth are identical.

[1] *Op. cit.*, pp. 11 f.　　[2] *Ibid.*, pp. 11-14.　　[3] *Foi et Vie, op. cit.*, p. 78.

a

II

THE RELATION BETWEEN THE WORD AND THE SACRAMENTS

THE CONSTITUTIVE ELEMENTS OF THE SACRAMENTS

A. PRIORITY OF THE WORD

The question of the relation between the Word and the sacraments now demands consideration. By the Word, the Word *of God* preached in Scripture and today in the Church should be understood. Our concern, then, is with the *written* Word of God, read or heard and believed, and with the *preached* Word of God, heard and believed by the faithful; but *here* the emphasis is quite decidedly placed on the latter, for *here* it is necessary to lay hold of the relationship of the sacraments to the Word in their common ecclesiastical relevance today. And it is a very substantial relevance. To deal with this question will allow us at the same time to clear the ground for treating subsequently of the *efficacy* of the sacraments.

The Roman Church commences from the premiss that the sacraments contain all that is necessary for the salvation of sinners, and that they require no further explanation. If not in theory, at least in practice, it amounts to considering that the Word is superfluous as a means of grace. On the contrary, the Reformed Churches jealously place the emphasis on the supremacy of God's Word and regard it as absolutely essential, and as preceding the sacraments in order and in dignity. If this is correct, what need is there for sacraments to be added to the Word ?

The Reformed theologians [1] insist on the fact that God has created man in such way that he acquires knowledge

---

[1] With the exception of some Scottish theologians and the Dutch theologian Dr. Kuyper, who, with certain Lutherans, maintain that a specific grace, different from that which is conferred by the Word, is transmitted by the sacraments. The following may also be consulted : P.-Ch. Marcel, *A l'Ecole de Dieu* and *A l'Ecoute de Dieu*, the section devoted to the sacraments.

specially by mediation of the senses. The Word is adapted to the hearing ; the sacraments to sight and touch, etc. In bringing into play the activity of the other senses which have been given to us, in adding the sacraments to the Word, one can say that God comes to the aid of sinful man. He addresses Himself to his entire being. The truth reaching the ear through the Word is symbolically represented to the other senses through the sacraments.

Thus each sacrament offers *a visible external sign*, a material element which is palpable to the senses. The external matter of the sacrament does not consist solely in the elements employed, namely, water, bread and wine, but in all that accompanies them. Sprinkling or immersion in baptism, the blessing of the cup, the breaking of the bread, the distribution and reception of bread and wine in the Lord's supper, are not arbitrary or indifferent formalities : they are an integral part of the sacraments and they assist us to a better understanding of the promises and benefits of the covenant. The elements themselves of the sacraments constitute signs and seals of the invisible benefits of salvation. However, one must never lose sight of the fact that, if the Word can exist and be complete without the sacraments, the sacraments can never be complete without the Word. " A sacrament never exists unless the Word of God precedes it," says Calvin [1] ;   " the sacrament is added as an appendix intended to subscribe and confirm the Word and to make it all the more sure to us : for our Lord sees that it is an assistance to the ignorance of our sense and also to the sluggishness and infirmity of our flesh."

B. POINTS OF RESEMBLANCE BETWEEN THE WORD AND THE SACRAMENTS

Between the Word and the sacraments there exists a number of points of resemblance.

1. *Their Author is the same*

God constitutes them together as means of grace. Men, in fact, cannot create sacraments, nor anything which is related to the worship which they render to God. It behoves

[1] *Instt.* IV. xiv. 3.

them to receive and to guard that which has been ordained by God. It belongs only to God to seal His Word.[1]

2. *Word and sacraments have the same content*

Christ is the central content of the Word ; He is at the same time the central content of the sacraments.

(a) *Christ is the central content of the Word*

Reformed theologians insist most vigorously on the fact that the sacraments can confer no benefit which cannot be equally received from the Word of God, by *faith* alone. Holy Scripture, in fact, affirms that he who *believes* enters into possession of all the gifts of grace. " He who *believes* has eternal life " (Jn. iii. 36) ; he who believes " is justified by *faith* " (Rom. iii. 38); he is at peace with God (Rom. v. 1) ; he is sanctified (Jn. xv. 3), and purified (Acts xv. 9) ; he is even glorified (Rom. viii. 30).

He who *believes* is in communion with Christ (1 Jn. i. 3) ; it is by *faith* that Christ dwells in our hearts (Eph. iii. 17) ; he who *believes* partakes of the flesh and blood of Christ (Jn. vi. 47 ff.) ; he is in communion with the Father (1 Jn. i. 3) and with the Holy Spirit (Jn. vii. 39). The Spirit is communicated by the preaching of faith (Gal. iii. 2, 5), etc. All this is summed up in the general affirmation that he who believes becomes " a child of God " (Jn. i. 12).

Thus the Word contains *all* the promises of God and faith appropriates them *all*. The content of the Word is Christ, Christ whole and entire.[2]

(b) *Christ is the central content of the sacraments*

The signs and seals which, as we have said, constitute the primary element of the sacraments presuppose, in so far as they are *signs* and *seals*, something which is signified and sealed, an internal grace. This internal grace which is signified and sealed by the sacrament is the second constitutive element of a sacrament.

That each sacrament is a sign and seal of internal grace, freely offered and received by the believer, is something to which Scripture testifies in a number of important texts.

---

[1] 2nd Helv. Conf., xix. 3 ; Conf. of the Ref. Chh., para. 5, etc.
[2] Cf. *La source de la foi* in *A l'Ecole de Dieu*, pp. 131 ff. ; *A l'Ecoute de Dieu*, pp. 121 ff.

Sacraments are signs and seals *of the covenant of grace.* " This is the *sign* of the covenant which I make between you and Me. . . . I have set My bow in the clouds, and it shall become a *sign of covenant* between Me and the earth " (Gen. ix. 12 f.). " You shall circumcize your flesh, and it shall be *the sign of the covenant* between Me and you " (Gen. xvii. 11). The four texts relating to the institution of the Lord's supper speak of the " blood of the covenant."

The sacraments are signs and seals *of justification by faith.* " Then Abraham received the *sign* of circumcision, as a *seal* of the justification which he had obtained by faith " (Rom. iv. 11).

The sacraments are signs and seals *of the forgiveness of sins.* " John . . . was preaching the baptism of repentance for the remission of sins " (Mk. i. 4 ; Mt. iii. 11 *et al.*). " This is My blood of the new covenant, which is shed for many for the remission of sins " (Mt. xxvi. 28 *et al.*).

The sacraments are signs and seals *of faith and of conversion.* " He is a Jew who is one inwardly, and the true circumcision is that of the heart, performed by the Spirit " (Rom. ii. 29). " He that believes and is baptized shall be saved " (Mk. xvi. 16). They are signs and seals *of communion with Christ in His death and in His resurrection.* " All we who have been baptized into Jesus Christ were baptized into His death . . . in order that, as Christ was raised from the dead, . . . even so we also should live a new life " (Rom. vi. 3 f.). " All you who have been baptized into Christ have put on Christ " (Gal. iii. 27). " The cup of blessing which we bless, is it not the communion of the blood of Christ ? The bread which we break, is it not the communion of the body of Christ ? " (1 Cor. x. 16).

To sum up, the internal matter of a sacrament, the inward grace which is signified and sealed, is Jesus Christ and His spiritual riches—the covenant of grace, justification by faith, remission of sins, faith and conversion, communion with Christ, etc. It is Christ, whole and entire, in all His fulness and with all His riches, according to His divine nature and His human nature, with His person and His work, in His state of humiliation and in His glorification. Christ and Christ alone is the " heavenly thing " signified in the sacrament—Christ who, with all His benefits and blessings, is the Mediator of the covenant of grace, the Head

of the Church, the Yea and Amen of all God's promises,
the content of His Word and of His Testimony—Christ :
Wisdom, Justification, Sanctification, and Redemption of
believers, Prophet, Priest, and King, through whom alone
God conveys all His grace, who remains the same yesterday
and to-day and for ever. Jesus Christ, He who was, and who is,
and who is coming, is the truth of the sacraments without whom
they are nothing, just as He is also the truth of the Word.[1]

There is thus not a single benefit of grace which might be
missing from the Word and communicated in a special and
particular manner to believers through the sacraments.
There is no *special* baptismal grace, nor a *special* eucharistic
grace. The content of the Word and of the sacraments is
exactly the same. Word and sacraments contain, present,
and offer the same Mediator, Jesus Christ, the same covenant
of grace, the same benefits, the same communion with God,
the same redemption.

The sacraments are joined to the Word for the purpose
of signifying not simply a general truth, a general promise,
a general event of free grace, but a promise which has been
made *to me*, individually to myself and to each separate
believer, the truth that God has shown *me* grace in Jesus
Christ, the event of *my* adoption, of *my* election which I
ought to receive ; they serve to strengthen the faith of each
one of us in view of the realization of this promise, this
truth, this event, in each one of us. The sacraments visibly
represent and amplify the awareness which we have of the
spiritual blessings of the covenant of grace, of the cleansing
of our sins, of our participation in the life which is in
Christ.

As signs and as seals the sacraments are, in the same
manner as the preaching of the Word, *means of grace*, that
is to say, means whereby the internal grace operating through
the Holy Spirit in the heart is strengthened. " On the one
hand," says Professor Lecerf,[2] " there is the Word—a promise
of goodwill in Jesus Christ affirmed to all those who believe in
Him ; on the other hand, there are the sacraments—a divine
seal set upon this promise made to all who believe, and to them
alone, and offered to all the members of the covenant of

[1] Conf. of the Netherlands, para. 33.   [2] Bull. of the Calv. Soc., No. 44, p. 9.

grace in order to confirm this promise to them individually." [1]

3. *Connection between the material elements and the internal grace*

What has just been said leads us to the third point of resemblance between the Word and the sacraments and, at the same time, to the third characteristic of a sacrament. In calling the sacraments signs and seals Scripture indicates of itself that there exists a close and precise connection between the material elements and the internal grace which they signify, between the sign and the thing signified.[2] What is the nature of this connection ? The almost unanimous opinion of Reformed theologians is that this connection is in the first place *relative*, and then *moral and spiritual*.

(a) *The connection is relative*

It is similar to that which exists between Christ and the Word, between the benefits of the covenant of grace and the Word of God. We say that this connection is relative,[3] because if the words in the vocabulary of the language which

---

[1] One may remark that in what has been written above there is no question of justifying the existence of the sacraments by implying a dualism of nature and grace of Greek origin (cf. Th. Preiss : *Le Baptême des enfants et le Nouveau Testament*, Verbum Caro, Aug. 1947, pp. 114 f.). Is it really necessary to prove yet once again that the dualism of Calvin is not that of *nature* and grace, but of *sin* and grace, of *sinful flesh* and the spirit, and that this dualism is of biblical origin ? " It is not that the Word is of itself insufficiently certain or that, as far as itself is concerned, it could have any better confirmation—for the truth of God is ·by itself alone so sure and certain that it cannot have a better confirmation from any other quarter than from itself—but the purpose of a sacrament is to confirm us in the Word. For our faith is so slight and feeble that if it is not propped up on every side, and supported by every means, it is suddenly altogether shaken and upset and unsteady. And just as we are so ignorant, and so addicted and attached to earthly and carnal things, that we have no thought of, nor can we understand or conceive, anything which is spiritual ; so the merciful Lord accommodates Himself in this to the rudeness of our sense, so that He leads us to Himself even by means of earthly elements and causes us to contemplate in the flesh, as in a mirror, His spiritual Gifts " (Calvin, *Instt.* IV. xiv. 3). Further, it seems to us impossible to hunt out here all God's intentions and reasons. There are certainly motives connected with the existence of the sacraments which we are not capable of grasping at present and which will only be revealed to us hereafter. Let us confess that we make nothing more than an approach to the question, and let us humbly admit our incapacity for defining the mysteries of God in a perfectly adequate manner. We experience them more than we are able to speak of them.   [2] Westminster Conf., xxvii. 2.   [3] 2nd Helv. Conf., xix. 10.

we speak themselves indicate the relation which binds them to the things which they designate, then the water, the bread, and the wine in the sacraments are not *by nature* the signs and seals of Christ and His benefits. No one could see them there if God had not categorically declared it to be so, which is not to say that these signs have been chosen by God in an arbitrary manner. On the contrary ! As this is told us in the Word, we discover the closest harmony between the sign and the thing signified. Is it not the same God and the same Father who rules over the realm of nature as well as over that of grace ? Has He not created the visible world in such a manner that by it we can understand the invisible world ? For the believer, the world of nature is an image of the spiritual world : Christ constantly refers to this. A particular Word of God, however, was necessary in order that we might discern in the signs of baptism and of the Lord's supper an image of the spiritual blessings of redemption. And this necessity was, moreover, all the more imperative through the fact that the water, the bread, and the wine are not only the image of grace, but also the seals of it, and that, in the purpose of God, they serve to strengthen our faith. It is only when the relationship which we have just defined exists between the sign and the thing signified, and when the divine intention which established such a relationship is perceived, that there is, properly speaking, a *sacrament*. " That which beforehand was by no means a sacrament is made a sacrament by the Word of God." [1]

It is for this reason that, amongst Reformed Christians, the words of institution pronounced by the officiant possess no hidden, mysterious, or magical power ; they do not cause, nor are they intended to cause, the incorporation of the thing signified into the sign. Furthermore, these words of institution are a proclamation which introduces not the least change into the sign, but which, in a perfectly simple manner, distinguishes for the perception of the hearers and sets apart from their common use the elements employed, and confers upon them, then and there, a particular religious significance. Without the Word, and in separation from it, the bread and wine of the Lord's supper, and the water of

[1] 2nd Helv. Conf., **xix.** 8.

baptism, are nothing other than what they ordinarily are, namely, common daily amenities. As Augustine says : " Take away the Word, and the water is neither more nor less than water : the Word is added to the element, and there results the sacrament, as if itself also a kind of visible Word."[1]

Having pronounced the words of institution, the minister holds in his hands nothing more than a *sign*, and he distributes to the *believers* nothing more than a *sign*. But the promise is bound to the command, and where the sacrament is administered in accordance with this command and received with faith in virtue of this promise, there God Himself has undertaken to give, by His Holy Spirit, the invisible grace which is signified by it. It is God, and God alone, who remains the dispenser of grace. Therefore, at the time of the reception of the sacraments Christians do not depend upon the minister, but upon God alone ; they ought to give all their attention to Him and to His Word.[2]

(b) The connection is moral and spiritual

It is, however, no less objective and real.[3] Reformed theologians deny that the thing signified is *physically* or *locally* united to the sign ; but they affirm that, for him who believes, it is *spiritually* united to it. In the biblical economy grace can only be communicated in a spiritual manner, that is to say, by the Holy Spirit effecting faith. A physical communication of the grace of Christ and of His gifts is contradictory of the nature of the Christian religion, the nature of grace, the nature of regeneration (Jn. vi. 63). It is thus in a spiritual manner that Christ and His gifts are communicated by the Holy Spirit through the sacraments, just as also it is in a moral and spiritual manner that the

[1] Tract. lxxx on Jn. xv. 1-3.
[2] See the very interesting passage in the Second Helvetic Confession (xix. 8) : " When the Word of the Lord is added to them (i.e., the signs), with the invocation of His Name, then, by the renewing of their original institution and sanctification, these things are consecrated and declared to be sanctified by Christ. For the original institution and consecration of the sacraments performed by Jesus Christ always remain in force in the Church, in such a way that those who celebrate the sacraments just as the Lord instituted them possess still today this excellent original consecration in common with all. And this is the reason why in the celebration of the sacraments only the words of our Saviour Jesus Christ are recited."
[3] Cf. 2nd Helv. Conf., xix. 11.

same Christ and the same gifts are communicated by the Holy Spirit through the Word. This spirituality is so far from being contradictory of true reality that, on the contrary, it is from it that this reality receives all its meaning and by it that it is safeguarded. " Morality is not a synonym for laxity," says Lecerf, " and what is spiritual does not signify something imaginary. Nothing is more real than the Spirit of God; nothing is stronger than the truth, the fidelity of God."

In this respect, too, the sacraments are not different from the Word. Through the Word Christ is truly and really presented and offered to whoever believes. And He is just as really communicated to believers through the sacraments. The sacrament conveys the same Christ in His fulness as the Word, and in the same manner, that is to say, a spiritual manner, even though the means differ : the Word is audible, the sacraments are visible.[1]

(c) Both Word and sacraments must be received by faith

This is the third resemblance which unites sacraments and the Word : their respective contents are appropriated *by the believer* in the same manner—*by faith.* Faith is the sole way in which the sinner can become a participant of the grace which is offered both in the Word and in the sacraments. Word and sacraments are identical as regards the mode and the organ of perception and reception : *faith alone.* Even in the sacraments Christ is not received corporeally, but spiritually, by faith alone. The recipient of the sacraments receives them *as* he receives the Word. The Word is a gift of God, and so also are the sacraments. The attitude of the believer should, in the first place, be one of receptivity. " It follows," says Calvin,[2] " that in receiving the sacraments we do not deserve any commendation and even, because this action is passive as regards us, that it is not right to attribute anything at all to ourselves. I call the action passive because God does everything and we only receive."

This is an assertion of capital importance upon which the emphasis needs to be placed today, and to which we shall have

[1] For this reason the use of the inopportune expression " sacramental union " should be avoided.

[2] *Instt.* IV. xiv. 26 ; cf. Westminster Conf., xxvii. 2 ; 2nd Helv. Conf., xix. 10 ; etc.

occasion to return. It is summed up by the Confession of Faith
of the Reformed Churches of France (para. 37): " We believe
that equally in the Lord's supper and in baptism God really and
effectively gives us that which is figured by them. It is for this
reason that we associate with the signs the true possession and
enjoyment of that which is there presented to us."

The symbolical documents of the Reformation define the
sacraments in the following manner :

Confession of the Reformed Churches of France, para. 34 :

" We believe that the sacraments are added to the Word
for its more ample confirmation, so that they may be pledges
and seals to us of the grace of God and by this means aid and
support our faith because of our infirmity and immaturity ;
and that they are external signs through which God works by
virtue of His Spirit, in order that they should not be empty
signs to us ; yet we hold that all their substance and truth
is in Jesus Christ, and that if they are separated from Him
they remain nothing more than a shadow and a vapour."

Confession of the Netherlands, para. 33 :

" We believe that our good God, looking upon our immaturity and infirmity, has ordained sacraments for us, in order
that they might seal for us the promises and be pledges to us
of the good will and grace of God towards us, and also to
nourish and sustain our faith, for He has joined them to the
Word of the Gospel, so that all that He causes us to hear by
His Word, and which He performs internally in our hearts,
may be better represented to our external senses by ratifying
to us the redemption which He has communicated to us."

The Heidelberg Catechism, para. 66 :

" The sacraments are visible signs and seals instituted
by God to the end that, by their use, He may cause us to
understand better and seal to us the promise of the Gospel,
namely, that, because of the one sacrifice of Christ accomplished on the cross, He grants by His grace forgiveness
of sins and everlasting life—not only to all believers taken
together, but to each one separately."

Calvin's Catechism, para. 45 :

" A sacrament is an external testimony of the love of God who, by a visible sign, represents spiritual graces to us in order to seal the divine promises more firmly to our hearts, and to make us more certain of them."

The Catechism of the Church of England :

" A sacrament is an outward and visible sign of an inward and spiritual grace given unto us, ordained by Christ Himself as a means whereby we receive the same, and a pledge to assure us thereof."

The Westminster Shorter Catechism, Q. 92 :

" A sacrament is an holy ordinance instituted by Christ, wherein, by sensible signs, Christ, and the benefits of the new covenant, are represented, sealed, and applied to believers."

C. THE EFFICACY OF THE SACRAMENTS

It is now time for us to discuss the question of the efficacy of the sacraments. This new subject for consideration is bound to the preceding notion of the efficacy of the Word. Faithful to the principle of the *Soli Deo Gloria*, Reformed theology arranges its teaching on this question under three essential points :

　1. Like the Word, the sacraments are true means of grace.

　2. Like the Word, the source of the efficacy of the sacraments is due only to the grace of Christ and to the action of the Holy Spirit.

　3. Even as the Word is efficacious (in the positive sense of saving or redemptive efficacy) only for him who receives it with faith, similarly the sacraments, as far as they concern adults, are only efficacious as means of grace for those who receive them with faith.

Let us take these three points in turn.

1. *The sacraments are true means of grace*

That is to say, the sacraments are means instituted and utilized by Christ for making His people participants of the

benefits of redemption. Sacraments are not, as the Roman
Catholic Church teaches, the *exclusive* channels of grace,
but, like the Word, they are none the less channels. The
promise made to those who rightly receive the sacraments
is the same as that made to those who rightly receive the
Word : it is that, thanks to their means, they will be made
participants of the benefits of which the sacraments are the
divinely instituted signs and seals.

What is a means of grace ? In saying that the sacraments
are seals of grace, by grace we mean here the supernatural
and invincible action in the soul of the sinner by which God
leads him finally to glory by way of justifying faith. " It is
quite certain," says Calvin,[1] " that our Lord, equally in His
holy Word as in His sacraments, offers us all His mercy and
the grace of His good will ; but it is only apprehended by
those who receive the Word and sacraments with firm faith,
just as Christ, though offered and held forth for salvation
to all, is not, however, acknowledged and received by all.
Augustine, wishing to intimate this, has said that the
efficacy of the Word which is in the sacrament does not rest
in its being pronounced, but in its being believed and
received. It is for this reason that St. Paul, addressing
believers, expresses himself in such a way that he associates
communion with Jesus Christ with the sacraments, as
when he says : ' You all have been baptized and have put
on Christ ' (Gal. iii. 27) ; and again : ' We are one body
and one spirit, since we have been baptized into Christ '
(1 Cor. xii. 13). By God's good pleasure the sacraments
bring true testimony of communion with Jesus Christ,
and the Holy Spirit confirms the truth which they promise.
We conclude, therefore, that the sacraments are truly termed
testimonies of the grace of God, and, as seals of the favour
which He displays towards us, they signify it to us, confirming, nourishing, and increasing our faith by this means."

We see that Scripture makes not the least difference
between the sanctifying grace which is given in the sacrament and a sacramental grace which is distinct from it, for
the grace which is sealed in the sacrament is nothing more
nor less than that which is received from the Word by faith

[1] *Instt.*, IV. xiv. 7.

and which consists, in the first place, of justifying grace and, thereafter, of sanctifying grace.

2. *The source of the efficacy of the sacraments*

The efficacy of the sacraments is due only to the grace of Christ and to the action of His Spirit whom He sends. " The sacraments are visible signs and seals of the internal and invisible thing, by means of which God works in us by virtue of the Holy Spirit." [1]

Let us never forget that the Spirit is a personal agent who acts as and when He wills. God has promised that His Spirit will accompany His Word, and consequently God makes His Word an effective means of the sanctification of those who are His. The Word read or preached can only be effective if he to whom it is addressed believes that it comes from God, and then embraces it and applies it to himself. The faith which clings to the promises, the intelligence which lays hold of them, the trust which attaches itself to them—all this is performed by the Holy Spirit alone, all this is the work of grace.

Similarly, God has promised to make the sacraments— the visible Word, the Word in action—efficacious to the same end, by means of the activity of His Spirit, at the time of their distribution. The lordship of the Spirit is complete over the sacraments, as it is also over the Word when it is preached.

It is important to beware of certain errors, and this is why we also affirm *negatively* that the sacraments do not possess in themselves any *particular* power nor any *original* efficacy. The sacraments are not the efficient cause of the beneficent effects which they produce. Their efficiency, their efficacy, does not reside in the elements—in the water employed at baptism or in the bread and the wine of the Lord's Supper. No more is it in the sacramental action, nor in the distribution or the reception of the consecrated elements. Nor yet does the efficiency of the sacraments reside in the person through whom they are administered, nor does it proceed from the position or office of him who administers them. The minister does not by virtue of his position wield any supernatural power by which he renders the sacraments efficacious. No more does their efficiency

[1] Conf. of the Netherlands, para. 33.

depend on the character of the administrant before God, nor on his intention, that is to say, his resolve to render the sacrament efficacious. The man who administers the sacraments is not a performer of miracles. The Apostles and others were formerly granted a supernatural power of which they were bound to make use for the purpose of producing its legitimate effects ; but it is not the same with ministers of the Church in the administration of the sacraments.[1]

Calvin expresses himself admirably on this subject of the efficacy of the sacraments : " We recognize three graces of God," he says. " For, firstly, our Lord teaches and instructs us by His Word ; secondly, He confirms us by His sacraments ; and thirdly, He illumines our understanding by the light of His Holy Spirit and gives both Word and sacraments an entrance into our hearts, for otherwise they would only strike against our ears and appear before our eyes, but would by no means penetrate and move us inwardly. . . . The sacraments produce their effect only when the internal Master of souls adds to them His power by which alone hearts are pierced and affections touched so that an entrance into them is given to the sacraments. If He is missing, the sacraments can convey no more to our spirits than the light of the sun to blind eyes or a voice sounding on deaf ears. That is why I make the distinction between the Spirit and the sacraments whereby I recognize that the power resides in the Spirit, while nothing else is left to the sacraments except that they are instruments which the Lord uses towards us—instruments, moreover, which without the operation of the Spirit are useless and empty : nevertheless, they are full of efficacy when the Spirit is active within. . . . To the end that the Word may not fall in vain upon the ears, nor the sacraments be presented in vain to the eyes, the Spirit declares that it is God who there speaks to us and softens the hardness of our heart in order to prepare them for the obedience which is due to His Word. Then He transmits both His words and His sacraments to the ears of the spirit. There is thus no doubt that both the Word and the sacraments confirm our faith by presenting to our notice the good

[1] Cf. Westm. Conf., xxvii. 3 ; 2nd Helv. Conf., xix. 11 ; Art. XXVI of the Ch. of England.

will of our heavenly Father towards us ; and in this knowledge consists the assurance of our faith and reposes all its
force. The Spirit also confirms our faith in that He impresses
on our hearts this assurance in order to render it effective.
Meanwhile, the Father of lights has no difficulty in illuminat-
ing our souls by means of the sacraments, just as He is
able to illuminate our bodily eyes by the rays of the sun. . . .
In the water and by the blood we have the witness of our
cleansing and redemption ; and the Holy Spirit, who is the
principal witness, assures us certainly of this testimony,
causes us to believe, understand, and recognise it ; for
otherwise it is impossible for us to comprehend it.'' [1]

Here, then, is the reason why the Holy Spirit is as inti-
mately linked to the sacraments as He is to the Word.

3. *The condition of the efficacy of the sacraments*

The sacraments are not efficacious as means of grace—
that is to say, they are not signs and seals of the covenant of
grace—except, as far as adults are concerned, for those who
receive them with faith.

The sacraments can exercise a *natural* influence upon
others than believers in presenting the truth and in stirring
up feeling, but their saving or sanctifying influence is
experienced only by believers, for whom alone they become
means in God's hands whereby the invisible benefits of His
grace are signified and sealed (Mk. xvi. 16 ; Acts viii. 36-38 ;
ix. 11, 17 f. ; x. 34 ; Rom. iv. 11, and Acts ii. 38, xxii. 16 ;
Eph. v. 26).

In His Word and in His sacraments our heavenly Father
offers His mercy, His good will, and His grace to us all. But
this grace is only accepted by those who receive this Word
and these sacraments with an assured faith.   Experience
shows that today a very large number of men reject this
grace; and similarly in the days of His first coming Christ
was offered and presented by the Father to *all*, so that *all*
might be saved, but He was not recognized and received by
all.

How do the sacraments strengthen our faith ?—in the
same way as our eyes see when the light of the sun shines

[1] *Instt.* IV. xiv. 8, 9, 10, 22.

and our ears hear when a voice is uttered.[1] But to what
purpose does the light shine for us to see, if our eyes are
blind ? To what purpose is a voice uttered, if our ears are
deaf ? Now, our eyes and ears possess naturally the faculty
of seeing and hearing. But it is not so with our souls which,
if they are to hear plainly what the Word says and to see
clearly what the sacraments represent, must be given
spiritual sight and hearing. This particular grace is precisely
that which is given by the Holy Spirit ; and this is the reason
why, apart from the action of the Holy Spirit, the sacraments
—like the Word—have not the least efficacy.[2]

" All those who bring to the sacred table of Christ a pure
faith, as though a vessel, truly receive that to which the signs
there testify, namely, that the body and blood of Jesus
Christ serve as food and drink for the soul no less than do
bread and wine for the body. Thus we hold that the water,
though a frail element, does not fail to testify to us truly
of the internal washing of our soul by the blood of Jesus
Christ, and that the bread and the wine which are given to us
in the Lord's Supper truly provide us with spiritual nourishment, inasmuch as they show, as it were visibly, that the
flesh of Christ is our food and His blood our drink." [3]

A sacrament received without faith confers nothing more
than the Word heard without faith : neither the one nor
the other is of value except by virtue of the promise which
they contain, and both the hearer of the Word and the
recipient of the sacraments receive nothing other than that
which they accept by faith. The assurance of salvation
depends on participating in the sacraments—as though
justification were thereby communicated to us—no more than

[1] We should point out that we are not describing a psychological process.
No one can " grasp " or " comprehend " the *how* of God's action in man's
heart. We are describing the *experience* of him who, in faith, complies with
the decrees of God. God commands : He knows why. The believer obeys ;
by experience and in faith he verifies the dependability of the decree which
he has received and of the promises which have been made to him. The
believer can neither explain nor justify this experience ; nor, indeed, ought
he to. He can only refer to the Holy Spirit, who is the sovereign Author
of this experience and to whom belongs its proper explanation.
[2] Nowhere does Scripture make the slightest allusion to an " indelible "
character which is imprinted by a sacrament.
[3] Conf. of the Ref. Churches, paras. 37, 38 ; cf. 2nd Helv. Conf., xix. 10.

it does upon the hearing of the Word, *but it depends upon it no less.* In the one case as in the other, the justification of redemption is found neither in the Word taken by itself, nor in the sacraments taken by themselves : it is found only in Jesus Christ, who communicates it to us at the same time by the preaching of the Gospel and by the confirmation which the sacraments bring to the Word.

Thus, from the subjective point of view of the recipient, it is only faith which causes the visible sign and the grace signified by it to coincide. He who hears the Word without faith, he who participates in the sacraments without faith, participates only in a visible sign without participating in the internal and invisible sanctification. Faithlessness dissociates and separates the sign from the grace signified and destroys the sacrament which, in man's eyes, is nothing apart from its truth. It is only the believer who, in receiving the sign, receives also the grace which the sign represents and offers. Moreover, the sign and the thing signified are not so closely linked to each other that the one cannot exist without the other. Thus it is that believers, receiving the Word with faith, receive justification and life without participating—should circumstances make it impossible— in the signs of the sacraments.[1]

But it is from the subjective point of view *of the recipient alone* that unbelief renders the sacrament void of its significance and its efficacy. If by the manner of his receiving the unbeliever renders what he receives ineffective, God, on His side, still does not cease to *offer*, and what He offers preserves no less its property and its nature. Notwithstanding the internal dispositions of the recipient, the sacrament *offered* remains truly what it *is*, just as the Word itself remains what it is. The unbeliever receives carnally a sacrament which none the less remains spiritual ; but it ceases to be spiritual for the unbeliever, who takes the sign instead of the thing signified and derives no benefit from it.

" Just as we do not judge the integrity and worth of the sacraments in accordance with the worthiness or unworthiness of the ministers, so let us not value them in accordance with the condition of those who receive them : for we know

[1] 2nd Helv. Conf., xix. 9, 10

that the integrity of the sacraments depends on the faithfulness or truth and sheer benevolence of God. And just as the Word of God remains the true Word of God, by which it is not just bare words that are recited in preaching, but since also the things signified by these words are offered to us by God, despite the fact that the wicked and unbelievers who hear the words fail to enjoy the things signified, inasmuch as they have not received them with true faith : so also the sacraments, composed of the Word, of signs, and the things signified, remain true and entire sacraments, not only because they signify sacred things but because it is God who offers and presents the things signified, despite the fact that unbelievers in no sense receive them, even though they are offered to them : and this results from the fault of men, taking the sacrament illegitimately and without faith, and not at all from the fault of God who gives and offers it ; so that unbelief can never render void or destroy the faithfulness and truth of God." [1]

We must beware of two errors : firstly, that of taking the signs as though they signify and convey nothing, for, in doing this, we wither the fruit that ought to be gathered by us from them ; secondly, that of thinking that in receiving invisible grace *through* and *by means of* a visible sign we may stop at the signs, without lifting our hearts and spirits up to Christ, who alone, through His Spirit, communicates these graces to us with the aid of external signs. It is Christ alone who confers on the signs their value and their efficacy. [2]

The interval between the reception and the effect of the sacraments

Is there a coincidence, a simultaneousness, between the reception of the sacraments and their effects ? This is the last question which we must briefly examine.

Since the sacraments are a visible *Word*, the problem of the moment of the action and efficacy of the sacraments is identical with that of the moment of the efficacy of the Word, as also are the source and the conditions of their respective efficacy. The rules regarding the reception and the

[1] 2nd Helv. Conf., xix. 12.
[2] Cf. Calvin, *Instt.*, IV. xiv. 14 ; 2nd Helv. Conf., xix. 11. On all these points there is absolute agreement in all the Reformed confessions of faith and in all their symbolical documents.

effect of the Word are not different from those which govern
the efficacy of the sacraments. Short of making the sacraments something quite other than they are, it is impossible,
in this respect also, to separate them from the Word and to
concede to them modes of efficacy which are different from
those of the Word. In a Reformed view of the efficacy of the
sacraments it is not possible to posit connections between
reception and effect of such a kind as cannot equally be
attributed to the Word and its proper effects. Otherwise
the sacraments would become something altogether other
than a visible *Word* : a special sacramental *genre*, severed
and alien from the Word.

In a general sense, the Word is always efficacious (cf.
Isa. lv. 11 ; 2 Cor. ii. 14-16, etc.). As it concerns sinful man,
whether it be for saving believers and those who persevere
in faith, or for condemning unbelievers and those who
persevere in unbelief, the Word, during the period of life
granted here below by God to those who hear it, is always
efficacious and achieves its end. As far as the saving ministry
of the Word as it affects the individual is concerned, no one
will affirm that its saving effect, that is to say, faith, always
follows *immediately* upon the hearing of the Word. Children
and also adults at first often fail to realize the nature of
God's announcement to them. Amongst those who in the
end attain to faith many at first rebel and refuse to believe,
it may be over a long period. It is only later that they
believe ; and when they are converted they recognize
that their faith is, in fact, the fruit of the Word which had
previously been proclaimed to them. We discern here the
existence of an interval between the preaching of the Word
and the appearance of its saving effects. The final efficacy
is undoubtedly preceded by many anterior and preparatory
effects, but these effects, produced by the Spirit acting freely
together with the Word, frequently remain secret ; they
defy all analysis and subjective comprehension, just as the
activity of the Holy Spirit, through whom we live and move
and have our being, defies all analysis. The *remembrance*
of the Word which has been heard has much to do with its
final efficacy. Parents, teachers, and pastors in their dealings
with children and adults are constantly verifying, on the one

hand, this interval between the proclamation of the Word and its effects, and, on the other hand, the remarkable power of the Word when recalled by the memory. In order to be effective with that final efficacy which results in the receiving of free pardon and salvation, the Word is active in general over a long period of time which is fundamentally, for each one, the period of God's patience, on the duration of which it is consequently forbidden to speculate, and which brings into play all man's faculties. Moreover, in accordance with God's decree it is necessary for the Word to be constantly *repeated*, so that its efficacy may be continuous and its action intensified throughout the life of the believer.

We observe the same connection between the reception and the effect of the sacraments. The sacrament of circumcision, for example, administered to the newly-born babe, is in advance the sign and seal for the child of an objective reality concerning himself, the covenant which *will be* announced to him. The efficacy of the sacrament will only be perceived subjectively when the child, having believed the Word, will be able to relate himself to it by faith. The *remembrance* of the sacrament received will play a part of the greatest importance. From the viewpoint of the individual who receives it, we have here the example of a sacrament, which is the sign and seal of the promise, but which has been received *previously to the Word*, which it ought always to confirm and seal as quickly as possible. And in this instance the interval between the reception and the conscious effects is still more marked than with the Word, since the latter *follows* the administration of the sacrament. We shall see that the same is the case with baptism. Remarks which are analogous, though not entirely similar, could be made concerning the efficacy of the Lord's Supper and the necessity for its frequent repetition.

The " collective " efficacy of the sacraments

However, the efficacy of the sacraments cannot, any more than that of the Word, be summed up by stating that the individual perceives it in his subjective consciousness ; in the first place because the real and objective effects of the sacraments—like those of the Word—far surpass the possibility of our introspection or subjective analysis ; and then also because it would be a serious mistake to envisage the efficacy of the Word and the sacraments only in so far as they affect each separate individual. The individual is *always* part and parcel of a number of collectivities, those, for example, of the covenant of grace, the Christian family, and the Church. The Word preserves and edifies the Church, Christ's body, as such, just as it preserves and edifies the Christian family as such. Here the link between the Word and its effects produced by the Spirit is much closer and can be compared to the food which sustains the life of every organism. Because of the permanence from generation to generation of the organism which is the Church, the body of Christ, comparable to an ever-living tree giving its fruits at all seasons, or to a body whose heart beats without cessation, the Word is *ceaselessly* efficacious for the strengthening of the whole body, for its sanctification and its perseverance in faith, whatever may be the " moment " of its decisive efficacy in this or that isolated individual. The two aspects, individual and collective, of the efficacy of the Word, cannot be separated or isolated from each other. One cannot study the one without the other. The individual hears the Word in the covenant, in the Church, and the same Word which is addressed to him is *also and at the same time* addressed effectively to the family as such, to the Church as such, and even to the world. Its effects are many and various.

Similarly, no one receives a sacrament *alone* : nor does anyone participate in a sacrament *alone*. The effects of the sacraments have application also beyond the individual to entire collectivities, taken as such, who participate in them in faith. Like the Word, the sacraments—the visible Word —render the covenant efficacious from generation to generation and edify the body of Christ. These collectivities participate in their efficacy and, in a certain sense, do so *immediately*, even when their effects on them are prolonged in time or when for this or that individual an interval intervenes. We shall return later to this important point in the section devoted to the spiritual solidarity and efficacy of baptism. It is sufficient here to display this last resemblance between the Word and the sacraments.

D. POINTS OF DISSIMILARITY BETWEEN THE WORD AND THE
SACRAMENTS

Though, as we have seen, there exists, according to Reformed
doctrine, a very close analogy between the Word and the sacraments as means of grace, yet there are, none the less, certain
differences between them which we shall now briefly describe.

(a) Word and sacraments differ in their necessity

The Word is indispensable to salvation, but the sacraments
are not. The sacraments, in fact, are subordinated to the Word:
they are *signs* of the content of the Word, and *seals* which
God adds to His testimony; they are, as Calvin says, columns
or pillars of our faith, helps which accompany the Word and
are joined to it. The Word, therefore, is definitely something
apart from the sacraments, but the sacraments apart from the
Word are nothing: apart from it they have neither value nor
power. The sacraments are nothing less than, but nothing
more than, a *visible Word*. All the benefits of redemption
come to us from the Word and only through faith, but there
is not a single benefit which can be received through the
sacraments alone, apart from the Word and without faith.

It is for this reason that the preaching of the Word should
precede the administration of the sacraments in order to
teach us and bring to our knowledge the significance of the
visible sign. The words which are called " sacramental "
are nothing other than a summary preaching of the promise
of the Gospel, which ought to be proclaimed by the minister
with force and clarity so that believers may be brought to
the end for which the sign was prescribed.[1]

The Word is thus indispensable to salvation, whereas the
sacraments are not. In affirming this, Reformed theologians
are conscious that their teaching is founded upon Scripture
in which the following emphases are constantly found :

1. The free and spiritual character of the Gospel in which
God does not link His grace to the use of certain external
forms (cf. Jn. iv. 21, 23 ; Lk. xviii. 14 ; etc.).

2. The fact that faith alone is the instrumental cause of
salvation (cf. Jn. v. 24 ; vi. 29 ; Acts xvi. 31).

[1] Calvin, *Instt.*, IV. xiv. 4.

3. The fact that, as far as adults are concerned, the sacraments do not produce faith but presuppose it, and are only administered when faith is present (cf. Acts ii. 41 ; xvi. 14, 15, 30, 33 ; 1 Cor. xi. 23-32 ; etc.).

4. The fact that some have been truly saved without the use of sacraments, for example, believers before the time of Abraham and the penitent thief on the cross. Sins can be forgiven and the soul regenerated and saved without ever having received a sacrament.

According to the Reformed view of a sacrament, sacraments are not means necessary for salvation. The *necessity of means* is in general an absolute necessity, a condition *sine qua non*. In this sense, food is a vital necessity for the body, light is necessary for the use of sight, the Word for the exercise of faith. In our opinion, the sacraments possess a *necessity of precept*. It is a duty to make use of them, but they are not means *necessary* for salvation. One *can* be saved without them. The benefits which they signify, and of which they are the organs of signification for sealing and applying them to believers, do not depend on their use in such a way that these benefits cannot be received apart from them.[1]

Christ, however, has ordered His disciples to baptize all those who are received as members of His Church, and He has required that His disciples should regularly commemorate His death by the celebration of the Lord's supper ; thus His people find themselves under a compelling moral obligation to obey these commandments of His. But it may happen that the exercise of this duty is counteracted by external circumstances (such as the great distances which separate Christians in some sparsely populated territories) which hinder the obedience even of those who are disposed and desire to practise their Saviour's injunction. Even where obedience is not opposed by external circumstances the observance of these commands may be neglected through ignorance or through scruples of conscience which are unjustifiable. We believe that if such people possess faith through the Word alone their salvation is in no way compromised.

It is not the *privation* but the *contempt* of the sacraments

[1] Cf. F.-J. Leenhardt, *op. cit.*, pp. 44, 62, 65 ; K. Barth, *op. cit.*, pp. 23-25.

which renders us culpable before God. Let us not forget that we are not spirits, but sensible and earthly creatures who cannot understand spiritual things otherwise than by sensible forms ; nor that God has instituted the sacraments in order that, by gazing upon signs, we might acquire a better notion of His benefits and be more firmly assured of His promises, and thus sustained and strengthened in our faith. No one can neglect the use of the sacraments *deliberately* without exposing himself to grave spiritual consequences.[1] The believer has no right to rely upon the operation of grace apart from the conditions upon which the promise of help has been made, and these conditions are : the hearing of the Word *and* the participation of the sacraments. It is for this reason that the faithful Christian, even at the cost of the greatest sacrifices, will go to hear the Word preached and will partake of the Lord's supper. In dispensing with these, excuses valid *before God* will alone be admissible.

(b) Word and sacraments differ in their extent

The Word is spread throughout the whole world, while the sacraments are only administered to those who are in the visible Church. To those who are not within the Church the sacraments mean nothing.

(c) Word and sacraments differ in their object

The object of the Word is to engender and strengthen faith, while the sacraments contribute only to its strengthening. " The sacraments," says Calvin, " do not fail to confirm Scripture and to render it more certain and more authentic, when they are added to it. . . . The promise is sealed by the sacraments, since it is plain that where promises are concerned the one is confirmed by the other. For that which is the most evident is the most suitable for assuring our faith. Now, the sacraments convey to us the clearest promises and, compared with the Word, have this peculiarity, that they represent to us the promises in a lifelike form, as though in a picture. . . . The sacraments, as we have already remarked, are to us from God's side just what messengers of good news are from man's side—not for the purpose of conferring grace

[1] Cf. Irish Art., para. 88.

upon us, but only for announcing and exhibiting the things which are given to us by God's liberality : they are a pledge which ratifies these gifts to us."[1]

(d) Word and sacraments differ in their external form, in the manner in which they present the same Christ to us

In a certain sense the Word itself is a sign and seal—a sign which attracts and holds our attention to the thing which it presents and explains, and a seal which ratifies that which exists in the true reality, although (or rather, because) this reality still remains in certain respects external to ourselves. This is generally true of every word, but it is very particularly true of the Word of God : he who does not believe it makes God a liar (1 Jn. v. 10), while, on the contrary, the believer, having been sealed in the truth of the Word, by the Word itself, gives his seal, in accepting its testimony, that God is true (Jn. iii. 33).

Word and sacraments present Christ and His blessings to us by means of the senses which God has given man, but by means of different senses. The Word signifies Christ to us and seals Him to us by the sense of hearing, whereas the sacraments do this by the sense of sight, in association with smell, taste, and touch. The sacraments are a visible Word, a mirror. " We can also use other similitudes," says Calvin, " for plainly describing the sacraments, as by calling them pillars of our faith. For just as a building stands and is supported on its foundation and is made more secure and firm by the adding of pillars underneath, so also our faith rests and is supported on the Word of God, as on its foundation ; but when the sacraments are added to it they act like pillars, on which it rests more firmly and by which it is still further strengthened." [2]

The bringing into play of these new senses brings to light a further difference in the manner in which Christ is presented to us. Apart from occasions when the Word is directly proclaimed to a single person in a private conversation, which is the exception, the Word preached is always addressed to a group of persons, sometimes even to a crowd. It is the privilege of the Word which is apprehended by hearing to be addressed to a community. But the individual is then taken

[1] *Instt.*, IV. xiv. 5, 17.   [2] *Instt.*, IV. xiv. 6.

in the mass, and one knows with what difficulty each separate person appropriates *to himself* the words spoken and the promises made. Frequently the hearer considers that the words are addressed to the mass, and not to himself : " Good sermon, but . . . it's for the others ! It's too strong for me, it's too good ; I'm not worthy of it ! It's not for *me* personally, etc. . . ." In other words, he *escapes* from the Word. He does not realize that he himself is singled out ; he does not know, or does not wish to know, that he himself is the object of God's love and mercy. Who has not passed through this experience ?

It is now that the sacrament intervenes. The sacraments, the visible Word, are addressed to each one taken separately, to each one for himself. They individualize and make the Word concrete for each one. Each one receives the promise for himself ; each one is personally marked out by God as the object, the precise addressee of the promises and of salvation. In the sacraments God engages in a solemn private conversation with each one. It is truly a special interview " face to face " : " To thee, here present, I promise, I give, I convey, I confirm. . . . Take, receive, believe, . . . *thou personally.*" Through the sacraments God lays His hand on each one, so that it is impossible to escape and impossible to say that the Word is addressed to others. The visible Word besieges the man who receives it, that very man at that very moment. God offers everything *to him*, and it behoves him to lay hold of everything *for himself.* We discover here once more the truth of what we have already emphasized, namely, that Christ is the central content of the sacraments.

(e) The sacraments renew in a concrete manner the covenant between believers and God as though being the seal of their eternal election

They strengthen believers in the communion of Christ, draw them into fellowship with each other, separate them from the world, and testify to angels and to men that they are the people of God, the Church of Christ, the communion of the saints. They signify to us that which God requires from us.

Consequently, the sacraments place those who receive them under the obligation of serving God ; they commit them, pledge them. They set the recipients apart as witnesses of God before men. "The sacraments are the signs and the marks of our profession, so that by these marks we testify that we belong to the people of God and we profess to be Christians."[1]

" The sacraments have been given (to the people of the Old Testament as to the people of the New Testament) as signs and recognizances of the grace and promises of God in recalling to them His great blessings, and for separating the faithful from all the other religions of the world ; briefly, to be received spiritually by faith, *and to bind to the Church those who receive them and to admonish them of their duty.*"[2] The words we have here emphasized are very important and the idea will be further developed when we deal with the subject of baptism.

In order to mark out the characteristic features of Reformed theology as distinct from the Romish doctrine of the sacraments (or any other doctrine), it is most important to maintain, on the one hand, the resemblances and, on the other, the differences which we have just defined between the Word and the sacraments. He who assigns to the sacraments a special and particular action of grace, different from that which the Word performs, divides Christ and His blessings, sunders the unity of the covenant of grace, introduces a materialistic concept of grace, elevates the sacraments into an autonomous institution in opposition and superior to the Word, upsets the relation existing between Scripture and the Church, makes the sacrament absolutely necessary for salvation, and places the believer in a position of dependence on the minister, the priest, or the pastor.

For this reason Reformed theologians did not and do not cease to emphasize and re-emphasize constantly the true relationship between the Word and the sacraments, as assigned by Scripture, namely, that, as signs and as seals, the sacraments are subordinate to the Word, and that Word and sacraments have the *common* object of exhibiting to us that the only foundation of our redemption is to believe in the sacrifice which Christ offered for us on the cross. In consequence the Reformed confessions of faith affirm this indissoluble connection between the Word and the sacraments.

---

[1] Reformed Catechism, para. 54.

[2] 2nd Helv. Conf., xix. 5 ; cf. also *ibid.*, xix. 1 ; Art. XXV of the Ch. of England ; Westm. Conf., xxvii. 1 ; Genev. Conf., para. 14 ; Calvin, *Instt.*, IV. xiv. 1, 19.

THE COVENANT OF GRACE

PRELIMINARY REMARKS

On several occasions hitherto we have used the expression
"covenant of grace." We have said that the sacraments are
the signs and seals of the covenant of grace. Now we must
justify this assertion and develop its implications.

Scripture, as we have already remarked, establishes that
Christ is the central content of both Word and sacraments.
We shall see that the principal office of Christ is to be both
the Revealer and also the Mediator, the Executor, and the
Guarantor of the covenant of grace which has been concluded
between God and men. Of this covenant Christ is today the
Dispenser. Christ came by reason and in virtue of a promise,
a promise so important that it is called *the* promise. Thus our
present task is to go back to the *divine cause* of Christ's
coming, whereby God willed and wills that there should be
a Gospel—a Word and sacraments of which Christ Himself
is the unique content. To neglect to go back to this cause is
to stop half-way in the study of the sacraments. To consider *Christ* as a gift which comes from Himself, who finds
in Himself and brings by Himself His explanation and justification, to establish the doctrine of the sacraments, and to
give them their content, by a method which is simply and
only *Christo*-centric, is to neglect the essential aspect of the
problem. Exegetes of the New Testament often fail to give
sufficient consideration to this fact.[1] As with every biblical
doctrine, the sacraments must be and are established in a
*theo*logical, that is to say, trinitarian, manner, and their
true content can only be defined in a manner that is *theological and trinitarian*. The work of the Son, if it is to be
intelligible to the mind, grasped by the heart, accepted by
the will—and consequently the sacraments which are the

---

[1] F. -J. Leenhardt, *op. cit.*, pp. 47, 48, justly says : " The true nature of
these issues should be sought in the divine intention which is historically
fulfilled in them."

signs and seals of it—must be related to the will and to the decrees of the Father. Christ took care to say and to preach this. It is not, on our part a begging of the question. It results from the most serious study, even the study of the texts.

I

THE OBJECTIVE ASPECTS OF THE COVENANT OF GRACE

A. THE COVENANT IN HISTORY

1. *The will of God to save fallen mankind*

It would have been possible for God to have inflicted eternal punishment upon man immediately after the fall as a just consequence of his disobedience. But in His mercy God decided not to cause judgment to intervene immediately. In His fatherly good will He wished to produce good from the evil that men do and to make use of Adam's fall and of sin as a means whereby a new and fuller revelation of His Divinity might be displayed. He resolved, therefore, to turn to the fallen world with all the splendour of His redemptive love and His saving grace. In doing this, God was concerned for His own glory as much as for the good of His creatures—*His own glory* : for He had created the world in order to make known to it the splendour of His Divinity, which, prior to the fall, had not been manifested in all its perfection—*the good of His creatures* : for, instead of leaving them to suffer death, the consequence and wages of sin, God took His fallen creatures in order to bestow upon them the revelation of His grace and the free gift of life.

God decided to substitute His patience and His grace for the demands of His justice. This is the eternal " covenant " of the Father. Holy Scripture reveals to us the conditions on which this grace would be and has been promised, realized, and acquired. An immediate destruction of sin was just as impossible as an arbitrary pardon which the offended majesty of God had not authorized. On the one hand, the sin was in man, and God's justice must finally have its course ; on the other hand, the majesty of God must be announced in its fulness to sinful man. Moreover,

God wished to pardon sin. While the sinner finds himself quite unable to expiate his sin for himself, God decides that it will be expiated by a Mediator who will acquire the justice which man has need of, and that man shall receive this justice as a free gift. God Himself, in the person of His Son, offers Himself so that this mediation may be effectively brought to fulfilment. The Son will be the Mediator, the expiatory Victim, the Ransom, the Saviour. The Father and the Son *together* resolve to cause the unique glory of God and the free salvation of His fallen creatures to shine forth at one and the same time. In theology this resolution is called " the pact of salvation " or "the covenant of redemption." [1]   " God has from all eternity determined and predestined the salvation of the world by Christ, and He has proclaimed this eternal predestination and counsel of His to the world by the Gospel ; whence it is quite plain that the religion and doctrine of the Gospel is the most ancient of all the religions and doctrines which have been, are, and shall be." [2]

As revealed in time and in the course of history, this will of God to save man from ruin and to give him justification and life is given the name of the " covenant of grace." It is first disclosed in Genesis iii. 15. From the very beginning grace is implicitly offered to all, to Adam and to his posterity, to Noah and to his posterity, according to rules and conditions of which we are largely ignorant.[3] Up till the time of Abraham Holy Scripture tells us nothing of a formal establishment of the covenant of grace in the sense which it assumed from that time on.

2. *The formation of the covenant*

With the appearance of Abraham, we enter into a most important period of the dispensation of grace, that of the covenant of grace. Let us turn to Genesis xvii. Having already made Abraham a participant in His promises (Gen. xii. 1-3, 7), *God makes a covenant with him* (Gen. xv. 1-18) of a most solemn nature : " *Abraham believed the Lord, who imputed it to him for righteousness* " (xv. 6). A little later,

---

[1] Cf. Ps. lxxxix. 2-5. We make a mere reference to this notion, without being able to develop it here.

[2] 2nd. Helv. Conf., xiii.   [3] Westm. Conf., vii. 3.

God renews this covenant with His elect in a still more precise and definite form. " The Lord appeared to Abraham and said to him : I am the Almighty God ; walk before Me and be upright. I will make a covenant with you, and I will multiply you exceedingly. . . . This is My covenant which I make with you : you will be the father of a multitude of nations. . . . Kings shall descend from you. I will establish My covenant with you and with your posterity after you, from generation to generation ; it will be an everlasting covenant, whereby I shall be your God and the God of your posterity after you. To you will I give the land where you sojourn as a stranger, and to your posterity after you . . ., and I will be their God. . . . See that you keep My covenant, you and your posterity after you, from generation to generation. This is the covenant which you must keep, the covenant established between Me and you and your descendants after you : every manchild among you shall be circumcized. You shall circumcize your flesh and it will be a sign of the covenant between Me and you. At the age of eight days, every male among you shall be circumcized, from generation to generation, whether he is born in the house, or has been bought for money from a stranger and is not of your race. He who is born in the house and he who is bought for money must be circumcized ; and My covenant shall be in your flesh the sign of an everlasting covenant. The uncircumcized male shall be cut off from his people, because he has violated My covenant " (Gen. xvii. 1-14). And God adds (xvii. 19) : " I will establish My covenant with Isaac, and it will be an everlasting covenant with his posterity after him."

Again, God says (xviii. 18, 19) : " Abraham shall become a great and mighty nation, and in him all the nations of the earth shall be blessed. I have chosen him in order that he may command his children and his house after him to follow the way of the Lord in doing that which is just and right, so that the Lord may accomplish for Abraham the promises which he has made to him. . . . I have sworn by Myself " (cf. xxii. 15-18).

This covenant was confirmed to Isaac, to Jacob, to Joseph, and to their posterity. In every age believers have trusted in this covenant of grace and its promises ; its sound echoes through all Scriptures, and God also makes constant reference to it as He progressively brings it to its full development.

3. *Unity and immutability of the covenant throughout the Old Testament*

The covenant concluded with Abraham was not annulled by the covenant made with Moses at Sinai ; on the contrary, it persists in all its force (Gal. iii. 17 f.). God Himself reminds his people of the promise made to Abraham and his posterity (Ex. vi. 3-8 ; Dt. i. 8). It is for the sake of the covenant that He will deliver His people (Ex. ii. 24), that He will be gracious to them (Lev. xxvi. 42), and that He will remain faithful (Dt. iv. 31, vii. 9, 12, xxix. 12 f.). The law of Horeb could only cause the grace of the covenant made with Abraham to shine more brightly (Gal. iii. 19-25). The intercession of Moses is based on his faith in the God of the covenant who remains faithful (Ex. xxxii. 13 f.). Moses recalls to mind the promises and the requirements of the covenant of grace concluded with Abraham and the patriarchs (Dt. vii. 12, viii. 18). A careful study, such as would exceed the plan and object of this résumé, would show that the covenant of grace with Abraham and his posterity and the Sinaitic covenant are *essentially* the same, the latter differing from the former only by reason of a new dispensation and different and temporary modes of application (Ps. cv. 8 ff.).

Through the succeeding centuries the people all too frequently attempted to break this covenant.[1] When it might seem that the unfaithfulness of men had cancelled out the faithfulness of God, God recalls in solemn terms the immutability of His decision, of His grace, and of the benefits of the covenant [2] ; and men, constantly being reminded that God

[1] Cf. Gen. xvii. 14 ; Lev. xxvi. 25 ; Dt. xvii. 2, xxix. 25, xxxi. 16-18, 20 ; Josh. vii. 11, 15, xxiii. 14-16 ; Jud. ii. 20 ; 1 Ki. xi. 11, xix. 10 ; 2 Ki. xvii. 15, xviii. 12 ; Pss. xliv. 18, l. 16, lxxviii. 10, 37 ; Prov. ii. 17 ; Is. xxiv. 5, xxviii. 18 ; Jer. xi. 2, 3, 10, xxii. 9, xxxi. 32, xxxiv. 18 ; Ez. xvi. 59, xvii. 15 f., 18 f., xliv. 7 ; Dan. xi. 28, 30, 32 ; Hos. vi. 7, viii. 1 ; Zech. xi. 10 ; Mal. ii. 8, 10.

[2] Cf. Lev. xxvi. 9, 42-45 ; 2 Ki. xvii. 38 ; 1 Chr. xvi. 14-18 ; Neh. ix. 7, 8 ff. ; Ps. xxv. 10, lxxxix. 31-38, ciii. 18, cv. 8-10, cvi. 45, cxi. 5, 9, cxxxii. 11 f. ; Is. l. 1, liv. 10, lv. 3, lix. 21, lxi. 8 ; Jer. xxxi. 32-34, xxxii. 38-41, xxxiii. 20 f., 25 ; Ez. xvi. 8, 60, 62, xx. 37, xxxiv. 23, 25, 30 f., xxxvi. 25-28, xxxvii. 26 f. ; Hos. ii. 18-20 ; Hag. ii. 5 ; Mal. ii. 5; 2 Cor. vi. 16-18 ; Heb. viii. 8-13.

is faithful, are exhorted to renew the terms of the covenant and to claim and enjoy once more the benefits of its blessings.[1]

The revelation of the covenant is so important that the words of God are called " the words of the covenant " (2 Ki. xxiii. 3 ; 2 Chr. xxxiv. 31), and the Scriptures are referred to as " the book of the covenant." Moreover, the offerings, the observation of the sabbath, and so on, are instituted as signs of the perpetual covenant (Num. xviii. 19 ; Ex. xxxi. 16 f.). The blood of the sacrifices is the blood of the covenant (Ex. xxiv. 8 ; Heb. ix. 18-20). The tables are the tables of the covenant (Dt. ix. 9, etc.), and the ark is " the ark of the covenant of the Lord " (Num. x. 33, etc.). But we should never finish if we wished to cite all the texts ; and the passages which refer to this covenant and promise without using the word itself in the text are still more numerous.

The efficacy and validity of the covenant of grace and its promises are apparent at every important stage of God's revelation. In the time of the Judges the theme of the covenant is present (Jud. ii. 1, 20, etc.). During the course of his life and in his last song David sings of the covenant with emotion (1 Chr. xvi. 14 ff. ; 2 Sam. xxiii. 3-5), and with him God renews His covenant (2 Chr. xiii. 5, etc.). Solomon celebrates the faithfulness of the God of the covenant (1 Ki. viii. 23 ff.). It is in virtue of the covenant that, during the reign of Jehoahaz, God is gracious to the Israelites (2 Ki. xiii. 22, 23). In recalling the covenant and its promises, God—through the mouth of Isaiah—exhorts His people to " look to the rock whence they were hewn and to the hole of the pit whence they were digged," and to receive the blessings of the covenant (Is. li. 1, ff.). The intercessions both of Jeremiah and of Daniel are based on the covenant (Jer. xiv. 20 f. ; Dan. ix. 4 ff.).

" We affirm that the ancient Fathers had two sorts of promises, as we also have to this day. The one sort concerned present or terrestrial things, such as the promises respecting the land of Canaan and victories, and such we still have today respecting our daily bread. The other sort concerned

---

[1] Cf. 2 Ki. xi. 17, xxiii. 3 ; 1 Chr. xvi. 14-18 ; 2 Chr. xxix. 10, xxxiv. 31 ; Ezra x. 3 ; Neh. ix. 38 ; Pss. l. 5, lxxiv. 20, lxxvii. 8-10 ; Jer. xiv. 20 f., l. 4, 5 ; Dan. ix. 4.

then, as is also the case now, heavenly and eternal things, namely, the divine grace, the forgiveness of sins, and eternal life, through faith in Jesus Christ. The ancient Fathers had not only external or terrestrial promises, but also spiritual and heavenly ones in Christ." [1] We shall soon return to this important question.

4. *The Covenant of grace in the New Testament*

The Virgin Mary sees in the birth of her Son a mark of the faithfulness of God in connection with His promises and rejoices in the fulfilment of the covenant made with Abraham (Lk. i. 50-55). Zacharias, after the birth of Christ, sings of the accomplishment of the covenant, ever present and efficacious (Lk. i. 72-75). And rightly so! For Christ had been announced beforehand as the one who would fulfil the covenant with the people (Is. xlii. 6 f.) ; He is the promised Mediator of the covenant (Is. xlix. 8 f.) ; He is " the messenger of the covenant " who was expected in faith (Mal. iii. 1). The promise having been fulfilled, He *is* the Mediator of the covenant and is confessed as such (Heb. viii. 6, ix. 15, xii. 24) ; He is the Guarantor of the covenant (Heb. vii. 22) ; He introduces His own into the covenant (Rom. v. 2). Christ Himself described His blood shed for the remission of sins as " the blood of the covenant " (Mt. xxvi. 28 ; Mk. xiv. 24 ; Lk. xxii. 20 ; 1 Cor. xi. 25).[2] It is by the blood of the everlasting covenant that Christ has become " the great Shepherd of the sheep " (Heb. xiii. 20) ; and His resurrection from the dead took place in virtue of the promise of the covenant (Acts xiii. 32 f.).

The exegesis of these texts shows that Christ's work is twofold. On the one hand, He endures the just punishment inflicted on the sinner by God, He intercedes for those whom the Father has given Him, and He causes their persons and their service to be actually acceptable to God. On the other hand, He reveals to man the truth concerning God and his relationship to Him, and also the conditions of acceptable service ; Christ persuades men to receive the truth, and

[1] 2nd Helv. Conf., xiii.
[2] We explain below in what sense the adjective " new " in the two last texts cited should be understood.

renders them capable of doing so ; and He directs and sustains them in all circumstances, in order that their salvation may be brought to perfection.

The theology of the covenant of grace is constantly presented to us in the thought of the Apostles and disciples. It forms the central theme of Peter's first sermon after Pentecost : it is the promises of the covenant and their fulfilment which are expounded (Acts ii. 14-41, iii. 12-26). From beginning to end these sermons are an exposition of the theology of the covenant. It is the theme of the covenant again which serves as the starting-point for Stephen's address (Acts vii. 2-8), and for Paul's defence before Agrippa (Acts xxvi. 6 f.).

Paul affirms the permanence of the covenant and the real vitality of its promises (Gal. iii. 17). Christians are the children born according to the promise (Gal. iv. 21, 23, 28) ; they are the children of Abraham (Gal. iii. 7, 26, 29) ; those who believe to-day are blessed together with faithful Abraham (Gal. iii. 9). The believer is justified by faith, like Abraham, and he enters into the same covenant and receives the same promises (Rom. iv.). The adoption, the glory, the covenants, the law, the service of God, and the promises belong to Paul's fellow-countrymen and kinsfolk according to the flesh, because of the covenant, even though they continue in unbelief (Rom. ix. 3 f.). They continue to be loved by God for the sake of their fathers (Rom. xi. 28) ; although they have rebelled, the people have not been rejected, because of the covenant (Rom. xi. 1 f.). The Gentiles, on the contrary, being strangers to the covenants of promise, are without God and without hope in the world (Eph. ii. 12). The author of the Epistle to the Hebrews speaks of the immutable covenant sworn by God, in which believers find their encouragement and refuge by appropriating the promises which it offers (Heb. vi. 13-20). Then, at the end of time, when the new Jerusalem descends from heaven, from the presence of God, and the tabernacle of God is established among men—then the promise of the covenant, " I will be your God and you shall be My people," is completely fulfilled. This last echo of the covenant is found in Rev. xxi. 3.

5. *The pastoral ministry is the ministry of the covenant*

In proclaiming the Gospel, the Apostles were nothing more than " ministers of the covenant " (2 Cor. iii. 6). This is said in a particular context, but it follows directly from the position of Christ relative to the covenant. The function of the covenant of grace consists in the effective calling of the elect from the misery of sin and death to the knowledge of the Son of God, to the appropriation of His righteousness and eternal life, and to the regeneration of their being as originally created in the image of God. This covenant is administered and this calling is made externally by means of the Word and the sacraments. The apostolic and pastoral ministry is that of the covenant.

In Scripture the covenant is regarded as the supreme " secret " of God, the mystery which He reveals to those only who fear Him : " The secret of the Lord is for those who fear Him, and He causes them to know His covenant " (Ps. xxv. 14). The doctrine of the covenant is the germ, the root, the pith of all revelation, and consequently of all theology ; it is the clue to the whole history of redemption. Every other doctrine, no matter what it may be, is in some manner connected with it, and, as we shall see, especially and primarily the doctrine of the sacraments.

B. THE PROMISES AND CHARACTERISTICS OF THE COVENANT

The reader who refers carefully to the biblical passages previously cited in the text and in the notes will easily arrive at the following conclusions which we are about to present in a systematic manner. In this matter it serves no purpose at all to quibble over this or that little detail.

1. *The promises of the covenant*

(*a*) The promises of the covenant are those of various temporal blessings which, more often than not, are symbolical of blessings of a spiritual nature.

(*b*) The covenant contains *the promise* of justification, that of the adoption of sons, and of the right to eternal life.

(*c*) The covenant contains *the promise* of the Spirit of God with a view to the full and free application of the work of redemption and of all the benefits of salvation.

(*d*) The covenant contains *the promise* of final glorification in a life which shall never end.

(*e*) The covenant contains *the promise* that God will be equally the God of the posterity of believers.

2. *The characteristics of the covenant*

(*a*) *It is a covenant of grace*, that is to say, freely given. It does not depend upon any human condition, it is not a gift in exchange for some service, it does not answer to any fulfilment of the law on the part of man. God Himself, in the person of His Son, provides the surety of the covenant, whereby all our obligations are met at the same time as the demands of the divine justice.

Again, it is a covenant of grace, a free covenant, because God by His grace, *rendered efficacious by the working of the Holy Spirit*, makes man capable of living in conformity with the requirements prescribed by the very terms of the covenant. The covenant of grace has its origin *in* the grace of God, it is put into execution *by* the grace of God, and it is experienced in the life of sinners *through* the grace of God. From beginning to end it is pure grace for the sinner. It is God who descends to man and raises him to Himself. It is He who disannuls the covenant of sinful man *with Satan and with death* (Is. xxviii. 18), who places enmity between man and Satan, who destroys death, and who, taking man for His possession, promises him victory over every adverse power. It is the work of God, only His work, and all His work. Man cannot lay claim to any personal glory : all the glory emanates from the Father, the Son, and the Holy Spirit.

(*b*) *It is a trinitarian covenant.* It is the full trinitarian God who operates in the covenant of grace and who, having planned the work of regeneration, brings it to fulfilment. It has its origin in the electing love and grace of the Father, finds its judicial basis in the surety of the Son, and is only fully experienced in the life of sinners by the efficacious working of the Holy Spirit (Jn. i. 16 ; Eph. i. 1-14 ; 1 Pet. i. 2). The doctrine of the covenant of grace admirably maintains and emphasizes the sovereignty of God in the whole work of redemption.

(c) *The covenant of grace is eternal and irrevocable.* God remains eternally faithful to His covenant and will never fail to bring it to full realization in His elect. Despite the fall, and despite sin, revelation affirms ever more strongly and clearly the irrevocable nature of the covenant given for a thousand generations. Men may be unfaithful to it, but God is not unmindful of His promises : the covenant depends and rests only upon His mercy. God has freely committed Himself to it, of His own accord and with an oath. His Name, His honour, His very being, are bound to it. It is irrevocable also because it is founded upon Jesus Christ, God's only-begotten Son in whom He is well pleased. Christ, the only true foundation, abides for ever.[1]

(d) *The covenant is particular and not universalistic,* that is to say, it will not be realized in *all* men, as universalists maintain. Scripture clearly reveals that God does not envisage its being realized in *all*, numerically, as when, for example, it limits its scope to Abraham and his descendants and to the proselytes who shall join the elect people. Again, the covenant is particular in the sense that many of those to whom the Gospel is preached have no desire to be incorporated into the covenant. But, in its New Testament dispensation, the covenant of grace can be called " universal " in the sense that it is now extended to all nations without limitation.

(e) *The covenant of grace is essentially the same in all its dispensations, although its form of administration changes.* This is a point of great importance. From time to time, in both Old and New Testaments, a " new " covenant is spoken of.[2] In what sense should this adjective be understood ? The answer to this depends on the texts.

1. The author may desire to emphasize the contrast with

---

[1] Cf. Ex. xx. 6 ; Lev. xxiv. 8, xxvi. 9, 42-45 ; Dt. iv. 31, v. 10, vii. 9, 12 ; Jud. ii. 1 ; 2 Sam. xxiii. 3-5 ; 1 Ki. viii. 23 ff. ; 1 Chr. xvi 14-18 ; Pss. lxxxix. 31-38, cxi. 9 ; Is. liv. 10, lv. 3, lxi. 8 ; Jer. xxxii. 40, xxxiii. 25 ; Ez. xvi. 60 ; Lk. i. 72-75 ; Rom. xi. 29 ; 1 Cor. iii. 11 ; Gal. iii. 17 ; Heb. vi. 13 f., xiii. 20.

[2] Jer. xxxi. 31 ; Lk. xxii. 20 ; 2 Cor. iii. 6 ; Heb. viii. 8 f., 13, ix. 15, xii. 24.

the Pharisaic or Judaic conception of the covenant, a conception which has perverted the Mosaic covenant into a covenant of *works*, implying *justification by works*. The prophets themselves emphasize this contrast and this opposition. In this connection it is not concerned with a *new* attitude of the New Testament. " The lying pen of the scribes has made this law a vanity," says God by the mouth of Jeremiah (viii. 8). This outlook has no concern for the authentic and original nature of the covenant of grace. Paul, in turn, follows on the prophets by making similar affirmations, notably in Romans ix. 31 f. and Galatians v. 4 : " The Israelites who sought after the law of righteousness have failed to attain to this law. Why ? Because they have not sought it by faith, but by works. They have stumbled against the stone of stumbling." " All you who wish to be justified by the law are separated from Christ ; you have fallen from grace." Here is the key which permits us to understand the angle from which Paul makes his criticisms of the " law " ; it is not that of the covenant, but in particular that of pre-Christian legalistic Judaism which misused the sign of circumcision.[1] Israel after the flesh has always endeavoured to appropriate in as carnal a manner as possible the promises of the covenant and to use the Sinaitic covenant as a covenant of works. The Apostle's criticisms are addressed to carnal Israel who have corrupted the spiritual covenant into a carnal covenant ; they are not intended to strike at the very foundation and the profound import of the covenant of grace, but at its perversion and deplorable misuse by sinful man. Similarly also today, criticisms directed against the false confidence which unbelievers might place in their baptism, and against a perversion of the administration of baptism in the Church, are not intended to strike at the New Testament institution itself, but, on the contrary, to restore to it its value and meaning.

" The Letter which is opposed to the Spirit denotes every external thing, but principally the doctrine of the Law, which, without the Spirit and without faith, engenders wrath and kindles sin in the hearts of those who do not believe with a true and living faith. For this reason it is

[1] Cf. O. Cullmann, *op. cit.*, pp. 66-70.

also called by the Apostle the administration of death."[1] When they applied themselves to Scripture, our fathers gathered the sense and the significance of *nuances* !

2. The adjective may be employed to emphasize that the forms of administration of the covenant differ, after Christ, from those which were before Him. This is the concern of the author of the Epistle to the Hebrews, in chapters viii, ix, and x. The " Mosaic law " has performed its function, but *the covenant* pursues and achieves its own end.

3. Finally, despite the irrevocable character of the covenant of grace of which we have already spoken, it is important to do justice to the complete liberty of God in His faithfulness. For those to whom it is addressed, the faithfulness of God, the covenant offered at each instant, is an event in itself altogether stupendous, which we can never lay hold of in advance for our own appropriation. In itself, and for us, this event of the free grace of God, of His free covenant, is at each instant something altogether *new*. The covenant, it is true, is eternal and irrevocable. But it is precisely when God wishes to attract our attention to this fact, when He wishes to convince us that He is faithful and stands by what He has promised, that, in achieving its accomplishment, He declares the *renewal* of His covenant. And this is also connected with the *newness* of heart whereby men trust in the promise. Here there is, objectively, something which recalls the subjective " Sing unto the Lord a *new* song " of him to whom the grace, the benefits, and the blessings received from God are always *new*. The Reformed theologians, and Karl Barth with them, have been careful to emphasize the *free* character of the grace of God. In this connection we must draw the necessary conclusions concerning the covenant *of grace*.

We hope we are not mistaken in finding, in the four accounts which we possess of the institution of the Lord's Supper, confirmation of the three orders of ideas which we are about to describe. In Matthew xxvi. 28 and Mark xiv. 24 Christ says : " This is My blood, the blood of the covenant "; in Luke xxii. 20 and in Paul's account in 1 Corinthians xi. 25

---

[1] 2nd. Helv. Conf., xiii.

Christ says : " This cup is the new covenant in My blood."
The exegetes may search for the historical reasons for the
differing forms and significances of these passages ; but from
the dogmatic point of view it seems that there we have a *new*
attestation of the identity of the covenant in its accomplishment, of its newness in its permanence, and of its freedom
in its trustworthiness. The unity of the covenant throughout
its different dispensations [1] is demonstrated by the following
considerations:

(i) The summary expression of the covenant is the same
throughout both Old and New Testaments : " I will be your
God ! " It is characteristic of the covenant made with
Abraham (Gen. xvii. 7), of that made on Mount Sinai
(Ex. xix. 5, xx. 1), or in the plains of Moab (Dt. xxix. 13),
of that made with David (2 Sam. vii. 14), as well as of the
covenant which is called " new " (Jer. xxxi. 44 ; Heb. viii.
10). In all the dispensations of the covenant God reveals
that He wishes to re-establish the sinner in blessed communion with Himself, and that those who believe are saved
and inherit eternal life. From the fact that God is called the
God of Abraham, of Isaac, and of Jacob, Christ deduces that
the patriarchs are in possession of eternal life (Mt. xxii. 32).

(ii) In the Scriptures the word " Gospel " or " Evangel "
has a very particular significance. It signifies the announcement of the plan of salvation through Christ, and it offers
salvation to whoever believes. Christ affirms that Abraham
rejoiced to see His day (Jn. viii. 55 f. ; cf. Lk. xxiv. 27).
Paul also asserts that this Gospel was preached to Abraham.
Consequently, the Hebrew believers are described as those
who hoped in Christ before His coming, because they
received *the Gospel* (Gal. iii. 8, Eph. i. 12). This promise
made to Abraham was none other, says Paul, than that " of

[1] The reader is requested to refer to the texts which we have already
cited. Cf. also O. Cullmann, *op. cit.*, pp. 68 f. In connection with this
subject one must vigorously denounce the most fallacious habit of designa-
ting the Old Testament by the term " the old covenant." This leads to
regrettable confusions. Even Cullmann, whose vocabulary is generally
so notably precise, uses language regarding this matter which is dog-
matically unprecise : " Circumcision is reception into the Old Covenant "
(*op. cit.*, p. 57, etc.), which should mean that the Abrahamic and Mosaic
covenants are confused ; but that is certainly not what Cullmann means.

which our twelve tribes, who fervently serve God night and
day, await the fulfilment " (Acts xxvi. 7). Faith was the
condition associated with all these Abrahamic promises
(Rom. iv. ; Gal. iii.). Those of his descendants who believed
in the promises of national blessings to the Hebrews received
those blessings, and those who believed in the promise of
redemption through Christ were made participants in that
redemption. Scripture, indeed, teaches that there is but one
Gospel only whereby man can be saved. The good news
is nothing other than that of the covenant of grace, and it
follows equally that this covenant is unique. Galatians i. 8 f.
shows that it is always the same Gospel that is in force.

(iii) Paul carefully demonstrates, in opposition to the
Judaizers, that the method by which Abraham obtained
salvation is the type, the model of the method in accordance
with which the believers of the New Testament must believe,
whether they be Jews or pagans. Abraham is *the father of
believers* (Rom. iv. 9-25 ; Gal. iii. 7-9, 17 f., 26-29). The
law has neither annulled nor altered the covenant of grace
(cf. Heb. vi. 13-18). Such being the nature of the covenant
made with Abraham, it is clear that, in the degree to which it
has reference to what is of an essential nature, it remains
always in force. We still live today under this covenant
of grace ; the Christian Church is founded upon it. Even at
this present moment man is justified by faith just as Abraham was. Christians are called the *children and heirs of
Abraham*, because faith in the promise of redemption assures
their redemption exactly as faith in the same promise
assured Abraham's redemption. " If you are Christ's," says
Paul, " then you are Abraham's posterity and heirs according to the promise " (Gal. iii. 29).[1]

(iv) The Mediator of the covenant, who brought about the
salvation of Old Testament believers and who brings about
that of New Testament believers, is the same yesterday,
today, and for ever (Heb. xiii. 8). There is no salvation in
anyone else (Jn. xiv. 6). " There is no other name under
heaven given among men whereby we must be saved "
(Acts iv. 12). The seed promised to Abraham is *Christ*

---

[1] O. Cullmann, *op. cit.*, p. 69, emphasizes that the place occupied by faith
in circumcision and in baptism is the same.

(Gal. iii. 16) and those who are identified with Christ as the true heirs of the covenant (Gal. iii. 16-29).

God, in fact, did not conclude His covenant in the first place with Adam, then with Noah, then with Abraham, then with Israel, and only last of all with Christ. His covenant was revealed from the fall onwards. Christ did not commence to act only through and after His incarnation, and the Holy Spirit did not commence to work only after the Pentecostal outpouring. All grace granted since the fall comes from the Father, through the Son, by the Holy Spirit. Subsequently to the fall the Son appeared as the Mediator, the second and the last Adam, and at the same time the Holy Spirit appeared as the Comforter, the one who applies the salvation won by Christ. Every modification, every development, every progression from this notion and from this concept through the course of the different dispensations of the covenant exists solely in relation to the creature himself. In God there is not the slightest modification, nor is there the least change. The Father is eternally the Father, the Son is eternally the Mediator, and the Holy Spirit is eternally the Comforter.

For this reason it is necessary to understand the Old Testament as being one in essence and substance with the New. Even though God communicates His revelation to us in the course of the unfolding of history and in a progressive manner, and though consequently mankind progresses in the knowledge, possession, and enjoyment of the revelation, yet God is always identical with Himself, and remains so. The sun lights up the earth progressively, but, evening and morning, day and night, it remains unaltered and identical with itself.

(v) The conditions of salvation revealed in the covenant always remain the same (Gen. xv. 6 ; cf. Rom. iv. 11 ; Heb. ii. 4 ; Acts xv. 11 ; Gal. iii. 6 f. ; Heb. xi. 9). The promises whose fulfilment is awaited by believers are the same (Gen. xv. 6 ; Ps. li. 12 ; Mt. xiii. 17 ; Jn. viii. 56 ; Acts xxvi. 5-7 ; Gal. iii. 14).

(vi) Finally, and this is most important for our subject. the sacraments—although differing in form—have essentially the same significance in the two dispensations, for the sacraments are always the signs and the seals of the covenant of grace (Rom. vi. 11 ; 1 Cor. v. 7 ; Col. ii. 11 f.). The covenant is to the sacraments what the palm of the hand is to the fingers.

Such is the subject which we must now study.

C. THE SACRAMENTS OF THE COVENANT
COMPARISON OF THE SACRAMENTS OF THE OLD AND NEW TESTAMENTS

1. *The essential unity of the sacraments*

Roman Catholic theology affirms that there is an essential difference between the sacraments of the Old Testament and those of the New. It assimilates the sacraments of the Old Testament to the ritual of the Mosaic covenant and affirms that their significance is purely typical. The sanctification resulting from them was not internal (it maintains), but only legal, and prefigured the grace which was subsequently to be conferred on man in virtue of Christ's passion. This does not mean that no internal grace accompanied their usage, but simply that it was not effected *by* and *through* the sacraments as such, as, according to Roman Catholic teaching, is the case since the coming of Christ. They had no objective efficacy, they did not sanctify the recipient *ex opere operato*, but only by reason of the faith and charity with which they were received—*ex opere operantis*. Because the full experience of the grace typified by these sacraments depended on the coming of Christ, the saints of the Old Testament were received into the *limbus patrum* until Christ brought about their deliverance.

Such affirmations, and all others connected with them, have for their background a particular conception of the relationship between the Old and the New Testaments which flows in general from *a priori* philosophical notions. It places the two Testaments in opposition to each other without discerning, as the Reformed theologians habitually did, their internal unity, equally concerning the divine Person who inspired them as concerning their respective contents.[1] This anti-legalism, surpassing the limits of a legitimate

---

[1] Cullmann is careful to note most vigorously, and on exegetical grounds, the unity, the permanence, and the continuity of the covenant of grace in its various sacraments ; *op. cit.*, pp. 45 f.

protest against Judaism and Pharisaism, produces and unwarranted opposition between the Old and the New Testaments, destroys the unity of revelation, devalues the teaching provided in the Old Testament, and finishes by making it, in the name of the dignity of the New Testament, a factor of negligible proportions for faith and for piety, and consequently for theology.

Certain forms of Protestantism have frequently constituted themselves the champions of such principles, and they have been tirelessly refuted by those who are persuaded by the Holy Spirit of the internal unity of the Holy Scriptures taken in their entirety. The *a priori* philosophical and religious premisses of such an attitude are numerous : a Hegelian view of philosophy, an erroneous conception of " progress " which is termed " historical," Christocentrism which is confined to the New Testament, and so on ; and, whether one wishes it or not, consciously or unconsciously, both in the Roman Catholic Church and in present-day Protestantism, instead of a *Christian* anti-Judaism or anti-Pharisaism there arises a kind of Old Testament antisemitism. Such tendencies have an importance greater than one might think in the relation of their conclusions to the subject of baptism.

Following Calvin, orthodox Reformed theologians have taken trouble to correct this attitude of mind in certain of their critics. " In asserting a difference of covenant they corrupt and destroy Scripture with rough audacity," says Calvin of such critics. " They depict the Jews as a carnal and brutish people who had no other covenant with God than one concerning only this temporal life, and no other promise than one offering merely present and corruptible benefits. If such was the case what remains to us other than to regard this nation as a herd of swine whom our Lord wished to nourish in their sty for a while in order to let them perish eternally ? "[1] This historical antisemitism, which makes no more difference between the law and the Gospel in the Old Testament than it does between the Gospel and the law in the New Testament, plays a very important part in the question of the baptism of infants through the *a priori*

[1] *Instt.* IV. xvi. 10.

F

opposition which it sets up between circumcision and baptism.[1]

Circumcision

It is, in fact, affirmed that circumcision, was, firstly, a purely *carnal* ordinance, and, secondly, the carnal sign of the race of Israel having reference to *natural* birth. Its relevance was thus bound to the transitory ceremonies of the Mosaic law, and after the birth of the Messiah its significance ceased. Thus Karl Barth writes : " Circumcision refers to natural birth, it is the sign of the election of the holy lineage of Israel, which, with the birth of the Messiah, achieved its goal, so that therewith this sign lost its meaning, since then it had no further significance." [2] He cites two texts, namely, Rom. iv. 2 and John i. 12; and the problem of circumcision is dealt with (?) in sixteen lines. Oscar Cullmann offers the following rejoinder : " The way in which Barth deals with this question is probably the weakest point in his doctrine of Baptism. . . . It is inexplicable to me how Barth, while conceding that Baptism is the fulfilment of circumcision, yet denies at the crucial point the inner relationship between the two, and can affirm that circumcision is in itself something quite different; so that the fact that children were circumcised has no bearing on the question of Christian infant Baptism." [3]

These judgments concerning circumcision are formulated in general by New Testament " spiritualizers," by American " dispensationalists " of the present day, by certain Baptists, and others. F.-J. Leenhardt, in his work *Le Baptême chrétien* and in the complementary article in *Foi et Vie*, adopts these views integrally. The eagerness with which he seeks to establish this point well shows that, in his eyes, this is one of the essential elements of his theory. But he assimilates circumcision to the Mosaic law, and the consequences of this

[1] We leave to the reader the task of referring to the literary works and chapters which treat of the relations, the unity, and the differences which exist between the Old and the New Testaments. Reformed dogmaticians cannot fail to rejoice at the change of theological climate which is apparent in this respect in numerous recent publications that indicate a welcome revaluation of the Old Testament, most often in line with historical Reformed thought.

[2] *Op. cit.*, pp. 43 f.

[3] *Op. cit.*, p. 57. Reference should also be made to his argument as developed on the two succeeding pages.

unfortunate error make themselves felt throughout his exposition and deprive it of the force of conviction which the author had wished to give it. Let us produce evidence for this affirmation. " No one," says Leenhardt, " dreams of denying the continuity of the two covenants, their essential kinship. But are they—this kinship and this continuity— exempt from the profound diversities in the mode of the dispensations ? Such diversity cannot be denied for the sake of a word."[1] By the two covenants Leenhardt means the *Mosaic* covenant and the New Testament covenant. After what we have already said, and shall yet say, it will be recognized that it is difficult to affirm that one's only concern is a " word." " This dialectic," says Leenhardt again— namely, the dialectic which he imputes to the Apostle Paul (but Paul is speaking effectively of the *Mosaic* covenant— here also each word has its weight—and not of the *Abrahamic* covenant of grace) between the covenant of the letter and death and the covenant of the Spirit and life—" this dialectic corresponds to the dialectic of the rule of law and of the rule of Jesus Christ."[2] But in the Abrahamic covenant it is precisely a question of the rule of the promise in Jesus Christ, which the Mosaic covenant does not annul.

" It is on this dialectic," proceeds Leenhardt, " that the judgment rests which Paul introduces concerning circum- cision in the Epistle to the Colossians (ii. 11) . . . I wish only to read in this text what is there ; now, in the light of all that Paul says about the law, *to which circumcision belongs*, I can see nothing else in what he says about circumcision in Col. ii. 11 than a simple protestation against a false concep- tion of circumcision. Here there is a faithful echo of the constant thought of St. Paul, who *never* spoke favourably of circumcision." We reply : (a) that the light which Paul provides for our understanding of Col. ii. 11 is very different (cf. Cullmann, *op. cit.*, pp. 58 ff.) ; (b) that circumcision belonged originally neither to the law nor to the covenant of works, but to the covenant made with Abraham, 430 years before Moses ; (c) that Paul speaks very favourably of circumcision when he is dealing with circumcision " in Christ," the very same which Abraham received and which

[1] *Op. cit.*, Foi et Vie, p. 87. [2] *Ibid.*, p. 88.

is fulfilled under the New Testament, the very same to which it behoves every true Jew to conform.

"The constant thought of the Apostle," Leenhardt continues, " is not only that the covenant of the law has been abolished and *together with it circumcision which was part and parcel of it*, but also that circumcision, *like the law*, is *essentially inferior to faith and cannot have a place in the thought of the believer*. Paul opposes *the law* to *the promise*, in order to emphasize the opposition of justification by works to justification by faith." We reply : (*a*) Paul is careful to tell us that the promise is precisely that made to Abraham and his posterity. It is this promise which he opposes to the law ; (*b*) In origin, circumcision is not part and parcel of the law, but, on the contrary, of *the promise*, of which it is the sign and the seal, just as it is the sign and seal of *righteousness obtained by faith* ; (*c*) How can it be said that circumcision has no place in the thought of the believer, when it is *the sign and seal of the righteousness obtained by faith*, and when Abraham was the first to receive this sign because of his faith ?

"The economy of faith has *nothing in common* with circumcision, which only intervened very late," says Leenhardt. This " very late," applied to the sacraments which have reference to the promise, anterior by definition, is from the psychological point of view precisely the whole question of the sacraments. But how can it be said that circumcision has nothing in common with the economy of faith and of justification by faith, when it is the sign and seal of it ? Faith remains, while the signs and seals of faith have been changed by Christ. The promise was not only for the circumcised. Rom. iv. 13-15 shows clearly that the law *in its dispensation* has no fundamental connection with the promise, nor, consequently, with circumcision.

Leenhardt further asserts that " Paul justly wished to insist on the fact that this faith preceded circumcision (Rom. iv. 11, 12) and is in consequence *substantially* foreign to it." [1] It is truly impossible for us to follow Leenhardt in his interpretation (fragmentary in other respects) of Romans iv. Furthermore, how is it that Leenhardt does not see that what he wishes to make Paul say recoils immediately

[1] For this and preceding quotations see *op. cit.*, pp. 88-90.

against his own argument concerning the meaning of baptism? For him, as a matter of principle, faith must precede baptism : "Baptism never precedes faith."[1] Would he, therefore, accept that, because faith precedes baptism, baptism is *substantially* foreign to faith ? Leenhardt's reasoning, when applied to baptism, shows that it is impossible to take it as conclusive. Theo Preiss has remarked that Leenhardt's conception is ill-defined. It seems that here baptism is the sign of something which is *on its way*—that it is accomplishing something undefined that the Word would not and could not accomplish, despite the author's denials—and not the *seal* of something which has been accomplished. We shall return to this point. We have already shown that in Leenhardt's view the sacraments are not seals.

In his pamphlet on Christian baptism Leenhardt says again : " Paul *opposes* one sacrament to the other. . . . In this parallel (Col. ii. 12), the term of comparison is only the idea of ' putting off,' a *carnal* reality in circumcision, a *spiritual* reality in baptism." [2] And : " This latter (*sc.* circumcision) marked *the children of Abraham* for obedience *to the law* . . . (Baptism) sets the converted Christian free from the *obligations* of which *circumcision was the sign.* . . . Paul can also define the setting free of *the son of Abraham* according to the flesh : You have become dead to the law by the body of Christ (Rom. vii. 4) "—and so on.[3] It seems useless for us to insist on bringing forward other proofs. From end to end there is confusion between Abraham and Moses, between the son of Abraham and the son of Moses (in the sense of Judaism), between the circumcision of the covenant of grace and the law. What Leenhardt has himself called " arguments of structure "[4] cannot stand up to an examination which is objective, exegetical, *and* historical. The moment the " structure " vanishes the building tumbles, and with it his conclusion, formulated in such precise terms : " The apology for circumcision which we read from the pen of O. Cullmann, pp. 50, 51, thus signifies an arbitrary and incomprehensible overturning of all (!) that we read from the pen of St. Paul in Romans and Galatians."

[1] *Le Baptême chrétien*, p. 62. [2] *Ibid.*, p. 58.
[3] *Ibid.*, pp. 67, 68. [4] *Foi et Vie, op. cit.*, p. 89.

Such affirmations, even if they enjoy the advantage of conciseness, are unfortunately—we repeat it—*a priori* in character and absolutely incompatible with the texts, whether of Old or New Testaments. Let us bring forward further proof of our contention.

(a) Circumcision is a spiritual sacrament

(i) Historically, there is no justification for placing circumcision on the same plane with the " carnal " ordinances of the Mosaic law. By its origin circumcision is independent both of the promulgation and of the abolition of the law of Moses, which it antedates by more than four centuries.

(ii) Circumcision was given to Abraham (and not to Moses !) as a sign and seal of the justification which he obtained through faith by believing in the promises of the covenant of grace, and thus as a sign of the cleansing away of sins in the same way as is expressed by baptism today. As we have seen, the significance of the covenant of grace was *spiritual*. The promise made to Abraham is *spiritual*, and the Apostle calls it the *Gospel* (Gal. iii. 8). The significance of the rite of circumcision was thus *spiritual* also, not only because the sign was in harmony with the promise (of which it is precisely the sign and seal), but because of the spiritual meaning attributed to circumcision as representing at the same time the promise of God to circumcize the heart of the people and of their children : " The Lord your God will circumcize your heart and the heart of your posterity, so that you may love the Lord your God with all your heart and with all your soul, and that you may live " (Deut. xxx. 6). Circumcision thus represents the obligation resting upon him who had received this sign, in authentication of this promise, to circumcize his heart and to live according to the covenant. It is essential that Deuteronomy vi. 5-9, xxx. 6, and Matthew xxii. 36, 37 should be linked with each other, and parallel passages. It is simply a matter of a summary of the law ! The law and the prophets, and not only the Apostle Paul, proclaim that it is not sufficient to be distinguished externally by the circumcision of the flesh, if the circumcision of the heart is lacking. From this it follows that uncircumcized lips are impure lips, and that an uncircumcized heart is a heart stained with sin.[1] It is not by chance that the terms " circumcize " and " circumcision " are employed to express yielding of the heart, obedience to God, conversion, and faith. Those who are circumcized outwardly but unconverted in their heart are called the " false circumcision," since it is only believers who participate in the *true* circumcision, which is according to the Spirit (Phil. iii. 2, 3 and Rom. ii. 28, 29). O. Cullmann establishes that circumcision is considered as a " being born again " : the circumcized are called " holy." [2]

Circumcision, therefore, truly has a spiritual meaning in perfect harmony with the covenant of grace, itself spiritual, of which it is the sign and seal. The device whereby an attempt is made to divide this Abrahamic covenant into two or three covenants distinct from each other, in order that, to suit the convenience of certain people, a " carnal " element may be inserted into it, has no justification, for when the Bible refers to the covenant with Abraham it always speaks of it in the singular.[3]

(iii) Furthermore, the New Testament interprets the promises made to Abraham in a spiritual manner, the material blessings being only the consequence of the spiritual blessings. Thus, circumcision, which was their sacrament, possesses equally from this angle a spiritual meaning.

(iv) Finally, the New Testament declares that " Christ was the minister of the circumcision for the sake of the truth of God, in order to confirm the promises made to our fathers" (Rom. xv. 8). If, in spite of the texts, it is insisted that the *true* circumcision—that is to say, circumcision as it was settled in the mind of God, and not as it has been deformed by the legalistic conceptions of certain Judaizers—is a *carnal* institution, then Christ was the minister of a carnal institution. If, however, it is impossible to attribute to

---

[1] Cf. in particular, Ex. vi. 2 ; Lev. xxvi. 41 ; Deut. vi, x. 16, xxx. 6 ; Is. i ; Jer. iv. 4, ix. 25 f. ; Ez. xliv. 7 ; Joel ii ; Acts vii. 51 ; Rom. ii. 26-29, iv. 11, etc.

[2] *Op. cit.*, p. 57.

[3] Cf. Ex. ii. 24 ; Lev. xxvi. 42 ; 2 Ki. xiii. 23 ; 1 Chr. xvi. 15 f. ; Ps. cv. 89, etc., etc.

[4] On this the following should be read again : Rom. iv. 16-18 ; 2 Cor. vi. 16-18 ; Gal. iii. 8 f., 14, 16 ; Heb. viii. 10, xi. 9 f., 13.

Christ a carnal ministry, then it follows that the true circumcision is spiritual.[1]

(b) Circumcision was not exclusively the sign of the national covenant with the Hebrews

This follows clearly from the fact that it was concluded with Abraham and that its usage prevailed for hundreds of years before the law was given on Mount Sinai, the moment when the people began to be a nation. Even from the text of the covenant itself it is quite evident that, in principle, this covenant was not national, but rather the contrary.

(i) Mention is made of proselytes from foreign nations who will themselves receive circumcision and who by it will be incorporated, in the first place, into the house of Abraham, and, thereafter, into the people of Israel; and the recruiting of these strangers, based on faith in the God of the covenant, had in itself an *international* character. From the time of its institution circumcision was the seal of a covenant open to all peoples.

(ii) This is further shown by the fact that these passages receive notice in the New Testament, not only in connection with temporal or national blessings, but in connection with the blessings of *redemption*, and their international character is most plainly emphasized. The New Testament interpretation of circumcision is a universalist interpretation.[2] The Jewish missionary spirit prior to Christ's coming affords another proof.

(iii) Abraham is the father of members of the Church of Christ. What we have already observed above finds here a fresh application. Cullman affirms[3] that according to the New Testament " Abraham, not in the sense of natural succession but of divine salvation-history, is the ancestor of the members of the Church of Christ. What holds for Abraham holds also for circumcision, which he received on

---

[1] We know beforehand that there are some who will vigorously contest this point of exegesis. But we hasten to add that we are not confined to this argument. We are not reduced to searching restlessly for proof-texts. On this particular point the Word of God is adequately generous in supplying other texts and other proofs which are beyond dispute.

[2] Cf., for example : Rom. xv. 7-13 ; Gal. iii. 6 ff., 13, 14, 17, 18, iv. 21 ff. And see O. Cullmann, *op. cit.*, pp. 58 f.

[3] *Op. cit.*, p. 59.

the basis of the righteousness of his faith in the promise of this succession." Hence Cullmann adds that circumcision has its meaning for salvation-history, inasmuch as it relates not only to the natural succession but also, from its inception, to the nations of the world.

(iv) The fact remarked above must also be taken into account—so far as some weight is accorded to it—that Christ was the " minister of circumcision."

The New Testament shows that the covenant made with Abraham and the promises which it contained found their fulfilment in Jesus Christ. And of this covenant circumcision was the specific sign and seal. Circumcision is a *spiritual* sacrament both from the point of view of doctrine and from the point of view of practice. Certain pedobaptists have been very much at fault in speaking of circumcision and seeking to support their case with it by considering it *by itself*, without studying it as a sacrament *of the covenant of grace*. In the light of these observations it is obvious that there is a very close kinship between circumcision, a spiritual sacrament of the covenant of grace, and baptism, which is also a spiritual sacrament of the same covenant.

That there is no *essential* or *fundamental* difference between the sacraments of the Old Testament and those of the New is equally apparent from the following considerations.

In 1 Corinthians x. 1-4 Paul attributes to the Church of the Old Testament what is essential in the New Testament sacraments of baptism and the Lord's supper : " Our fathers," he says, " were all *baptized* in Moses in the cloud and in the sea ; they all ate *the same spiritual food*, and they all drank *the same spiritual drink*, for they drank of that spiritual Rock which followed them ; and *that Rock was Christ.*"[1]

Since they represent the same spiritual realities, the names

---

[1] F. -J. Leenhardt, *Le Baptême chrétien*, pp. 49 f., in expounding this text affirms that Paul here causes Moses to play the part of Christ and that Israel " was saved " (!) by the faith which united them to him whom God had placed at their head, etc. Is there any need for us to say that we are obliged to reject completely such an interpretation ?—and we do so primarily because of the clear teaching of Scripture concerning the manner in which men can be " saved." It is not union with Moses that saves people, but union with Christ. Though Moses was a *liberator*, he was not a *saviour*, but simply the mediator through whom the law was given.

of the sacraments of the Old and New Testaments are employed, in texts which have received insufficient notice, *in an interchangeable manner.* Circumcision and the passover are attributed to the Church of the New Testament, baptism and the Lord's supper to the Church of the Old Testament. " Christ *our Passover* has been sacrificed " (1 Cor. v. 7). " In Christ we have been *circumcized*, not with the circumcision made by the hand of man, but with *the circumcision of Christ*, in putting off the body of the flesh " (Col. ii. 11). And this, it will be remembered, was precisely the meaning of the circumcision of Abraham, set in the perspective of the covenant of grace and not in that of the Mosaic covenant. Furthermore, in 1 Corinthians x. 1-4, which we cited above, baptism is attributed to the fathers of the Old Testament and the Lord's Supper is identified with the paschal feast, considered as spiritual food and drink received in Christ.[1]

The sacraments of the Jews tended to the same end as those of the Christians : they led to Jesus Christ, or, if it is preferred, they were images which presented Him to the view of believers and brought Him to their knowledge. Since the sacraments were seals (this is expressly stated of circumcision) by which the promises of God were sealed, and since no promise of God has been made to man *except in and through Jesus Christ* (2 Cor. i. 20), *all* the sacraments exhibit Christ to us, and teach and remind us of the promises of God.

All that we have today in our sacraments the Jews had formerly in theirs, namely, *Jesus Christ and His spiritual riches.* The efficacy of the sacraments of the Old Testament is identical with that of the sacraments of the New, because equally they are signs, seals, and confirmations of the good will of God for the salvation of men. There is, it is true, a difference between the sacraments as regards outward appearance, but they are identical as regards their internal and spiritual significance. *The signs have changed, while faith does not change.*[2]

Finally, the sacraments of the Old Testament imposed on those who received them the same religious and moral

---

[1] One could make analogous remarks regarding the Passover, but they would go beyond the scope of this exposition.
[2] Calvin, *Instt.* IV. xiv. 26 ; 2nd Helv. Conf., xix. 5.

obligations as are imposed today on those who receive the sacraments of the New Testament. " Faith holds the same place in circumcision as in Christian Baptism."[1]   It is, therefore, altogether improper to set a supposedly carnal circumcision over against a spiritual baptism.

2. *Differences between the sacraments of the Old and New Testaments*

Despite the essential unity of the various sacraments of the Old and New Testaments, there are certain differences between them.

(*a*) In the setting of Israel sacraments had a national aspect *in addition to* their spiritual significance as signs and seals of the covenant of grace.

(*b*) In line with the sacraments Israel had many other symbolical rites, such as sacrifices and purifications, which taken together were in harmony with their sacraments, whereas the sacraments of the New Testaments stand quite alone.

(*c*) The sacraments of the Old Testament pointed forward to the incarnate Christ and were the seals of the grace which was *subsequently* to be obtained through the sufferings and death of Christ, whereas those of the New Testament are concerned with and point back to Christ and His perfect redemptive sacrifice, which has now been *accomplished*. The ceremonies of the Old Testament are pointless and meaningless if their reference is not to Christ. Once again, the signs have been changed without faith having changed.

(*d*) In harmony with the whole economy of the Old Testament, a smaller measure of divine grace accompanied the usage of the sacraments than that which is now obtained through an entire faith by the reception of those of the New Testament. When the Word was made flesh the blessings and grace of God reached their plenitude. All our theologians affirm, with Calvin, that our sacraments are " more eminent in significance and more excellent in effect "[2] and that " by their means we obtain a fuller bounty of the Spirit."[3]   In other words, the gift of the Holy Spirit renders

---

[1] O. Cullmann, *op. cit.*, p. 65.   [2] *Instt.* IV. xiv. 22.
[3] 2nd Helv. Conf., xix. 6.

them more efficacious in the Church. But it is only a matter of *degree* that is here in question, of light which is more or less intense. Jesus Christ was offered to the Fathers through their signs, but He offers Himself more fully to us through those which He has now ordained for us, just as is demanded by the nature of the New Testament when compared with the Old. Our communion with God is more perfect.

(*e*) The sacraments of the Old Testament were provisional,[1] whereas those of the New are permanent until the time of Christ's return, when the promises, since they will then be fulfilled and realized, will have no further need to be sealed by the sacraments.[2]

(*f*) The sacraments of the Old Testament are bloody, but those of the New are not. It is, in fact, very remarkable that the two principal sacraments of the Old Testament, circumcision and the passover, were bloody, whereas the two sacraments of the New Testament are *not* bloody sacraments, because *the blood of the covenant has been shed once for all.* In all this there is a faultless harmony and homogeneity : " Where there is forgiveness, there is no further need of offerings (that is to say, bloody offerings) for sin."[3]

(*g*) The sacraments of the New Testament are addressed to a people greater than that of Israel, this people comprising all the Churches of the world.

In bringing this section on circumcision and the unity of the sacraments to a close, we shall offer one last remark of general import. It is a fact of the greatest significance that in all the works written in support of the Baptist position inevitably an attack is found, sooner or later, against circumcision *taken by itself,* or pronouncements which cannot fail to convey a depreciation of its importance, a minimizing of its meaning and value—and that too in spite of the clearest and most unmistakable biblical texts—which tends to pro-

---

[1] We must confine ourselves here to stating the fact, at least in so far as it concerns Christians who are not of Jewish stock. Jewish Christians declare today that their Christian children ought still to be circumcized. We cannot here embark on this vexed problem.
[2] Cf. Th. Preiss, *op. cit.*, p. 115.
[3] Heb. x. 18; cf. 2nd Helv. Conf., xix. 5, 6, and 7 Westm. Conf. xxvii. 5.

duce a crude and misshapen caricature of circumcision. But we do not wish to be misunderstood. Far be it from us to accuse our Baptist brethren of the least degree of bad faith or of wittingly neglecting important texts. Far rather do we believe that it is in all good conscience that they do not read the texts as we do—and this it is which makes the problem so serious !—and that they affirm that circumcision is merely carnal and national in significance.

How does this come about ? What is the subconscious cause which urges them, without their realising it, to deprive circumcision of its proper force ? If it is true that baptism is in essence so different from circumcision, is it then *impossible* for them to do justice to circumcision at the same time as they do justice to their conception of baptism ? Why, moreover, does the *objective* study of the two sacraments seem so difficult ? If the " two " covenants or their dispensations are in their opinion so opposite to each other, is it not *possible* for them to examine their respective contents objectively without radically transforming the content of one of them ? Again, why *is* it so difficult ? Are we not quite right to be very interested in this matter ? Does this not prove that *in reality* (biblical reality !) the thesis of those who oppose infant baptism does not stand so easily on its own feet ? That in order to appear valid it must be seen against an elaborate and meticulously prepared background ? That, in fact, it cannot be maintained except at the cost of distorting the content and the spirit of the Old Testament revelation, to which the New Testament itself bears the fullest testimony ?

The truth is that through the prism of these schematic *a priori* antitheses—namely, carnal and spiritual (which end by being applied to Old and New Testaments respectively by way of opposition), the Jewish nation and the community of professing Christians, the letter of the law (equated with the Old Testament) and the spirit of the Gospel (equated with the New Testament), and so on—the Scriptures, owing to the limitations thus imposed, undergo a general distortion. It seems that those who oppose infant baptism recognise intuitively that if they do justice to the true character of circumcision its affinity with the baptism of children would follow so plainly and so naturally that they would find it impossible to deny to pedobaptists the legitimacy of their conclusions, and would be obliged to revise their own premisses. This, in our opinion, would be the case because in dogmatics everything is interconnected, and such a conception of the sacraments depends on *anterior* theological principles and conclusions which are *exterior* to the texts themselves.

What other conclusion could we justly reach in assessing this attitude which is so surprising, but apparently necessary and inevitable where circumcision is concerned, except that of the internal feebleness of the " Baptist " thesis from the point of view of biblical theology ? If our Baptist brethren had succeeded in presenting their thesis *biblically*, and thereby *explicitly* doing justice to the circumcision of the covenant of grace, as the New Testament itself does justice to that circumcision, the force of their arguments would have been entirely different ! But the kinship between the circumcision of the covenant of grace and Christian baptism would then appear so obvious—we shall discover yet further reasons at the end of this study of the covenant—that it would no longer be possible to maintain with sufficient force the necessity for baptizing adults only, even if for other apparently legitimate and exellent reasons one persisted in wishing to do so.

Let there be no mistake, the line of cleavage between the two sides is traced by the manner, more or less faithful, in which one *respects* the biblical data concerning circumcision as a sacrament of the covenant of grace. In this debate, however, all does not depend upon circumcision, important though it is. It is but a fragment of the covenant of grace, and our Baptist brethren will only achieve their task if they succeed in carrying through a *theological*, that is to say, *scientific* and *biblical*, attack not only on the other constitutive elements of the covenant which we shall study, but *on the covenant itself*. They must attack the very *cause* itself and not simply—for that would be an error of method—one or other of its consequences. We shall permit those who oppose infant baptism to take refuge neither in the subjective conclusions of their personal sentiment, nor in the shadow of *history* and its impositions, nor again in criticism which is called modern and its self-styled "established" results, when, for reasons that are most disputable, they contradict or neglect data of Holy Scripture which are immediate and consequently of capital importance.

D. THE CHURCH IN THE COVENANT

Since the covenant is the same in both Old and New Testaments, and the sacraments have the same fundamental significance, another conclusion urges itself upon us where the objective elements of the covenant are concerned, namely, that through the course of history *the Church has been and remains one : the nation of Israel was the Church ; the Christian Church, since it also comes under the covenant of grace, is the same Church.*

1. *The Nation of Israel was the Church*

In the New Testament the people of Israel are called " the Church " (Acts vii. 38). God separated the Hebrews from all the nations of the earth so that they might become His own people and constitute His kingdom. It is to them that the oracles of God were entrusted. They were *Israelites* : it is to them that the adoption, the glory, the covenants, the giving of law, the service of God, and the promises belong (Rom. x. 4). One cannot say more than this of the Christian Church.

The Israelites were chosen with a view to forming a Church, that is to say, with a view to their being God's witnesses in the world on behalf of true religion, the promoters of His worship, and the keepers of His commandments. Their religious authorities, their prophets and their priests, were set apart by God and were His ministers. No one could become a member of the nation of Israel without taking the place of a disciple, without promising obedience to God's law revealed in His Word, and without submitting himself to the rite of circumcision which was the seal of the covenant. *No authentic definition of the Church can exclude the Church of the people of God in the Old Testament.*[1]

---

[1] Semantic researches in connection with the word *ecclesia* have confirmed this point and have shown that in the Septuagint version of the Old Testament *qahal* was translated by *ecclesia*. Cf. Kittel : *Theol. Wörterb. zum N.T.*, The Church (transl. by J. R. Coates).

Of course, Israel was also a State. But under the old
economy Church and State were identical. No one could be
a member of one without being a member of the other. In
the pure theocracy the chief priest was head of the State at
the same time as head of the Church. The priests and Levites
were civil as well as religious dignitaries. The sacrifices
and the feasts, and even the Passover, which was always
regarded as a sacrament, were simultaneously national and
religious ceremonies.

All this flows from the nature of God's covenant with
Abraham, which, as we have seen, comprised promises
of national as well as religious import. God chose the
descendants of this patriarch in order that they might
become His own people ; He made of them a nation which
was to be separated from all other nations and protected
against them ; He gave them a territory, and decreed for
them a code of laws which embraced at one and the same
time their civil, national, social, personal, and religious
duties. All these provisions were interwoven with each
other. The relations of the people with the civil power and
with God were not regarded as distinct. Whatever the nature
of their obligations, they were towards God. They were a
holy people, a Church constituted in a nation. The great
promise, as we have seen, was the promise of the redemption
of the world through the Messiah, to which all else was
subservient. Even the plan of forming the Hebrews into
a distinct nation, and the reasons for which they were
separated from other peoples, were intended to keep alive
the knowledge of this promise. Nearly all the significance
and value of the priesthood, the sacrifices and the temple
service lay in their prefiguration of the person, offices, and
work of the Messiah. The oracles of God entrusted to the
people were concerned with the special work of redemption.

It would be a contradiction to assume that a man could
have been a Jew without at least professing his belief in
these promises and prophecies and taking his place as a
disciple. Consequently, a man was a member of the Jewish
community solely in virtue of the fact that he was a member
of the Jewish Church. It was absolutely impossible for him to
be a member of the one without being a member of the other.

2. *The Christian Church is the continuation of the Church of Israel*

The Christian Church is not a *new* Church, but identical with that of Israel. There is but *one olive-tree* and it lives on (Rom. xi. 16 ff.). The Christian Church is founded on the same covenant and on the same Gospel: the promise of redemption by Christ. Because of the continuity of the covenant the new Israel is grafted into the old, and there is now but a single people.

This doctrine, according to which the Church is today founded on the Abrahamic covenant—in other words, that the plan of salvation revealed in the Gospel was revealed to Abraham and to the saints of the Old Testament, and that they were saved in exactly the same manner as has been the case with men since the coming of Christ, namely, by faith in Christ—this doctrine is not revealed to us in Scripture in an incidental manner. It forms an integral part of the very substance of the Gospel. It is present in the teaching of our Lord, who came to fulfil and not to abolish the promise (Lk. xxiv. 27), and who bade those who interrogated Him to search the Scriptures of the Old Testament if they wished to understand what He, the Christ, was teaching.

The Apostles did just the same. The Christians at Berea were praised because they examined the Scriptures every day in order to verify whether the doctrines taught by the Apostles accorded with this infallible norm (Acts xvii. 11). These messengers of Christ made constant reference to the Old Testament in support of their teaching. Paul said that the Gospel which he preached had already been taught in the law and the prophets (Rom. iii. 21 f.). He declared to the Gentiles that they were grafted into the old olive-tree so that they might partake of its root and sap (Rom. xi. 17).

It is thus entirely illegitimate to maintain that there is an *essential* contrast between the New Testament covenant of grace and that same covenant in the Old Testament. The Gospel covenant of grace is the prolongation of the Abrahamic covenant. The Christian Church is the continuation of the Church of Israel.

There are some who will not subscribe to these conclusions and, in view of principles which they esteem as superior, we shall say that they do not appear to regard themselves

G

as bound by the exegesis of the Apostles ! Theirs is an
easy-going attitude which permits the saying and affirming
of everything and equally the suppressing and denying of
everything. Do they wish to pretend that they possess a
greater measure of the Holy Spirit than the Apostles and a
better understanding of the " secrets " of God ? To reject
the authority of the Apostles on one point is to invalidate
any authoritative appeal to them when our opinion happens
to be in accordance with theirs ! If the exegesis of the
Apostles is not binding, what other exegesis can claim to be
able to bind our minds and hearts ? For ourselves, we feel
ourselves bound, and not only bound, but constrained and
persuaded by the exegesis of the Apostles, and at this point
of the debate we can only say to those who disagree with us :
Non possumus.

In conclusion, God has always had but a single Church
in the world. The God of the Old Testament is our Lord :
the God of Abraham, of Isaac, and of Jacob is the God of our
covenant and our Father. Our Saviour was the Saviour of
the saints who lived before His coming in the flesh. The
divine Person who brought the Israelites out of Egypt
and led them through the wilderness, who appeared in all
His glory to Isaiah in the temple, and towards whose coming
the eyes of the people of God have from the beginning been
turned in faith and hope, is the same whom we acknowledge
as God manifest in the flesh, our Lord and Saviour Jesus
Christ. Consequently, He who was the Head of the Theocracy is the Head of the Church. The blood which He shed
for us has been shed from the foundation of the world, as
well to atone for the transgressions committed under the
first Testament (Heb. ix. 15) as for us and our salvation.
The promise, whose fulfilment the twelve tribes who fervently served God night and day awaited (Acts xxvi. 7), is
precisely the promise upon which we rest. The faith which
saved Abraham was, as far as its nature and its object were
concerned, the very same as that which is the condition of
salvation under the Gospel. " The city which has secure
foundations, whose architect and maker is God " (Heb. xi. 10)
is the Jerusalem resplendent with glory, the new heavens,
to which we aspire.

II

THE SUBJECTIVE, INDIVIDUAL, AND ECCLESIAS-TICAL ASPECTS OF THE COVENANT OF GRACE

THE BENEFICIARIES OF THE COVENANT

A. TO WHOM IS THE COVENANT OF GRACE OFFERED ?

Wherever the Gospel is preached and complete salvation in Jesus Christ (and consequently the covenant of which Christ is the Mediator) is proclaimed, the covenant is offered to every man who, sinful and fallen, has perverted his ways and is incapable in himself of regaining communion with God and of holding to it. The condition on which " a man who has attained the age of discretion "[1] may *enter* into the covenant is that he should voluntarily accept its terms through faith. For the proselyte, the pagan, or the atheist to whom the Gospel is announced and the covenant offered, it is the acceptance by faith of the promises of the covenant and the confession of his faith which determine his entry *into* the covenant. In this case, faith is a condition *of* the covenant. Through the preaching of the. Gospel the covenant is thus offered to a considerable number of men and women amongst whom—thanks to the effective working in them of the Holy Spirit at the time of the preaching of the Word, and according to the inscrutable purposes of the grace of God—some believe in the promise and accept the terms of the salvation which is offered to them. To the promise of God, " I am your God and your Saviour," they reply by faith, " I am Thy child."

[1] Henceforward we shall use the simple term " adult." It is obvious that the word " adult " ought not to be taken in its judicial sense of legal majority. The age of spiritual maturity varies according to a number of factors. The constant changes of opinion concerning the age of catechumens in the Church are attempts at establishing accuracy in this matter. In the Old Testament it was generally fixed at about twelve years. There are also differences for girls and boys.

Under the Old Testament the conditions of *entry into* the covenant were a sincere profession of faith in the true religion, the promise of obedience, and submission to the rite of admission which was prescribed. The sincere proselyte really received Jehovah for his God, and placed his trust in all His promises and especially in the promise of redemption through the posterity of Abraham. He did not confine himself merely to obedience to the law of God such as was then revealed, but he strove sincerely to abide in the covenant and to keep its commandments. Thenceforth he occupied a place in the Church and nation of Israel equal to that of a son or daughter in the natural line of descent, and he participated in their sacraments.

In the New Testament the Christian Church demands from those whom it receives as members of its *visible* communion nothing more than a sincere profession of faith, the promise of obedience to Jesus Christ in repentance, and the submission to baptism regarded as the rite of admission.[1]

We therefore affirm that for *entering into* the covenant of grace there was no alteraticn in the conditions of the admission into the Church of proselytes subsequently to the proclamation of the Gospel. For remaining in the covenant, and consequently in the Church, the requisite conditions are exactly the same in the two Testaments. This confirms our conclusions concerning the unity of the covenant and the unity of the Church.

Apart from the eventuality of a false or hypocritical profession of faith, we observe that adults enter into the covenant considered as a legal relationship and as a communion of life. It behoves them not only to acquit themselves of certain external duties, and to promise further that they will thenceforward put their saving faith into practice ; they confess also that they accept the covenant with a living faith and that it is their desire and intention to persevere in this faith. They enter, consequently, at a single stroke into the life of the covenant taken in its fulness. This is, moreover, the only manner in which adults can *truly* enter into the covenant.

---

[1] We shall return later to certain aspects of this question and study them in greater detail.

B. THE COVENANT OF GRACE, PLACE OF VOCATION AND
ELECTION

However, it is only in the case of proselytes that the faith
of the believer is a condition *of* the covenant.

(a) The covenant imposed by God

The great revelation that Scripture affords us from the
time of Abraham onwards is precisely that God, in His
good pleasure and incomprehensible mercy, chose from the
universal mass of fallen men one family, one people, one
nation to be and to remain His own people, to establish
a covenant with them and their posterity, to communicate
to them the plenitude of His grace and salvation, and to
reveal to them His glory. God chose Abraham and his line,
Israel and his posterity. *This covenant is a relationship
which God imposes in His sovereignty.* Abraham did not
choose it ! *It pleased God* to make a covenant with him.
Israel was not consulted, generation by generation, regarding
the suitability and reality of this covenant. *It was imposed
upon them by the sovereign God.* God chose the heirs of the
promise according to His pleasure. The attitude of God is
independent of the behaviour of man, of his inclination
or his disinclination, of his love or his antipathy regarding
this relationship. Despite anything that man may do or
wish to do in order to destroy this relationship and to rid
himself of it, he can in no wise alter the immutable will of
God : " You are *My* people and I am *your* God." [1]

It is essential to emphasize this fundamental *objective*
character of the covenant. Here, the reality of the covenant
does not depend on the behaviour of man : it precedes it.
Judicially, man is placed *in* the covenant, whether he wishes
it or not. He cannot prevent God saying to him, " I am your
God." Here, the free decree of God is anterior to every human
proceeding, and *always* so. He deals with whom it pleases
Him to deal : *the covenant precedes faith.* Since *in this way*
the condition of participation in the covenant depends on God
alone, faith is no longer the requisite condition of membership.
The covenant of grace was not established with man in his

[1] Cf. the texts cited above.

capacity as believer, because faith is itself *the fruit* of the covenant. Faith not being a condition *of* the covenant, but a condition *in* the covenant, the covenant precedes faith.

(b) *Man must respond to it*

" I *shall be* your God, and you *shall be* My people." Here, there is no escape for man. He must respond. God speaks, decides, demands, and man *must* submit himself and respond. God offers to re-establish between Himself and man an intimate and deep relationship, a communion of life, and consequently to perform for him the promises which He has uttered.   God promises to establish an intimate union, compared in Scripture to that which unites husband and wife or a father and his children. And *here* the choice does not rest with man : he *must* respond and his response *must* be that of true, trusting, and consecrated love. God promises to be his God ; and man *must* respond that he wishes to belong to Him and to throw in his lot with that of His people. God promises him justification through the forgiveness of sins, filial adoption, eternal life ; and man *must* respond by saving faith in Jesus Christ and entrust himself to God for time and for eternity by a life of obedience and consecration.

The sinner is exhorted to repent and believe ; but his faith and repentance give him no meritorious claim to the blessings of the covenant. For he is, in fact, incapable of responding to it by himself, and God does not expect him to fulfil in his own strength the demands made by the covenant. Confronted with the demands of the covenant, it is only from God that man can obtain the power necessary for the fulfilment of its duties, in accordance with the promise which has been made to him : " The Lord your God will circumcize your heart and the heart of your posterity, in order that you may love the Lord your God with all your heart and with all your soul and with all your life " (Dt. xxx. 6 ; cf. viii. 18).

(c) *Through the grace promised man can respond to it*

It is here that the richness of the promises of the covenant and their efficacy appear. Knowing that of himself man is incapable of responding to His order and of appropriating

His promises with faith, God does not content Himself
with decreeing the obligations of the covenant or announcing
the promises. What purpose do those promises serve which
man, in his inability to do good and to believe, cannot
receive because he fails to comprehend them ? The answer
is—and this is a point of prime importance—that with the
promise (and with its demands) God by His Holy Spirit
gives man that which is necessary before it can be welcomed,
received, and believed. *At the same time God makes the
promise that He will render man capable of receiving the
promise!* In a certain sense, God pledges Himself to
accomplish in man the conditions which He demands from
him. To the promise is joined the gift of God whereby man
can—and consequently *must*—respond by faith to the
promises heard (Dt. viii. 18 ; xxx. 6, 11-20). Faith, which
was not a condition *of* the covenant, becomes by the grace
of God the condition realized for abiding *in* the covenant.
To the covenant offered to sinful man God adds subjectively
in man the desire and the deed, in order that His fallen
creature maý voluntarily and freely accept this covenant and
confirm it, and be able to abide in it.[1]

The covenant of grace is a covenant in the name of which
God promises with an oath that if we wish it (the possibility
of thus wishing constitutes a dynamic part of the promise)
we shall feel and know Him to be our Father and our
Saviour, and that He will really be so : He will not leave us in
sin and in death. In virtue of this covenant we always have
a *right* before Him to His paternal welcome and to the
blessings of His promises, if we desire them (the possibility
of thus desiring forms part of the promise). It gives the
assurance that those who are born *in* the covenant will never
be excluded from grace if they desire and demand it.

(*d*) *The glory of God is exalted for the benefit of man in regeneration and liberation*

It is most important to observe that this doctrine of the
covenant which, as we have said, upholds so fully and

[1] In other texts which we have cited above, the affirmation, that God by
His Spirit will perform what is needful for man to be able to respond
positively to His advances, appears many times. It is also one of the
central affirmations of the New Testament.

rigorously the sovereignty of God in the work of salvation at the same time, precisely because it does so, equally and in a beautiful manner does justice to the rational and moral nature of man. In the covenant of grace man *must be* and *is* active. Although a fallen creature, God wishes to treat him as having been created in His image and to place him on the ground where, inasmuch as he is a responsible and inexcusable creature, he will be confronted with his eternal salvation or his eternal perdition ; and he is active : he must *choose* (Dt. xxx. 15-20). God wishes to make him enter into this covenant voluntarily and freely, and in doing so to break voluntarily and freely with sin. After having projected and established it, God Himself fulfils the covenant. It must be received and kept by man voluntarily and freely. God wishes that the work of grace should be reflected in the human conscience, and not only in the conscience, but in every part of man ; it excites man's will and man's faculties to act with a grand energy. By His Holy Spirit God makes it possible for fallen man to declare himself and to choose the life of the covenant when Christ is offered to him.

Let us not imagine, then, that God's decision to possess Himself of man by a decree leaves man passive and inert. It is the opposite that takes place ! The covenant of grace does not kill man ; it does not regard him as a block or a piece of wood, but it takes possession of the man, it lays hold of him in his entirety with all his faculties and powers of soul and body, for time and for eternity ; it does not annihilate his powers, but it removes his powerlessness ; it does not destroy his will, but frees it from sin ; it does not stifle or obliterate his conscience, but sets it free from darkness ; it regenerates and recreates man in his entirety and, in renewing him by grace, causes him to love and consecrate himself to God freely, spontaneously, voluntarily, with all his heart, all his soul, all his mind, and all his powers, both of spirit and of body.

The covenant of grace testifies to the fact that the honour and glory of God are not gained to the disadvantage of man, but on the contrary to his benefit, and reach their zenith in the regeneration of the entire man, in his enlightened conscience, in his restored liberty.

(e) As the seed-bed of election, the covenant edifies the body of Christ

The effects of the covenant are really and concretely applied to us to the glory of God which becomes our glory.

The death of Jesus Christ could not have been in vain : it is efficacious. God has promised to His Son that He will not be a King without a kingdom and subjects. As for these subjects, God takes them in the first place and normally in the covenant, thus in the Church, by promising to all those who are born in it that He wishes to be their Father, to justify them, and to lead them to life. All that is necessary for us truly to be able to have the conviction that He is our Father and Saviour in Jesus Christ has been accomplished by Him.

It is for this reason that, from the viewpoint of God's decision and consequently of the call which God addresses to the sons and daughters of the covenant, and because of the grace active in their hearts, all the sons and daughters of the covenant are obliged, in conscience, to enter into this covenant and to live by it. To adduce textual justification for this *obligation* of the children *of* the covenant to walk *in* the covenant and, after having confirmed it, to *abide* in it, would entail citing almost all the Scriptures. For those whom God inserts in His covenant justifying faith, sanctifying grace, and so on, are the *consequences* of the covenant and of the promise made by God : " I will be *your* God."

The covenant of grace reveals, therefore, that God does not choose His elect just anywhere. He chooses them *in the first place* and *normally* in the covenant. The biblical history of redemption confirms this fact with emphasis. The covenant of grace delimits one sort of inner circle whence the elect are called and lay hold of their vocation. The covenant is the seed-bed at whose centre election to life eternal is realized. In the covenant Christ is the Head, the Chief, and the Representative of His own, but in no wise does He supplant or annihilate them in their personality. He offers Himself to them in such a way that, instructed and prepared by His Spirit, they consent freely to this covenant. The covenant of grace has certainly been concluded with Christ in this pact of salvation or covenant of redemption to which we have made allusion, but beyond the Head and through Him it is extended to all those who are His own, and it lays hold of them completely, body and soul. Election is realized *in* and *through* the covenant which demands faith and conversion of its own.

It is very important not to consider the covenant from the sole angle of its *final* efficacy or as an end in itself : the covenant is a means administered in view of an end, namely, the salvation of the greatest number.

(f) *The organic character of the covenant*

Scripture teaches us that the covenant of grace has an organic character. In the two Testaments it is realized by means of an historic process ; it perpetuates itself in the midst of successive generations and brings together believers in a new *organism*, which is the Church, with Christ as Head.

In the covenant Christ appears as having taken the place of Adam, as the second Head of the human race. Adam has been replaced by Christ. Humanity which fell in Adam is restored in Christ. It is not simply individuals, separate from each other, who are saved, but rather, through Christ, the *organism* of humanity and of the universe itself which is saved in the person of the elect. The structure of the new organism is assumed from the original creation in Adam, regenerated and restored. The covenant of grace is the organization of the new humanity, with Christ as Head, attaching itself to the order of creation, ceaselessly relating itself to it, and thereby making the whole of this creation qualitatively and intensively secure.[1]

(g) *The historic character of the covenant :* " *From generation to generation* "

Here is the reason why the covenant of grace does not jump from one individual to another : it displays itself

[1] Cf. F. -J. Leenhardt, *op. cit.*, p. 25 : " The fulfilment of messianic prophecy in Jesus is a resumption of the original work. Redemption is related to creation. It has a cosmic significance ; it concerns the relationships of God not only with men, but with the world." O. Cullmann, *op. cit.*, p. 34 : " In the New Testament there is on the one side a humanity redeemed by Christ, and on the other a Church, a universal *Regnum Christi* and a narrower body of Christ." This idea, which is very pregnant, needs to be developed. It exceeds the scope of our subject and we have not the leisure to deal with it here.

organically and historically; it travels through history and it has different dispensations. It is conformed to the times and occasions determined by the Father who, as Creator, is by His providence sovereign over history. It was never simply concluded with one or other person taken individually—always *his posterity* is included in it: it is a covenant "*from generation to generation.*" It never embraces the mere personality of believers considered abstractly in its individuality, but concretely with respect to the concrete personality as it exists and lives historically; not this particular person, not this person *alone,* but *with him* all that belongs to him; not only for *his own* sake, but this person as a father, with his posterity, with everything connected with him, with his money and goods, with his influence and authority, his profession and his relationships, with his intelligence and his heart, his science and his art, with his social life and his political life.

C. THE CHILDREN OF THE COVENANT

(a) The heirs of the promise

It is the will of God, clearly revealed in Scripture, to count the children of believers amongst the members of the covenant which He freely established in His sovereignty: "I will be your God and the God of your posterity after you ; I will circumcize your heart and the heart of your posterity."

Scripture contains very precise and specific promises concerning the *children* of believers, the posterity of those whom God has introduced into His covenant—promises made to children and for children in their capacity as children or " little children," who are regarded by God and by Christ in a particularly benevolent manner—promises made to children as posterity which in its turn arrives at adult age.[1]

Scripture teaches us that children born in the covenant are *heirs.* But their heritage is *that of the promise,* of which the Holy Spirit is the pledge. We can never insist too much on this point in opposition to those who obstinately maintain

[1] Cf. Gen. ix. 8 ff. ; xvii. 7, 9-12 ; Dt. v. 2 f. ; xxix. 29 ; Num. xviii. 19 ; xxv. 10-12 ; Ps. xc. 16 ; cii. 28 f. ; ciii. 18 ; cxii. 1 f. ; cxv. 14 f. ; Is. xliv. 2-5 ; lix. 21 ; lxv. 23 ; Jer. xxxii. 38-41 ; Hag. ii. 5 ; Lk. i. 50, 54 f. ; Gal. iii. 16 ; Heb. xi. 9, etc.

that according to us the heritage has to do with salvation. These children do not inherit salvation and eternal life. Salvation is not hereditary ! They inherit only the promises. It behoves them thereafter to receive the *content* of the promise by faith and repentance, and thus by regeneration and conversion, and to live a life consecrated to the Lord. Then, and then only, will they be heirs of *the things promised*. The heritage is only communicated to the heir who receives the promise *with faith*.[1]

The promises of God concerning the little children of the covenant are all the same considerable, and one must needs be blind not to comprehend their importance. Are we not obliged to believe in the universality of the condemnation of sinners, unless it should please God to remove this condemnation ? He says that He has removed it for the children of the covenant. Are we not obliged to believe in salvation by grace, that is to say, in the liberty of God to call whom He wishes ? Now, it is here that God reveals the methods of His grace. He does not leave us in doubt. He *will call* us sons and daughters, and He will circumcize the heart. He reveals to us that He wishes to choose His elect in the covenant, and that the children for their part are treated with favour. This is indeed a sensational declaration ! Let us see what is its significance both for parents and for children.

(b) The promises made to parents

God promises to parents, to future parents of the covenant, that He considers their children in the covenant and, consequently, in His kingdom and in His Church, and that He wishes thereafter to make them living members of the covenant.

What does this mean except that He promises that, when the time has come that they have reached the age of discretion and the Gospel of the covenant has been presented to them, their children will have the *possibility* of freely,

---

[1] Ps. xvi. 6 ; lxi. 6 ; cxix. 111 ; Is. lviii. 14. It is very remarkable that this concept of heirs and of heritage is valued above all in the New Testament : cf. Rom. iv. 13-17 ; viii. 17 ; Gal. iii. 18-29 ; iv. 7 ; Eph. i. 11, 14, 18 ; Col. i. 12 ; iii. 24 ; Tit. iii. 7 ; Heb. vi. 17 f. ; ix. 15 ; xi. 7 ; Jam. ii. 5. These ideas of heredity and of heritage are linked and associated with those of *sonship* and, consequently, with *the paternity of God*, and there is nothing astonishing in the fact that they are frequently found in Scripture.

voluntarily, and consciously choosing between good and evil, blessing and cursing, life and death (Dt. xxx. 11-20, and all similar texts), the possibility and the liberty of confirming the covenant offered by God and of loving and serving their Redeemer.[1] And all this is so because God wishes to make them living members of the covenant. To parents He promises that He wishes to be the God of their children and to bring them to Himself. He sets parents free from the fearful unrest which would haunt them if they were obliged to ask themselves : " Does God wish to be the Father of my child ? " without any reply being afforded them. In the economy of salvation which ever assigns the chief prominence to the sovereign freedom of God, who loves whom He wills, who has mercy on whom He wills, and who shows grace to whom He wills, who is revealed to whom He wills and chooses whom He wills, this is a question which every Christian parent should be obliged to ask. But God sets parents free from the anguish of this uncertainty and from the hazards of a subjective and human reply. To this question which every converted parent ought, within the free economy of free grace, to ask : " Does God wish to be the Father of my child *also* ? " God Himself in His amazing goodness provides the divine and paternal answer, which confirms the whole biblical revelation of the plan of salvation : " Yes, it is My wish ! I will be your God and the God of your posterity after you. You will be saved, together with your family." He keeps the promise He has made : " Choose life, in order that you may live, together with your posterity " (Dt. xxx. 19).

Consequently, God in His grace undertakes with an oath to receive the children of believers as long as they live, on condition that these children in turn appropriate the promise by faith. If they ask Him to be their Father, He will be. Moreover, God is not content simply to have made this promise : He produces the conditions necessary for the promise to become effective. The covenant is more than a

[1] Viewed from the angle of man's corruption and his inability to do good, this possibility is in itself something altogether extraordinary which ought justly to excite our wonderment. This possibility and this liberty are already the work of the special grace of God.

simple offer of salvation, and more also than an offer of salvation to which the promise concerning faith in the Gospel has been added. It affords the assurance, founded on the promises of God, that God will work within the children of the covenant when, where, and as it pleases Him.

God, according to the promise, restores liberty of choice to the children of the covenant,[1] with the result that, confronted with the alternative of life or death, they are able voluntarily and freely to embrace the one or the other. God assures believers that they will not beget sons and daughters in order to see them perish eternally : He wishes to be their Father. If they are lost, if they refuse the grace of the covenant, it is because they themselves have *chosen* the way of perdition. They will not be lost for the reason that the divine grace has never been offered to them, but, on the contrary, for the reason that this grace has been offered to them with the possibility of their receiving it, and they have despised and rejected it. Christian parents cannot avoid envisaging and accepting the risk of such a free decision on the part of their children. But God will have spoken to these children. He makes this promise to parents in virtue, not of their merits, but of His grace, to which He has given expression in a covenant from generation to generation.

(c) *The promises made to children*

Independently of what has just been said, God assures the children of the covenant that He loves them for the sake of their fathers and the promise made to them. His gifts and His calling are irrevocable. He is solemnly committed to help them each time that they ask Him for help.[2] He assures them that if, after their backslidings and failures, they repent and believe in the promise, they can present themselves before Him with the assurance of being heard and pardoned. The child of the covenant can say to *his* God : " Remember Thou Thy covenant " (Ps. lxxiv. 20).

---

[1] How ? When ? By internal regeneration and by making the proclamation of the Gospel efficacious for them. The promises are sufficient for us and we do not need to construct hazardous psychological explanations.

[2] Reference should be made on this point to all the texts where God entreats His rebellious children to ask Him for help because He will hear them *in accordance with the promise.*

" Do not cast me off ! Do not forget to have pity ! Do not cause Thy mercies to cease" (Ps. lxxvii. 7-10). " Turn Thou me according to Thy promise and I shall truly be turned : for Thou art the Lord my God " (cf. Jer. xxxi. 18). God promises that He will hear and grant and dispense the riches of His mercy.

If they so wish, the children of the covenant can thus confirm this covenant and break with sin, for God gives them the possibility of doing so. He has provided and will provide them with sufficient grace so that they may not necessarily succumb to temptation and may choose and hold to the path which leads to life.

(d) The responsibility of children, parents, and the Church

Will all the children *of* the covenant enter *into* the covenant and confirm it ? Although the children of believers enter by birth into the covenant, considered as a legal relationship, and, although they continue throughout their lives to be legally bound by its demands, Scripture on the one hand and experience on the other teaches us that this does not mean to say that *all* are or will be likewise *in* the covenant considered as a communion of life.

Because of the liberty granted to man of giving or with-holding his heart the covenant does not always attain to full realization. It has not been promised that all the children of the covenant are of the number of the elect. But, on the basis of what we have said above, parents and the Church in the exercise of its ministry ought to be reasonably assured that the covenant is not and will not be, as far as they are concerned, a mere legal relationship with its external obligations and its privileges, only showing what *ought* to be, but that it is also or will in time become a *living reality*. As long as the children of the covenant do not by their conduct give evidence of the contrary, we ought to consider them as being in possession of the life of the covenant. The grace of the covenant, in fact, is not always saving grace, absolutely efficacious and infallibly conducive to salvation ; it is resistible grace which may suffer revolt and which involves the full responsibility of him who rejects it and consciously, voluntarily, and freely chooses the road which leads to perdition. "The possession by a child of Christian parentage is indeed," as Cullmann points out, "no guarantee of subsequent faith," but a "divine indication" of its probability.[1]

From this angle the promises of God regarding efficacious and saving grace are not given to the posterity of believers as separate individuals, but in a collective sense. The promise that the covenant will be given its full accomplishment in the children of believers does not indicate that God wishes, strictly speaking, to endow *all* the children of believers with saving faith. A certain number of them will voluntarily choose unbelief or rebellion despite the work of God in their hearts by the Holy Spirit, despite the Gospel offer of grace and pardon in Jesus Christ, despite the liberty —a fruit of grace—which is theirs to believe and confirm the covenant. It is not all Israel which is the true Israel and the children of believers are not all the children of the promise in the perfection of its fulfilment.

There is, indeed, another important element which enters into the effectiveness of the covenant. The fulfilment of its promises in the hearts of the children depends *also* on an express condition of the covenant, namely, the teaching by parents of their children from their earliest years, the expounding to them of the promise, and, consequently, the announcing to them, of the Gospel at the family hearth as well as in the Church. It is here that the faithfulness of parents and of the Church comes into play. "Hear, O Israel, the Lord our God is one God ! You shall love the Lord your God with all your heart, with all your soul, and with all your strength. The commandments which I enjoin upon you this day shall be engraved in your hearts, and *you shall teach them diligently to your children* ; you shall speak of them when you are in your house, when you are travelling, when you lie down, and when you rise up. You shall bind them for a sign to your hand, and you shall carry them as frontlets between your eyes. You shall also inscribe them upon the posts of your house and on your gates. . . . Therefore lay up the words I have spoken to you in your hearts and in your souls " (Dt. vi. 4-9 ; xi. 18 ; cf. 19 ff. ; Gen. xvii. 19).

[1] O. Cullmann, *op. cit.*, p. 51.

This emphasizes once more the dynamic character of the covenant and man's active rôle. All Christian pedagogy ought to be founded on the injunctions and promises of the covenant. This implies the need for a profound reform of all pedagogy which professes to be Christian but which is not founded upon the covenant of grace.

For this reason it is absolutely essential for parents and the Church, whose common ministry is that of the covenant, to remind the children of the covenant ceaselessly of the necessity for regeneration and conversion, while at the same time presenting to them the Gospel of grace. If parents or the Church (how disastrous when it is *both* !) neglect to do this, they despise one of the conditions governing the effectiveness of the promise which has been made to them *and* to their posterity. Faith comes through the Word preached. Where this preaching has no place the covenant, short of a miracle of God, is not and cannot be confirmed.

One cannot emphasize enough the fact that the faith of parents in the promise of the covenant is one of the elements connected with the fulfilment of the covenant in their posterity. The reason for this is the " spiritual solidarity " which we shall study below, and also God's promise, in Scripture, to grant to him who believes and prays that which He Himself has bidden him to believe and ask for in accordance with His promise. Beyond doubt the promises of the covenant will be fulfilled when parents, clinging to these promises by faith, entreat and supplicate God, in the name of these promises, to be faithful to His promises in regard to their posterity. Here is the rule of the prayer of faith, based upon the promises, uttered by God's order : the granting of such prayer is assured.[1]

If it were possible to know exactly the reason why numerous children of the covenant have not confirmed the covenant and have not been saved, one might discover that the reason is very frequently the incredulity of the parents who have not taken the promises seriously and who, consequently, in a certain sense, have disowned one of the essential conditions of the covenant. They have, it is true, believed for

---

[1] Cf. P.-Ch. Marcel, *A l'Ecoute de Dieu*, pp. 309 ff., on the granting of prayer.

H

themselves, but not for their children. Here again individualism results in dreadful catastrophe. The promise, however, is explicit : " Believe in the Lord Jesus Christ and thou shalt be saved, thou *and thy family* " (Acts xvi. 31).

The same remark applies to the *sanctification* of parents *for* their children in the spiritual solidarity of the family (of this more below). " Enter into the ark," said God to Noah, " thou and *all thy family*, for I have seen that *thou* art righteous before Me in this generation " (Gen. vii. 1).

Thus when the children of believers arrive at the age of discretion, from the simple fact that they are *of* the covenant they cannot assume that they are the heirs of *salvation* : to them it belongs to be converted and, by a true confession of personal faith, to accept voluntarily the responsibilities of the covenant which are incumbent upon them. To refuse to do so is, strictly speaking, to destroy the covenant relationship between themselves and their God and Saviour.

The children of believers are associated with the covenant in such a way that the covenant, considered as a legal relationship with all the obligations and promises which it contains, is found to be the most effective means whereby this legal relationship is transformed into a communion of life. The covenant of grace is a means to an end, namely, to arouse and call the elect ; and, on the other hand, to render those who refuse salvation absolutely inexcusable.[1]

" In the time elapsing between the Resurrection and the Parousia of Jesus," says Karl Barth,[2] " the relationship between parents and children can no longer have the decisive significance which it had for pre-messianic Israel." In support of this important assertion Karl Barth has cited two texts [3] : Romans iv. 2 and John i. 12 f. " According to Romans iv. 2," he says, " the succession of those who

---

[1] In stressing the significance of the covenant considered as a means to an end we must beware of unduly exaggerating God's demands and the resulting human obligations. We ought, on the contrary, to stress the promise of the effective operation of the grace of God in the hearts of the children of the covenant. If we insist exclusively on the responsibilities of the covenant, if we exaggerate them even, and if we fail to give preeminence to the fact that, in the covenant, God gives what He demands of us, or, in other words, that *His promises cover all His demands*, we are in danger of falling into the snare of Arminianism.

[2] *Op. cit.*, p. 50.   [3] *Ibid.*, p. 44.

believed this promise and in this faith were true children of Abraham was, however, already in pre-messianic Israel in no way identical with the succession of the race and the circumcision or its (male !) members." To this O. Cullmann replies [1] that " the analogical affirmation is permissible for Baptism also, since attestation by faith is decisive *after* the reception of the gift of grace. If the succession of the circumcised is not coincident with that of the believing, this is due not to *circumcision* but to the *circumcized*. Hence Abraham was instituted as father of the circumcized and the uncircumcized according to God's determined plan to save. It is because of the way in which the circumcized have behaved themselves that circumcision . . . no longer constitutes the boundary line which separates between those who are and those who are not the children of Abraham." This observation is valuable, even where the practice of baptizing adults only is concerned.

Can one invoke the very text of the institution of the covenant against the covenant of grace and its organic principle of generation to generation ? In itself, Karl Barth's observation is very just. It demonstrates that the same will be the case in the sphere of the covenant under the New Testament ; and this is what we have already demonstrated and shall again demonstrate when we come to speak of the unregenerate in the Church.

Karl Barth proceeds to comment on John i. 12 f. : "The succession of those called to the Church of the new covenant is plainly not dependent on a racial succession, not on family or nation, but comes in this way : in the life of the individual, now here in this manner, now there in another, there comes an acceptance of Jesus, a faith in His name. It is this which gives him the power to become a child of God." (i) But verse 11 must not be forgotten : " The Word came to *His own* and *His own* received Him not." In conformity with the plan of the covenant, it is first announced and offered to " His own." It is a fact that the mass of them did not accept it, but to them it came first of all. Some of His own, however, did receive it, because they " believed in His name " and were " born of God." This is precisely the efficacy of the

[1] *Op. cit.,* p. 67.

covenant of grace. The work of election normally operates within the seed-bed of those who are called. (ii) In commenting thus Karl Barth identifies the Church with the community of those who are " born of God " and who " believe in His name," and thus with those who are regenerate. In the covenant, however, there are the called and the elect. What Karl Barth says is incontestably true of the elect. (iii) Short of making the relationship between parents and children in the Old Testament something which, in our opinion, corresponds neither to reality nor to what the Reformed theologians say of it, we hold, on the contrary, that in the light of these texts Karl Barth's argument against the succession of generations is not convincing. We shall see that the New Testament maintains this relationship just as we have defined it. (iv) Is it imagined that such an affirmation implies, in the Christian Church, a modification of the content of the decalogue (Ex. xx. 5 f.) ?

Besides, has not Karl Barth spoken a little earlier [1] of " the Church as *a manifestation of the covenant of grace* in the time between the Resurrection and Parousia of Jesus Christ " ? But what covenant does it manifest if it is equally the case, as we have seen Barth also says, that " in the time elapsing between the Resurrection and the Parousia of Jesus the relationship between parents and children can no longer have the decisive significance which it had for pre-messianic Israel " ? According to Karl Barth, and taking into account his comment on John i. 12 f., must one not conclude that this is a covenant with men " taken individually " by themselves and lacking any connection with this relationship ? But is it possible, in an individualistic conception of this nature, for the covenant to support its title, since it has been deprived of its organic and historic character and is confused with an individualistic " receiving of Jesus Christ " ? Can it even continue to exist ? In the face of all the texts which we have cited can such a conception of the New Testament covenant, fundamentally differing from that of the Old Testament, be maintained ? We think not, for in most of the texts cited in connection with the plan of the covenant's general characteristics and its unity the New Testament teaches,

[1] *Ibid.*, p. 34.

as we are about to see, a spiritual solidarity of the family, resulting from this relationship between parents and children, which obtains in the Christian Church.

(e) *The spiritual solidarity of the family*

The theology of the covenant is further confirmed by the concept of spiritual solidarity which is developed in the New Testament. In harmony with the concepts of the Old Testament, Christ and the Apostle Paul speak of the home and the family as a whole spiritually united under its head. The family forms a collective entity whose lot is bound to that of one of its members, for the present time and even for eternity.

This was so with the family of Zaccheus (Lk. xix. 9), with that of the nobleman (Jn. iv. 53), of Cornelius (Acts x. 2), of Lydia (Acts xvi. 14 f.), of the gaoler (Acts xvi. 30-33), of Crispus (Acts xviii. 8), and of Onesiphorus (2 Tim. i. 16). These families were saved and attained faith through the faith of one of their members, generally the father, but also the mother when she is a widow (Lk. vii. 11-17) ; that the mother is a widow is not always certain (Acts xvi. 14 f.)[1] In this way, too, the family of Noah was saved, for God said to him : " Enter into the ark, thou *and thy whole family*, for I have seen that *thou* art righteous before Me in this generation " (Gen. vii. 1 ; Heb. xi. 7-11).

In God's eyes parents and their children are *one*. By divine right parents are the authorized representatives of their children ; they act for them ; they engage in spiritual obligations because of them and for them, and also in their name. Such is the order of God. It is for this reason that in every case when parents enter into the covenant in the capacity of proselytes they do so together with their minor children. As with families placed within the covenant, so also with proselytes it is through hearing the Gospel preached and through the exercise of a free human decision that Christ becomes a name of contention and causes division in the family, between husband and wife, or between the parents and one or other of their children (Mt. x. 34-39 ;

---

[1] One may remark that historically these texts are placed both before *and after* the resurrection of Christ : a significant point when Karl Barth's views, quoted above, are recalled.

Lk. xii. 51-53 ; xiv. 26). It is then, according to the two Testaments, not merely at the time of the parousia, but in the present eschatological situation which determines the coming of the Son of man, that the community of the family submits or is disrupted—sometimes only for a while—before a superior community, that of the body of Christ.

The houses into which the Apostles and disciples go to proclaim the Gospel are considered by Christ as a whole. If the disciples are welcomed and the Word is listened to—obviously by those who are capable of it !—" the peace " of the Gospel rests on that *whole* house ; but if they are not welcomed and the Word is rejected, the *whole* house is excluded from this peace and is delivered over to judgment (Mt. x. 12-14). Thus beyond dispute the New Testament confirms the decalogue, and here in particular the passage where God says : " I will visit the iniquity of the fathers upon the children unto the third and fourth generation of those who hate Me, and I will show mercy unto a thousand generations of those who love Me and keep My commandments " (Ex. xx. 5 f.). This passage throws into bold relief the spiritual solidarity of the family in its successive generations (without, however, involving any compelling psychological necessity, as, for example, Ezekiel xviii shows), and at the same time it displays the radical kindliness of the covenant of grace.

This is the place to recall the miracles performed by Christ for such a child (Mt. ix. 18 f., 23-26 ; cf. xvii. 14-18 ; Lk. vii 11-17—and here it is a matter of being raised from the dead) and for such a person belonging to a household (Mt. viii. 5-13 ; Lk. vii. 2-10), *because of* the faith of the father or the mother of the family, or even because of the faith of a group of people interceding for a friend (Mt. ix. 1-8). These facts, New Testament manifestations of the covenant of grace, ought to hold our attention and to cause us, of necessity, to abandon any *a priori* individualistic philoso-phizings, since they are just as incompatible with the theology of the New Testament as with that of the Old. " Thanks to individualism and to philosophical idealism," says R. Mehl,[1] " we have ceased to consider the family as a

[1] *Faut-il continuer à baptiser nos enfants ?* Foi et Vie, Jan. 1949, p. 57.

spiritual reality, forgetting that Jesus regarded it as a unitary whole before God and that He performed His miracles for such or such a child or such a servant because of the faith alone of the father of the family."

A careful study of the idea of *conversion* would show that it is not a typically individual phenomenon. Christ used to speak of the conversion or of the failure to repent of a house, of a city, or of a people. In a number of passages " conversion " and " being converted " are terms used in a sense that is specifically collective.[1] In the conversion of an individual it is, thanks to the action of spiritual solidarity, the over-all collectivity which occupies the background, and the community is indissolubly linked to Christ. In this connection also we are much more interdependent and spiritually bound up with each other than we might think.

A serious study of *sanctification* would likewise show that the Christian is never sanctified for himself in so far as he is an individual, but as a member of communities (family, Church, etc.). There are collectivities which, in the person of each one of their members, are recipients of the personal sanctification of each one. All the occurrences of the " personal " Christian life are complex and impinge objectively, according to the purposes of God, and subjectively, according to the classic laws of collective psychology, upon the combined whole of the collectivities of which each person forms a part. The central text, in relation to which a multitude of biblical texts which we could cite here find their true perspective, is John xvii. 19 : " For their sakes I sanctify Myself in order that they also may be sanctified through the truth."

Paul sums up the fact and the consequences of this spiritual solidarity when he says to Christian parents, even to those living in a mixed home where only one of the two is a believer, " Your children are holy " (1 Cor. vii. 14) : *holy*, that is to say, set apart as belonging to the elect people and simultaneously the beneficiaries of the grace of the covenant.

---

[1] Cf. Mt. xi. 20 f. ; xii. 41 ; Acts v. 31 ; xiii. 24 ; xx. 21 ; Rev. ii. 5, 16 ; iii. 3, 19, etc. Similarly, Mt. i. 21 ; Rom. x. 1 ; xi. 26, where it is a matter of the salvation of a people ; and even Jn. iii. 17 ; xii. 47, where it is a matter of the whole world.

Children are not outside, they are *within* the circle of the elect people. They are not holy in the sense of a sanctity realized in their being, but *before God* because of the relationship which God establishes with them in the covenant which is imposed upon them and because they are the objects of His good will. This text is the *conclusion* of a theology which was then well known, and not, as some have wished to regard it, the point of departure for theological phantasies in the realm of conjecture. It sums up the covenant of grace and its consequences for those to whom it pertains; it is the outcome, not the origin of the covenant. In association with other texts, it is not the basis of the doctrine, but its confirmation.

The study of the texts shows that it is Christ, and Christ alone, who is the foundation of the Christian notion of collectivity, of " spiritual solidarity," of family " sanctity." This again is a confirmation of our conclusions relative to the covenant.

This spiritual solidarity, a heritage of the thought of the Old Testament, is one of the most characteristic elements of the thought of the New Testament. The individualism of post-Socratic Hellenic thought prevailing in the Greco-Roman empire clashed so violently with this concept that primitive Christianity was incapable of understanding these texts in a communal sense and sought persistently to interpret them in an individualistic sense or neglected their importance.   In the sixteenth century this communal thought had become so fundamentally alien to the very notion of religion that it was only with difficulty regained by the Reformation. Calvin in particular had a very clear appreciation of its importance, but not, however, to the point of systematically developing a theology of the covenant, although it may be discerned throughout his work.   The principal elements of this theology, which is termed *federal*, only came into their own much later. Before long it was the turn of modern individualism to combat this notion in theology or to refuse to recognize it in Scripture, on the part, in the West, both of Roman Catholicism and of Protestantism, whereas the Eastern Church remained faithful, on this point, to the primitive teaching. This is a matter which today should no longer be overlooked.

D. CHILDREN IN THE CHURCH

What we are about to say concerning the children of the covenant is largely corroborated by the fact that in the Old Testament children received the sacrament of circumcision. They were thus members of the visible Church.

(a) *Children were members of the Church of Israel*

After what we have said above regarding circumcision as a spiritual sacrament and the identity between the visible Church and Israel, the objection that the administration of the sacrament of circumcision to children was simply in recognition of their right to citizenship in the community of Israel immediately falls to the ground. Circumcision was the sign and seal of membership in the Hebrew Church. It follows that every child that was circumcized because of the fact that it was one of the members of the elect people was thereby sealed and marked as a member of the Church of God as it was at that time. Circumcision was the seal of the covenant of grace. If, therefore, children were circumcized by God's order, it was because they were incorporated into the covenant made with their fathers. Since the Abrahamic covenant was solemnly confirmed under the form of the Mosaic covenant, God required that the *little children* should be presented before Him together with all the people (Dt. xxix. 10-12).

(b) *Children are members of the Christian Church*

We have similarly established the unity of the Church of the New Testament with that of the Old. Seeing, therefore, that the Church is *one* under both Testaments, if children were members of the Church of Israel under the theocracy, they are also—unless the contrary is proved to us from the texts and writings of the New Testament—still today members of the Christian Church which, in accordance with the promise, is the continuation of the Church of Israel. Is there anything in the New Testament which can justify the exclusion of the children of believers from membership in the Church ? Upon those who affirm that these children are not members of the Church lies the onus of proving what they advance.

If children ought to be debarred from the birthright which they enjoyed ever since there was a Church on earth, for thousands of years in fact, then there is need for a positive commandment which enjoins their exclusion, or some clearly revealed modification of the conditions required for membership of the Church which shows their exclusion to be necessary and inevitable. We believe that it will be somewhat difficult to prove that Christ ever gave a commandment whereby it was forbidden to consider the children of believers any longer as members of the Church, or that there has been such a change in the conditions of admission into the Church that their exclusion must be regarded as inevitable.

We have seen that these conditions are today the same as they have been from the very beginning. Moreover, according to the terminology of the New Testament, membership of the Church does not depend upon a previous confession of faith.[1] Our Lord's attitude towards children is, in fact, very significant and ought to engage our full attention. So far from excluding children from the Church, in whose bosom they have always been cherished, Christ calls them the lambs of His flock, takes them in His arms and blesses them, and declares that the kingdom of heaven is for those who are like.them and that their angels always behold the face of the Father in heaven. Their purity is such that to cause one of these little ones to stumble is to deserve eternal punishment.[2] If they are members of the heavenly kingdom, is not this proof that they are in the covenant ? Why should they be excluded from the earthly kingdom, the visible Church, the place of the covenant ? We propound this question on exegetical as well as on dogmatic grounds.

Karl Barth [3] affirms that children, even of tender age, are in the kingdom of Christ, but not in the Church, and that parents ought to know this, or be informed of it. But how ought they to know it ? On the strength of what authority ought they to be informed ? How is it that their children are in the kingdom ? By what decree has it taken place ?

---

[1] O. Cullmann, *op. cit.*, p. 53.
[2] Mt. xviii. 1-6, 10, 14 ; xix. 13-15 ; Mk. x. 13-16 ; Lk. xvii. 1 f. ; xviii. 15-17 ; and, doubtless, also Mt. xi. 25.
[3] *Op. cit.*, pp. 43, 49 f.

They can be in the kingdom only if God has received them into it after having regenerated them and bestowed on them the benefits of Christ's sacrifice. How are they regenerated, and how is justification imputed to them ? Is it not precisely here that the whole doctrine of the covenant of grace comes in ? That certain persons, and even little children of unbelievers, form part of the kingdom without forming part of the visible Church, because it pleases God to call them, indeed, even to receive them into it otherwise than by the ministry of the Church, is what all theologians accord to the liberty of divine grace.[1] But *can* this be said of the children *of believers* and of the posterity of those who are found *in the Church* ? If the children of believers form part of the kingdom, are they not in Christ and Christ in them ? Christ Himself has said that whoever receives one of these little ones in His Name receives Him. Does not the exegesis of the New Testament demonstrate the perfect equivalence of the expressions " in Christ " and " in the Church " ? Is it possible to maintain the contrary on exegetical grounds ?

If the children of those who are in the Church do not belong to the Church, then we demand proof from the New Testament of the spiritual dissociation of the family as a religious community, on the one hand, and, on the other, that when the children of believers reach the age of discretion and embrace the faith of their fathers they do so in the capacity of *proselytes*. Without doubt this has been affirmed by certain people for *a priori* reasons, but we have no knowledge of its having been supported by scriptural texts.

Children, then, are members of the visible Church, not merely in virtue of a simple judicial determination of God, but in virtue of the work which He has promised to accomplish in their hearts by the Holy Spirit and by the ministry of the Church, and which He prosecutes effectively from generation to generation in accordance with the promise. Viewed thus, membership of the Church is something entirely objective. As far as God is concerned, the children of His people have a place in the covenant and thus in the visible Church. They bear His Name, not only through the sovereign

[1] Karl Barth : *ibid.*, pp. 23 f.

decision of their heavenly Father and Saviour, but because of the mercies of which they are the beneficiaries, and this too without their having been consulted, whether it pleases them or not when they reach adult years. So also the father of a family gives his name to his children from the time of their birth and lavishes his care upon them without their having been consulted. So also the state gives its nationality to newly-born babes and authoritatively places them under its power and protection without their being capable of expressing any preference. To deny to God the right of including children within the bounds of His covenant and of placing them within the sphere of His benefits and mercies even before they are conscious of them, it would be necessary to deny to the father of a family the right of giving his name to his children and of keeping and nurturing them at his hearth, and to the state the right of imposing upon them its nationality and of granting them its benefactions and its protection.

Later on, certain children under certain conditions may snap the bonds of family or nation and break away from their obligations. Then, free from the onus of its demands, they will do what they like. But they are, to begin with, held by this bond. Still, having reached the age of discretion, some of them may break, as far as they are concerned, the relationship which links them to the covenant of grace and, renouncing the mark of their origin, depart from the visible Church. In doing this they exercise all their responsibility ; but they must take into account the fact that they are traitors, renegades, covenant-breakers, and they must expect to suffer the consequences of their decision.

E. THE UNCONVERTED IN THE COVENANT AND IN THE CHURCH

A most important consequence arises from the manner in which the covenant of grace is administered: the covenant embraces also, in time, men and women who inwardly remain unbelievers and who do not participate in its spiritual benefits. In other words, the visible Church is not and never has been composed of only converted and regenerate people.

(a) *There are unregenerate in the Church*

This assertion is supported by the following facts concerning the Apostolic Church.[1] The New Testament shows us clearly that the primitive Church itself was not composed exclusively of true believers and regenerate persons. On the contrary, numbers of unregenerate individuals received baptism, partook of the Lord's Supper, and for longer or shorter periods exercised various ministries, holding sometimes the most important offices. Judas was one of the band of Apostles, and it seems that later other apostles were guilty of defection (2 Cor. xi. 4 f., 13; Gal. ii. 6). During our Lord's ministry disciples who had certainly received baptism went off and left Him (Jn. vi. 66). After Pentecost, two disciples, Ananias and Sapphira, showed that they had not been regenerated (Acts v. 1-6). Amongst the members of the Church who are named in the New Testament and proved themselves to be unregenerate we find the incestuous Corinthian (1 Cor. v. 1-11), Hymenæus and Philetus who deserted the truth in order to teach heresies (2 Tim. ii. 16-18), Demas and Alexander who fell away (1 Tim. i. 20 ; 2 Tim. iv. 10, 14), and Diotrephes, who set up a scandalous dictatorship in the Church of which he was the leader (3 Jn. 9-11).

In the Church and in the midst of the Christians there were *false* brethren, *false* teachers, and, amongst the most eminent, *false* apostles, who preached a *different* Christ, a *different* Gospel, a *different* Spirit (2 Cor. xi. 4 f., 13, 26 ; Gal. i. 6-9 ; ii. 4-6 ; 1 Tim. iv. 2 ; 2 Pet. ii., a chapter which is entirely devoted to them). Antichrists went out from the very *midst* of the Christians (1 Jn. ii. 18 f.). There were in the Church fomenters of division who did not serve Christ (Rom. xvi. 17-20), depraved persons who had been partakers of the Holy Ghost (Heb. vi. 4-6), impious individuals who crept in amongst the Christians, twisted the grace of God to serve their own irregularities, and denied the only Lordship of Jesus Christ (Jude 4-11, 12-16, 18 f.) ; also those who lived unruly lives (1 Thes. v. 14), those whose lives were corrupt (2 Tim. iii. 1-9), and those who deserted the faith

[1] As for the Old Testament, the fact is too well known for any useful purpose to be served by insisting on it here.

in order to adhere to a false science (1 Tim. vi. 20, 21). In the Church at Rome there were libertines—a fact which caused Paul to write Romans vi as well as other chapters ; and the Church at Corinth was composed largely of carnal Christians (1 Cor. iii. 1-4 ; cf. also Heb. v. 11-14 ; 1 Cor. vi. 12-20, etc.).

In every one of these cases it is members of the apostolic Church who are involved, baptized persons who in large measure had benefited from the grace of the Holy Spirit. These are facts the gravity of which cannot be underestimated, and they indicate how the membership of the Christian Church is made up in every age, as the following considerations bear out.

The visible Church is administered by men. If, then, the Church were composed only of regenerate individuals, it would be necessary for its ministers, or for the Church itself, to be able to read the very hearts of its members and to be absolutely infallible in their judgments concerning men's internal state. It is, indeed, true that the New Testament teaches that faithful ministers and members of the Church ought to " discern the spirits " as they manifest themselves, but nowhere has Christ promised to the Church or to any individual the gift of probing men's hearts in order to decide whether the regeneration of grace has been effective in them or not, and if so to what degree.

On the contrary, it is plain that Christ forbids us to make such judgments regarding men's hearts. Whenever the official religious authorities of the Church of His time passed judgment on the sin of some person or other in order to exclude them from the visible Church, Christ always made them feel that they were wrong. Where others were concerned, He taught His disciples constantly to entertain a favourable estimate, namely, one of love, in the hope of the internal and secret working of the Holy Spirit. He never committed to them the task of separating the tares from the wheat. Judgment belongs to God.

The covenant of grace is a unity ; its external and internal aspects, even though they cannot always be reconciled on this earth, cannot and ought not to be separated from or opposed to each other. There are, it is true, barren branches on the vine, there are tares amongst the wheat, there are vessels of gold and vessels of earth in the house. But we have neither the right nor the ability to draw the line of demarcation between them. God Himself will undertake that task on the day of the harvest. In accordance with the commandment of love, as long as they continue in the way of the covenant they ought to be considered and treated as members of the covenant. Although they are not of the covenant, they are none the less within the covenant : the day is coming when they will be judged. While upon earth, however, they are in many ways associated with the elect ; and the elect, since they are members of the Adamic race, can only be gathered together, as an organism, in a single body with Christ as Head by means of the covenant.

The conditions prescribed by God in the two Testaments for admission into the visible Church are such as a really unregenerate man could respond to. In that case such a man is only a Jew or a Christian " externally." These conditions, as we know, are adequate knowledge and a sincere profession of faith and obedience. Those only can be expelled who by their outward behaviour blatantly and scandalously contradict their profession of faith and obedience.

The conditions for admitting someone into the communion of the Church cannot be more severe than those which are required for remaining in this communion. If, in accordance with apostolic practice, the discipline of the holy table excludes from its fellowship those who cause public scandals, it is well known that the sacraments are none the less given to others than to truly regenerate persons. We simply demand of those who communicate an adequate knowledge, a sincere profession of faith and obedience, and a decent life in public. Hypocrites and unregenerate people can conduct themselves in such a manner as to appear to be sincere.

It is important to observe that, in both Old and New Testaments, it is not *regenerate* persons who compose the Church or enter it, but *disciples*. That is something very different ! Peter was not *converted* until after the death of Christ. For some years he had had his place in the band of *disciples* without being converted. It is Christ Himself who affirms this (Lk. xxii. 32). The words " regenerate " and " converted," used substantivally for denoting individuals, are not found in the New Testament. They are convenient terms which were later invented by the Church with a view to the systematic expression of certain ideas or facts. The substantive " regeneration " and the verb in the passive " to be regenerated " are applied only to the truly elect (e.g. Tit. iii. 5 ; 1 Pet. i. 3, 23). As for " conversion," it indicates the receiving of the pardon of sins, the giving of the Holy Spirit, in the full sense of that expression, the entering into the kingdom and the enjoyment of a heritage in it (Mt. xviii, 3 ; Acts ii. 38 ; iii. 19, etc.) ; it is never imposed as a condition of entry into the visible Church. The visible Church is composed of *disciples* amongst whose number are found those who are or will be truly regenerate, converted individuals destined for life eternal. It is obvious that all the moral exhortations of the prophets, of Christ, and of the Apostles place disciples under the obligation of being converted and regenerated by the Holy Spirit, by reason of their participation in the Church and its sacraments which they receive. The two most important passages devoted by Paul to the sacraments (Rom. vi. and 1 Cor. xi. 17-34) were written with this only in mind. In the visible Church the called and the elect are found side by side.

Even if in its first generation the apostolic Church comprised only members who had been baptized as adults, it did not possess the faculty of being composed entirely of regenerated and converted persons, whether they were of Israelite or pagan origin. In harmony with the dispensation of the covenant of grace, every attempt made to ensure that the Church should be composed entirely of regenerated individuals was ineffective. All who made such attempts met with failure. As far as we know, such a Church has never existed on the earth's surface. This fact alone indicates that such a Church does not form part of the divine plan.

The relationship between parents and children, says Karl Barth,[1] " certainly has not the right to make of ecclesiastical

---

[1] *Op. cit.*, p. 50.

order open disorder." Is it really the relationship between parents and children that ought to be condemned here ? Does this disorder result from this relationship ? Does it not rather result from the children who are implicated in it, who exchange good for evil and blessing for cursing because they prefer to be workers of iniquity (Is. v. 20) ? Does not Scripture instruct us that this relationship, when it unites children to their Christian parents, is on the contrary a relationship of order ? Is it not this that makes it possible for Christians to live *as families* in Christian order ? When confronted with disorder is it right for us to lay the blame on the liberality of God and on the breadth of His promises, thanks to the efficacy of which there still exists such order as we see in the Church ? And is it not our duty to ask other questions as well ? What is the definition, from the New Testament point of view, of ecclesiastical *order* ? On what texts is it based and whom does it concern ? What, likewise, is the definition of ecclesiastical *disorder* according to the texts ? In view of the presence of unregenerate persons in the Church of the New Testament, is there a single text which, with the purpose of limiting their number, suggests that the theological conception of the spiritual relationship between parents and children in the covenant ought to be modified, or that the principles of recruitment for the Church ought to be changed ? The covenant of grace and, with it, its organic principle of " from generation to generation," has been declared immutable, irrevocable, and eternal (as we have seen above) : would the same covenant have been conceived in the New Testament as a passing, transitory, and temporary covenant having force and validity only for and in the Old Testament ? A subjective definition of ecclesiastical order or disorder will never be theologically acceptable, and the fact of the imperfection of the visible Church, even in the New Testament, is something that cannot be gainsaid.

We must, then, accept this fact in faith. But *we* are ashamed of the presence of unconverted persons in the Church. The adversary, the world, Christian brothers even, make it a reproach to us. In our weakness as arrogant men we are ashamed of the pitifully weak state of the Church.

I

We wish it could have more effectiveness. We would be proud to belong to a Church composed entirely of true believers, of regenerate persons, a Church in which not only the power of the Word, but that of the kingdom of God were manifested. It is very tempting for us to proclaim that the Church will convert the world and that the world will no longer overwhelm us with insults. We should then be able to lift up our heads once more ! And it is very tempting for us to draw up plans for changing ecclesiastical disorder into order and an unhealthy Church into a healthy community. But what, then, is the practical import of these pious desires?

In the first place, to what New Testament definition of the sanctity or health of the Church are we to refer? Further, are we *sure* that if the Church were healthy we, the believers, the pastors, or the theologians, would today have a place in it ? Would we not have been excluded completely since there was a time when we were unconverted and unregenerate ? And if we had been excluded from it, would the Word of God have reached us to bring about our conversion and to declare our election ? Being unable to be disciples, would we have been elect ? If the Church today were healthy, are we really sure that we have the right to continue in it ? Which men, which ecclesiastical institutions, should, according to the New Testament, guarantee the health of the Church ?

Is this not, *in certain respects*, the business of God ? Is it not He who takes the risk ? Is it not He who overcomes it in His liberality ? Can we not lift our liberality to the height of the liberality of Him who has shown so much patience towards us ? Shall we not also show an equal patience towards others (those who have been born into the covenant but have not yet themselves entered into it), in the name of the promise, and because of our certainty that God makes it effective by means of those who are His own, precisely through the preaching of the Word which reaches them ? Since the Church is *for* the people, ought there not to be a people who hears, a point of contact between this people and the Church of the true believers ? In the covenant, God gives such a people to the Church. In face of the world which harasses us are we going to be obsessed with the false problem of the effectiveness of the Church, when our sole obsession ought to be that of the conditions in the Church governing the effectiveness of the Word ? Does not what we know of the covenant of grace demonstrate to us that the expression of the grace of God is such, and that we ought to acquiesce in it with all the risk that it implies ? Are we too feeble to make God's business ours as well and, just as He shoulders before the world the responsibility of His own apparent feebleness the limits of which He has Himself chosen, so also ourselves to shoulder before the world something of the responsibility of God, that is to say, of the weakness and disorder of the Church, bearing in mind the promised grace *which is coming* for a large number of those very people who today are a dishonour to the Church ? Let us explain our attitude by confessing in faith, in the name of the promises of the covenant, the necessity of this apparent weakness of the Church as a result of the love and patience of God. If contact is to be established with detractors, both without and within, will not the best proclamation be made in this sphere ? Let us not blush because of the love and patience of God towards the children of the covenant, the benefits of which we ourselves have enjoyed. Our attitude on this point has much importance in connection with our conception of the administration of baptism.

(b) *The position of the unregenerate in the covenant and in the visible Church*

The question now arises concerning the position of the unregenerate in the covenant and in the Church.

1. *Their spiritual responsibility is involved.* Whether they wish it or not, in virtue of God's sovereign decree and of His promises they are counted in the number of those on whom God wishes to bestow grace, and consequently they are *under obligation to repent and believe*. If when they arrive at the age of discretion they do not turn to God and accept Christ by faith, they will for their part have broken *freely*, *voluntarily* and *consciously* the covenant which God offers them. The fact of being born in the covenant with all the

promises and benefits that it conveys, lays an increased responsibility upon them. " If I had not come," says Christ, " and spoken to them, they would not have had sin ; *but now they have no excuse for their sin* ".(Jn. xv. 22). God comes to them, speaks to them, and speaks to them again !

2. *They can appeal to God's promises.* If the children of the covenant become conscious of their desperate situation and seek God, and if they feel the need of conversion and bemoan their weakness, *they can and should appeal to the promises* which God made when He established His covenant with believers and their posterity. They can and should cry to Him *with the assurance that He will hear and answer them, since this is exactly the request that He expects from them.* God always wishes to be their Father and their Saviour : man's unfaithfulness does not destroy His faithfulness.

3. *They are subject to the ministry of the covenant.* Provided they have not severed every bond with the visible Church and the parish in which they are domiciled, they are constantly being admonished and exhorted to live in harmony with the demands of the covenant by the preaching they hear, by the example of the brethren, by the visits of the pastor and other Christians, and by the instruction which they receive. The Church ought to treat them as children of the covenant, to present to them the seals of the covenant, and to exhort them to use these in a legitimate manner. They are priority guests invited to the supper, children of the Kingdom to whom the Word must first be preached (Mt. viii. 12 ; Lk. xiv. 16-24 ; Acts xiii. 46, etc.).

4. *They share in the communal blessings of the covenant.* Whether they wish it or not, because of the spiritual solidarity of which we have spoken they share—in so far as they concern them—in the communal blessings of the covenant, in the same way as a thankless son shares in the blessings of his family, the rebel Israelite in the advantages of the theocracy, and the unjust and wicked in the benefits of sun and rain. Even though they lack any experience of the regenerating influence of the Holy Spirit, they are none the less subject to certain special operations and influences of

the Holy Spirit. The Spirit (and the Church in the exercise of its ministry) strives in a very real and particular manner to convict them of sin, of righteousness, and of judgment, to give them some measure of enlightenment, and to enrich them with the blessings of common grace.

The considerable importance of these facts must be emphasized and some of their consequences briefly noted.

(i) *The Church's strategy.* If the Church pays attention to the demands of the administration of the covenant and considers those who have been born in it as being primarily entrusted to her care, if she knows how to avail herself of the theology of the covenant and of the psychological and pedagogical weapons which it affords, if she believes in God's promises and in His faithfulness, then she ought to reconsider her hasty judgments, too often formed without charity and with an altogether Pharisaic brutality—and which undoubtedly control her methods of work—against Protestants who are called " detached " or who have become " indifferent." She must learn once more to regard them lovingly as members of the covenant and of the people of God. She has an urgent and special ministry in respect of them, founded on the commands and promises of God. We shall return to this point in connection with baptism. All ecclesiastical strategy—in every sphere !—flows from the covenant of grace, and is something very different from that spoken of in most Church synods.

(ii) *The range of duties of the pastoral ministry.* The covenant of grace indicates to the pastor of each parish the order of urgency of the tasks which have been entrusted to him in the ministry.

He ought, in the first place, to strengthen and sustain in the covenant all those who—according to the judgment of charity—have not broken away from God. He ought by every influence of his ministry to confirm them in the faith and to cause them to advance in the Christian life. There should be a solid nucleus in the Church, for everything depends on it.

He ought, next, by order of priority and with great patience, to apply himself to the search for the rebellious and unregenerate children of the covenant, to proclaim to them their responsibility, to reprove them and make them aware of their voluntary and deliberate revolt, while at the same time presenting anew to them the promises and demands of the covenant. The ministry of the covenant ought primarily to be exercised in favour of those who have been born in the covenant, to the end that they may be converted and believe. The pastor who takes his stand on the power and faithfulness of God in the covenant of grace and who, with the patience of Christian love and the persistence of " the minister of the covenant," goes out to seek for the wandering " sheep " and the withered " branches," does not tarry to be astonished and confused by the results of this work which God has ordained and blessed according to the riches of His mercy, in conformity with the assurance that He will not be false to His promises.

When this work has been done, when it has been prosecuted and recommenced without cessation, the pastor can think of " evangelization " properly so called. In the place where the Church exists—a community living *by the covenant* —God adds proselytes to her number. According to the administration of the covenant, " conversions " of proselytes are only possible with reference to a true Church, living in grace and pardon, and conscious of her riches in the Gospel. The conversion of " individuals " takes place when the Church is alive—her numerical strength is of little importance ! Possible proselytes are not lacking in good sense. Who would associate with a dead body or merely eke out an existence ? People are not converted in a human and social vacuum, but by being incorporated into the body of Christ. Once more, it is necessary for its existence to be visibly manifest.

We are fully convinced that the serious setbacks suffered for a long time now in our methods of evangelization through the Churches [1] may be attributed in the majority of cases

---

[1] We are not speaking of itinerant evangelists whose vocation and ministry is to proclaim the Word, particularly in those places where no Church or parish has been established. Nor do we presume to lay down a rigid regulation. " Inspired " individuals can receive special directions from God for the organization of their work in accordance with particular circumstances.

to the fact that the theology of the covenant has been too much ignored in our Reformed Church and that, in order to bring about a change, attempts have been made to invert the order of the duties which have been entrusted to us. It has been a case of putting the cart before the horse.

It is not superfluous to add that, in the covenant, the administration of the parochial system is likewise very different from that which is most frequently practised. The Church has no right to ignore the " unattached " ; she ought, with an invincible persistence, in season and out of season, *always* to remain in contact with them, by means of the local magazine and of pamphlets, and so on. She ought ceaselessly and in a thousand different ways to remind them of her existence, right up to the day when they are carried to the cemetery, without ever acknowledging herself defeated or resigning herself to the loss of such persons.

(*iii*) *The care of the soul.* The theology of the covenant of grace—which is simply that of faith—when applied to the Sunday School, in religious instruction and the care of the soul, is remarkably effective. Since they have been born into the covenant, children and young people and also adults, although overtaken by the evil of life and tormented by religious questions, are not and should never be considered as proselytes. *For them the content of our message is not the same as that which we address to proselytes.* Since they are within the covenant, the promises which concern them, the demands of God, the possibility of their responding to them, and also their responsibility, are quite different. If the pastor does not depend upon the covenant of grace in preaching the Word to them, in persisting, reproving, rebuking, exhorting with great patience and without ceasing to instruct (cf. 2 Tim. iv. 2), he is defenceless when he hears people say : " It's not my fault ! One either has faith or does not have it ! God has never spoken to me ! " and so on. Nobody likes to admit that he has fought against God and voluntarily, consciously, and freely rejected His Word. It is a Word of God and not a word of man that is needed to overthrow the justification of their own unbelief The psychology of the covenant cuts these fallacious excuses to the quick. The covenant puts the sinner—whatever his age— face to face with his own responsibility. It causes him to take knowledge of his rebellion as a real and deliberate effect of his will. In the course of my ministry I have *never* encountered *a single* person who, when pressed by the preaching of the covenant, has not finished by acknowledging that God had *in fact* spoken to him, that he had *in fact* rebelled, that he was *in fact* responsible, and that it was he *in fact* who was the author of his actual distress ! Once a person has been brought this far and has then been confronted with the promise, he is not far from a true conversion.[1]

[1] Cf. P.-Ch. Marcel, *A l'Ecoute de Dieu*, p. 142.

BAPTISM: SACRAMENT OF THE COVENANT OF GRACE

PRELIMINARY REMARKS

In the First and Second Parts, the content of which we trust is still recollected by the reader, we have cleared the ground in such a way that it is now possible for us to proceed directly to the study of baptism. We have demonstrated in a general manner that the sacraments of the New Testament have *essentially* the same significance as those of the old : both are signs and seals of the covenant of grace ; their respective content has been and remains Jesus Christ and His spiritual riches ; the nature of their efficacy is the same ; the religious and moral demands imposed on those who receive them are identical. Before we verify these facts in detail for baptism, we shall offer three brief remarks.

(*a*) Having posed the question which actually confronts the Church concerning baptism—which is also the reason for this study—we are obliged to treat in the first place of the baptism of adults and of the manner in which adults ought to regard the baptism which they have received, and after that of the baptism of children. In a systematic treatise intended for Reformed Christians who have resolved the question of the baptism of children we should take care to avoid this method, which, in our opinion, involves great inconveniences. But as it is we are constrained to bring forward our proofs one by one. The classical method, which follows the chronological and historical order, leads inevitably to certain repetitions for which we apologize : it is not our fault that it was not otherwise.

(*b*) When a sacrament is studied it is not the sign and the outward ceremony which ought *in the first place* to receive our attention, but the promises and spiritual mysteries which our Lord wishes it to represent. " When one desires to speak of a sacrament it should be noted that the whole substance and propriety ought to be estimated in accordance with the doctrine which the sacrament confirms. Let us note, then, that the doctrine is the principal element, in relation to which the sacrament is an accessory." [1] It is not possible by commencing from the sign to " deduce " what it represents and signifies. If we wish, therefore, to know what baptism is, we must lift our spirits to the *promises* of God which are conveyed to us through it and to the internal and spiritual things which are displayed to us by it. These promises are anterior to it—for the Word precedes the sign and it alone is the instrumental cause of faith—and it is they which make the sacrament what it is. The content of the promises constitutes the content of the sign ; the truth of the promises constitutes the truth of the sign. When we know to what end the promises have been given to us we shall know equally to what end and within what limits the sign, which is the confirmation of the promises, was instituted, and how it serves and ought to serve us. From this it follows that a sacrament is not *in the first place* the sign of an action of man, but the sign and seal of a promise of God and of the Word announced. Above all, we must refer to the Word of God, in which the whole efficacy of the sign is found. It is an *objective* point from which we start.

(c) We shall in due course speak of the blessings, the benefits, and the efficacy of baptism. For the present we must beware of attributing to baptism any blessings and effects which cannot be attributed to the Word. For adults and proselytes, all the blessings of baptism are in reality offered to the baptized persons before baptism in the Word of the Gospel whereby Jesus Christ is presented to them. They can appropriate these blessings or have already appropriated them, at least in part, by faith. However small faith may be, it is capable of appropriating all the blessings of the Gospel, even if each one of them is only partially apprehended. But it is not sufficient that faith should have only a beginning in us ; it is necessary that it should be nourished and sustained, that it should grow and increaʳ ᵛ. It is for the purpose of nourishing, strengthening, and increasing this faith that the blessings of the Gospel will be declared afresh, presented, confirmed, signified, and

[1] Calvin : *Against the Anabaptists*, Opera, VII, 60.

sealed by baptism—a visible Word. Thus we should not represent matters as though only some blessings, or never all the blessings, are given or can be received in the case of faith which precedes baptism, and that those which are still lacking will be conferred by baptism. Once again, the Word heard and believed, before and after baptism, contains all the blessings and faith appropriates them all. There is not a single blessing which may be communicated by the sacrament and not also by the Word. Even the incorporation into Christ's body is effected by means of faith, and through baptism receives its sign and seal. According to Scripture the grace of baptism exists only as a *declaration* and a *confirmation* ; it cannot ever be anything else. It is essential that this point should be clearly grasped if one wishes to avoid warped views which cannot fail to lead to errors of interpretation.

I

THE BAPTISM OF ADULTS AND PROSELYTES

WHAT IS THE MEANING AND SIGNIFICANCE FOR ADULTS OF THE BAPTISM THEY HAVE RECEIVED ?

A. BAPTISM AS A SIGN AND SEAL

Of what is baptism the sign and the seal ? Such is our first question. We shall see in due course how it is a means of grace and we shall study the modes of its efficacy.

1. *Baptism is in the first place the sign and the seal of the remission of sins and, consequently, of our justification.* The fundamental proclamation of the Gospel is the promise of forgiveness of sins to everyone who believes. Preaching announces and attests the remission of sins. According to the command of God this promise requires to be signified and sealed by a sacrament (Mk. i. 4 ; Acts ii. 38 ; xxii. 16 ; etc.). Baptism signifies the important truth that the soul which believes is purified from the guilt of sin by the sprinkling of the blood of Christ. " Believers are assured by baptism that this condemnation (of sin) is entirely withdrawn from them, since our Lord promises us by this sign that a full and entire remission of sins has been made, equally of the guilt which ought to be imputed to us and of the penalty incurred by the guilt which we ought to bear. They also receive righteousness, but such righteousness as the people of God can receive in this life, namely, by imputation alone, because our Lord in His mercy regards them as righteous and innocent."[1]

[1] Calvin : *Instt.* IV. xv. 10. In the course of this third part we shall cite a number of passages from Calvin, because of their freshness and their inimitable vivacity and precision. Some of them are little known and we believe that in publishing them we are performing a useful service. But the fact of our citing these passages in no way implies that we are using them as a *norm* : we have no such idea ! *We cite them when we are convinced*

The conversion effected by the Holy Spirit on the occasion of the preaching of the Word is the road by which the pardon obtained through Christ comes into our possession ; but baptism, united to the Word, is precisely the proof and the guarantee that this pardon has *really* been granted to him who believes. It is in virtue of the preaching of the Gospel, according to which we are cleansed from our sins by the blood of Christ, that the sinner obtains the pardon of his sins : baptism is the sign and testimony of this cleansing.

In baptism, as in the preaching of the Word, all our sins together with their guilt and penalty are remitted to us— not only past sins, but also present and future sins, because justification is a judicial act, a change of state which is accomplished perfectly and once for all in a single moment. " Baptism has been granted to us from God as a letter patent *signed and sealed*, by which He informs, certifies, and assures us that all our sins have been remitted, covered, abolished, and effaced in such a way that they will *never* come before His scrutiny, *never* be called to remembrance, and *never* be imputed to us. For it is His will that all who believe should be baptized for the remission of their sins. . . . We ought to couple baptism with the promise that all those who believe and are baptized shall be saved (Mk. xvi. 16)."[1]

2. *Baptism is the sign and the seal of regeneration, of the death of the old man and of the resurrection of the new man, through communion in the death and resurrection of Christ.* The central texts on which this affirmation rests are as follows : Rom. vi. 3-6 ; 1 Cor. vi. 11 ; Gal. iii. 26 f. ; Col. ii. 12 ; Tit. iii. 5. It is essential to make reference to them. The examination of these texts calls forth the ensuing remarks.

that they are in accord with the only conceivable norm, namely, Holy Scripture. This is the only manner in which a Reformed Christian may justifiably make use of the literature of the " fathers." We adduce these citations also because a great many modern authors, even amongst those who are sympathetic with our viewpoint, have spoken of the doctrine expounded by Calvin in terms which are scientifically unacceptable. The citation of a number of passages will permit us to rectify this. We do not, however, return merely and simply to Calvin without taking into account the fruit of the labours of the Reformed Churches and theologians in the course of the succeeding centuries. The attentive reader will easily check this.

[1] Calvin : *Instt.* IV. xv. 1.

(a) One is not here concerned with a question of *imitation*, as though the death of Christ ought merely to serve as an *example* to us following which we ought to die to sin and rise to a new life. The question here is primarily one of *participation*. On the one hand, we are made *partakers* of His death : the death of Christ has power to extinguish the enmity of our flesh and to cause us to die to sin. On the other hand, we are made *partakers* of His resurrection, for His resurrection has power to arouse in us a new condition which makes it possible for us to live a new life. The efficacy of Christ's death and resurrection is *communicated* to us. " So long as we live in Adam and in our own nature we can only do evil and we are so depraved that within us there is nothing but rebellion against God. It is, therefore, needful that we should enter as it were into a death and into a sepulchre in order that we may be renewed and that our Lord may give us a new understanding and a new heart, and that He may reform us in such a way that we become no longer the persons we were previously, but that we become as it were refashioned and new creatures, just in the manner that Scripture employs this language." [1] Becoming dead to ourselves we are made new men : the two things are inseparable. The old man is put to death in order that we may become new creatures. It would be of no avail to us to die with Christ if we did not rise to live a new life.

(b) More precisely still, the question here is one of *incorporation*, of *implanting*, of *grafting*. We become one plant with Christ. " Paul says that we are grafted into the death and passion of our Lord Jesus Christ in order that we may also be partakers of His resurrection and life. . . . For one takes a shoot from a tree, cuts a branch or the trunk of another tree, and inserts this little twig which has been excised, and one sees that it becomes united into one common substance and that the root pumps its sap into this little shoot which has been taken from another tree. It is just in this way, says St. Paul, that we are grafted into our Lord Jesus Christ so that our old life may be crucified with Him and we may rise to newness of life." [2] To go to the heart of

[1] Calvin : *Sermon* on Deut. vi. 20-25, Opera, XXVI, pp. 487 f.
[2] Calvin : *Sermon* on Gal. iii. 26-29, Opera, L, p. 562.

the matter, the death of Christ and our own death, which is ultimately accomplished *in us*, are not two distinct and separate events. The two deaths are simultaneous in principle. We have been buried *with* Him (Rom. vi. 4) ; we have been crucified *with* Him (Rom. vi. 6) ; we have died *with* Him (Rom. vi. 8) ; we shall also live *with* Him (Rom. iv. 8).

(c) The believer *puts on* Christ and becomes *one* with Him (Gal. iii. 27). " It is beyond any question that we put on Christ in baptism and that we are baptized to the end that we may become one with Him." [1] Consequently we become " children of God by faith in Jesus Christ " (Gal. iii. 26). " Thus we are favoured as the elect of God and as possessing the promise by which He assures us that He is ready to receive us mercifully ; but above everything it is necessary that we should put on our Lord Jesus Christ. For if we look into ourselves it is evident that God must detest us and hold us in execration, which is also what we deserve." [2]

We are truly incorporated into Christ's body when His death displays its fruit within us. This communion, this conformity to His death is the principal element of baptism, whereby not only our cleansing, but also the death and destruction of our old man is figured. From the moment of our being received into Christ's grace the efficacy of His death and resurrection immediately manifests itself within us.' By faith, everything which the Lord offers by the visible sign is confirmed and realized in the believer. Those who believe and are baptized put on Christ. When the institutions of the Lord and our faith are conjoined and make contact we receive that which the promise offers us : never are the signs then "naked and empty." God is true when He promises us the grace of His Spirit in order to reform us in newness of life.[3]

(d) Being one with Christ, we are through the Holy Spirit made partakers of all His blessings. In a passage written concerning the Lord's Supper, but which is equally applicable here, Calvin declares : " I do not accept the trifling according to which we only receive Jesus Christ with the intelligence and the mind when we say that we receive

[1] Calvin : *Comm.* on Rom. vi. 3.
[2] Calvin : *Sermon* on Gal. iii. 26-29, Opera, L, p. 564.
[3] Cf. Calvin : *Instt.* IV. xv. 5 ; *Comm.* on Rom. vi.

Him by faith. For the promises offer Him to us, not just so that we may amuse ourselves by a mere contemplation of Him, but so that we may truly enjoy His communion. It is *through His Spirit* that the Lord Jesus grants us the grace of being made *one with Him in body, soul, and spirit*. The Spirit is the bond of this communion by which we are united to Christ, *the channel by which all that Christ is and has descends to us*. It is for this reason that Scripture, when it speaks of the participation which we have with Christ, refers the whole efficacy to His Spirit." [1]

Christ is thus the central content of baptism. The fulfilment of baptism is in Christ, who is the proper object of baptism and its end and purpose. The gifts of God which are offered us by baptism are found in Christ alone through the Holy Spirit. That is why the Apostles baptized in His name (Mt. xxviii. 19 ; Acts ii. 38 ; viii. 16 ; xix. 5) ; that is why in the Church all baptism ought to be administered in the name of Christ.

Original sin, however, is not completely nullified or eradicated by baptism.[2] The Word, and with it baptism, which is a visible Word, transforms and renews us, breaking the power of original sin within us, and enabling us to walk in newness of life, but in such a way that, contrary to our will, sin always abides in our flesh. Original sin is, indeed, partially and in principle nullified by baptism, though not totally so. While it is no longer a cause of condemnation to us, until our death it remains the impure source of all sorts of sins. " This corruption never ceases in us, but constantly produces new fruits, namely, the works of the flesh, just as a burning furnace perpetually sends forth flame and sparks, or a fountain continually pours forth its water. For concupiscence does not die nor is it ever fully extinguished in men until, freed by death from the body of death, they have altogether laid aside their own nature. Baptism, indeed, assures us that our Pharaoh is drowned and our flesh mortified, not, however, in such a way that it no longer causes us trouble, but only that *it does not have dominion over us*.

[1] *Instt.* IV. xvii. 12.
[2] Conf. of the French Reformed Churches, XI ; Conf. of the Netherlands, XV ; Art. IX of the Church of England.

For as long as we live shut up in this prison of our body the remains and relics of sin dwell within us ; but if we hold by faith to the promise which God has given us in baptism, *they will not dominate or reign at all.*"[1]

" In this manner (God) promises us in baptism, and shows and assures us by a sign, that by His grace and power *we are delivered from the captivity of Egypt, that is, from the bondage of sin*, and that our Pharaoh, who is the Devil, is drowned, although he does not cease to harass and annoy us. But as that Egyptian after being drowned did not remain at the bottom of the sea, but was cast up on the shore and alarmed the Israelites by the terror of his look, although he could not hurt them, so indeed our infernal enemy shows his arms and makes himself felt, *but he is unable to conquer.*" [2]

3. *Baptism is the sign and the seal of the believer's communion not only with Christ Himself, but also with the Church which is His body.*

(a) *The baptized person is removed from a corrupted race and separated from the world* (Acts ii. 40). We are not sufficiently conscious and mindful of this remarkable blessing ! According to the Gospel there are not three possibilities—unbelief, faith, and, between them, indifference ; there are not three kingdoms—one of Satan, one of God, and, between them, a large neutral zone occupied by " good pagans." We are taught by Christ that we cannot serve *two* masters : we serve God *or* Satan ; we can be citizens of the kingdom of Satan *or* of the kingdom of God. It is impossible simultaneously to serve these two masters or to belong to these two kingdoms : the one must be loved and the other hated, the one served and the other despised. We are the children of Satan, the liar, the murderer, who is our father and claims us for his own, *or* we are the adopted children of the Living, the True, the Holy God. *There is no middle position !* By nature we belong to the kingdom of Satan, who considers us as his own property, but God by a decree of His love and an act of His omnipotence, together with the faith which He causes to be born within us, separates and saves us, as Peter says, " from this perverse generation," regards us as

---

[1] Calvin : *Instt.* IV. xv. 11.   [2] *Ibid.*, IV. xv. 9.

His children, removes us from Satan's dominion, and brings us into His own kingdom. We pass from a condemned race into the holy assembly of the children of God : we are made citizens of heaven.

The believer is removed from error, unrighteousness, darkness, foolishness, and death, so that he may enter into truth, righteousness, light, wisdom and life. God causes wolves and goats to become doves and sheep ; tares are changed into wheat ; those who were " outside " are united to those " inside " ; the children of this age become the sons of the Kingdom ; those who were born of the flesh are born anew of the Spirit. The texts supporting this antithesis between these two kingdoms and these two " citizenships " display themselves throughout the length of the New Testament.

Baptism is the sign and the seal that we are " set apart," " saved from the midst of this corrupt generation." We ought indeed to extol the activities of grace in celebration of such a deliverance ! They are all too few who, having taken seriously the universality of sin and condemnation, also take seriously their detachment from this world of darkness and their transition to the light ! Whether one wishes it or not, to minimize the tragic condition of our natural state is also to minimize and depreciate the exceptional privilege of our new condition, our joy and our gratitude to the God of love who loves us so effectively. The Confessions of Faith do justice to this matter : " By the sign of baptism God separates us from all other religions and peoples, and consecrates us to Himself as His own inheritance and treasure."[1] " By baptism we are . . . (received into the Church of God and) separated from all other peoples and from all strange religions in order that we may be entirely dedicated to Him, carrying His mark and His standard, and it acts as a witness to us that He will be our God for ever, since He is a Father well-disposed to us." [2] " Baptism is not only a sign of profession and mark of difference, whereby Christian men are discerned from others that be not christened, but it is also a sign of regeneration or new birth, whereby, as by an instrument, they that receive baptism rightly are grafted into the Church ; the promises of forgiveness of sin, and of

[1] Helv. Conf., 20. 4.   [2] Conf. of the Netherlands, 34.

our adoption to be the sons of God by the Holy Ghost, are visibly signed and sealed. . . . "[1]

(*b*) *The baptized person is made a disciple of Jesus Christ* (Mt. xxviii. 19 ; Jn. iv. 1, etc.). It is a great honour and an outstanding distinction to receive the mark of Christ's disciple, to be enrolled in the number of those who confess His name, and marked as belonging to Him and not to the world and to Satan.

(*c*) *The baptized person is incorporated into the visible Church of Jesus Christ* (1 Cor. xii. 13 ; Acts ii. 41, etc.). It was not our Lord's object only to save us by the renewing of the Holy Spirit and to cause us to enter into the communion of His mystical body. He also wished to establish a visible Church, composed of all those who confess Him as their God and Saviour. He therefore instituted an external and visible sign which marks us as being of His people and enrols us in their number. Prior to baptism this sign was circumcision.

To belong to the visible Church is both an honour and a great advantage. The baptized person is incorporated, " added " to the visible Church ; he is the beneficiary of the blessings whose administration is entrusted to the Church which exercises to his benefit the " ministry of reconciliation." The Church in the New Testament, moreover, possesses greater riches than under the old theocracy. In Romans ix. 4 Paul speaks in glowing terms of the privileges of the Jews ; yet when he compares the present Church with that of the Old Testament (2 Cor. iii. 6-11 ; and the Epistle to the Galatians), or when the author of the Epistle to the Hebrews compares the Mosaic economy with that of the new dispensation, in each case the superiority of the New Testament Church is energetically maintained, and it is affirmed that the advantages enjoyed by the faithful through membership of the Church are much more to be envied. The oracles of God have been entrusted to the Church ; she is the depository of the Truth which makes man wise unto salvation, and the divinely instituted means of preserving and communicating this truth. It is a remarkable blessing to be in the bosom of the Church and not be

---

[1] Art. XXVII of the Church of England.

cast out into the " world." It is good to be in the place where
one can benefit from the oath of faithfulness sworn by God
to His Church. It is good to share in the care and protection
of the people of God. It is good to be able to appeal for her
prayers and efforts to cause us to enter or to keep us within
the way of salvation. It is good, above all, to be one of those
to whom God has made the special promise of grace and
salvation. Only those who renounce the privilege of being
members of the Church are deprived of all these blessings.

* * * *

We are now in a position to formulate some important
conclusions.

1. *The covenant of grace is the foundation of baptism*

When we seek the ultimate *foundation* of baptism it is not
sufficient to say that we find it in Christ. Christ is the
content of baptism and as such His place is one of eminence.
But the true foundation of this sacrament ought to be sought
higher still, namely, in the decree of God whereby Christ was
given to us, thanks to which the Almighty has become
" *God-with-us*," and which is revealed to us in the covenant
of grace.

We have already seen that Christ is the Mediator, the
Guarantor, and the Fulfiller of the covenant. His blood shed
is the blood of the covenant ; His sacrificial death fulfils
and completes the covenant ; His resurrection is the manifestation of the power of the promise of the covenant, thenceforth fully accomplished. If He gathers together His own into
His body, if He is the Great Shepherd of the sheep, it is by
the blood of the everlasting covenant. His entire ministry,
and that of the Apostles, is to administer the covenant in
conformity with the riches of God's plan of salvation.

By the preaching of the Gospel the covenant—fulfilled
in Christ—is offered to whosoever believes ; by the administration of the sacraments the covenant is signed and sealed.
The Lord's supper is a sacrament of the covenant because
the blood shed by Christ is that of the covenant. Baptism,
which has reference to the death of Christ, accomplished
according to the promises of the covenant, and to His
resurrection in virtue of the same promises of the same

covenant, is equally a sacrament of the covenant of grace. Here it is not a question of an arbitrary or *a priori* comparison. All that the New Testament says concerning baptism bears us out.

The covenant contains the promise of justification and forgiveness of sins ; the Gospel proclaims this ; the preaching of the Word effects belief in this ; baptism is the sign and seal of this. By baptism God reveals that He wishes through His justification to re-establish the sinner in blessed fellowship with Himself.

The covenant contains the promise of the adoption of sons, fellowship in the death and resurrection of Christ, and our incorporation into Christ. It makes us children of God. Baptism is the sign and seal of this adoption, this sonship, this fellowship, and this incorporation.

The covenant has reference to vocation and election, and so also has baptism. It contains the promise of life eternal and of glorification : " Whosoever believes and is baptized has everlasting life." The covenant is all of grace; it *is* grace in Jesus Christ ; baptism is the sign and seal of *this* grace.

The covenant conveys the promise of the gift of the Holy Spirit with a view to the full and free application of the work of redemption and of all the benefits of salvation ; baptism, which unites us to Christ and makes us partakers of all His blessings and mercies, is the sacrament of this. Together with the Word, it is the Spirit's means of action whereby all the riches of salvation are communicated to us by faith. The Spirit is at work in forming all the fruits which result from baptism, just as in those which are conveyed to us by the preaching of the Word.

The covenant is trinitarian: so also is baptism, in conformity to the command of Christ and the economy of salvation. It is the sign and seal of the mercy of the *Father* who wishes to receive us into His grace, who provides us with a *Mediator* through whose death and life we are regenerated, in order that by the sanctification of the *Spirit* a new spiritual nature may be built up in us. The *cause* of our cleansing and regeneration is in God, the *matter* is in Christ, and its *efficacy* is the fruit of the Spirit.[1]

[1] Cf. Calvin : *Instt*. IV. xv. 6.

The covenant and baptism are both entirely to the glory of God and intended for His glorification in us.

The object of the covenant is to remove sinful man from the corruptions of this age, to separate him from the wicked, and to incorporate him in God's people and Church : baptism signifies and *seals* the reality of this act of God which is fulfilled in whoever receives the promise with faith. Baptism is the sacrament of this setting apart, of this incorporation into the visible Church. The covenant builds up the Church, and so does baptism.

It is important to observe that, whatever are the New Testament texts which relate to baptism, or which make mention of it or speak of its nature and effects, all without exception are set down within the framework of the covenant of grace which has reached complete fulfilment. This fact is *objective*. With the scientific consciousness which characterizes them exegetes enumerate and analyse these spiritual realities signified and sealed by baptism, but they too often seem to add them to each other without any close organic bond. The covenant is precisely the spiritual cement which arranges them in relationship to each other and co-ordinates and unites them in a harmonious and majestic whole.

The fact that baptism confirms the economy of the covenant of grace in every point and even in the smallest details is a fresh proof from the New Testament that the eternal and irrevocable covenant is and remains essentially the same in the New Testament, which carries it to the peak of its power and, by the ministry of the Word and the sacraments, gives it all its efficacy in Jesus Christ.

The central promise of the covenant : " I will be your God and you shall be My people ; I will be your God and you shall be My son ; I shall call you My son and you shall call Me Father," is *the* promise of the Gospel of which baptism is the sign and seal, fulfilled for whoever believes the promise and repents. God declares to us by baptism that He wishes to possess us for His people and His heritage.

The primary condition of entry into the covenant is faith and repentance. According to the New Testament, since for adults faith and repentance are the condition for receiving 'it, *baptism is thus the sacrament of the believer's entry into the covenant of grace.*

As the washing of regeneration, the cleansing in the Saviour's blood, the putting on of Christ, the witness of our adoption as sons, the door into the visible Church and into the kingdom of heaven, the introduction to life eternal, *baptism is the sacrament of entry into the covenant of grace, the visible sign of our adoption:* " *In baptism we have the covenant of God as it were engraved in our bodies.*" [1]

Thus the covenant and it alone with its promise of adoption is the true foundation of baptism. Karl Barth, even though his conception of the covenant differs from ours, since he deprives it of its organic bond and individualizes it, yet establishes the same link between baptism and the covenant : " Baptism is the representation of man's association . . . with the covenant of grace which is concluded and realised in Him."[2] " That faith (of those baptized) has its ground and essence in the objective reality of the divine covenant of grace " [3] "In baptism He says to the candidate that He also for him and with him is dead and risen and a partner in the covenant,"[4] etc. No *a priori* argument, no reason, no motive, however valuable it may at first appear to be, no supposed demonstration can, according to the Scriptures, invalidate this vital point and cause the foundation of baptism to be anything other than the covenant of grace, or cause baptism to signify and seal anything else *in the first place* than our adoption and reception into the covenant : " There has always been but one adoption, there has always been but one Saviour, there has always been but one grace which God has promised to the ancients and to us." [5]

Recognizing these facts, the Confessions of the Reformed faith are unanimous and explicit in this connection, as also are the symbolical books. " Baptism has been given to us as a witness of our adoption . . . "; such is the opening statement of the Confession of the French Reformed Churches, para. 35. The Helvetic Confession affirms (20, 2) :

[1] Calvin : *Sermon* on Dt. x. 1-8, Opera, XXVII, 8.
[2] *Op. cit.*, p. 9.   [3] *Ibid.*, p. 21.   [4] *Ibid.*, p. 29.
[5] Calvin : *Sermon* on 1 Cor. x. 1-5, Opera, XLIX, p. 587.

" To be baptized in the name of Jesus Christ is nothing other than to be enrolled, introduced, and received into the covenant and family of God, that is, into the heritage of the children of God, and henceforward to be given the surname of God, that is to say, children of God. . . . Baptism thus reminds us and represents to us in a lifelike manner God's great beneficence and inestimable grace displayed to the human race." Again, the same Confession declares : " We are all born in the defilement of sin and are children of wrath ; but God, who is rich in mercy, freely cleanses and purges our sins by the blood of His Son, *adopting us in Him for His own children, and He even binds us to Himself with a holy and sacred covenant*, enriching us with a variety of gifts and bounties in order that we may be able to lead a new life." The Westminster Confession speaks as follows : " Baptism is a sacrament of the New Testament, instituted by Jesus Christ, not only for the solemn admission of the baptized person into the visible Church, *but also to be a sign and seal to him of the covenant of grace*. . . . " Article XXVII of the Church of England says that by baptism, " as by an instrument, they that receive baptism rightly are grafted into the Church, the promises of forgiveness of sin *and of our adoption to be the sons of God by the Holy Ghost* are visibly signed and sealed. . . . " The Heidelberg Catechism speaks of baptism as " the sign of the covenant," and Calvin's Catechism affirms that baptism " assures us that God receives us who were estranged to Him, as members of His own household."

2. *Baptism has taken the place of circumcision as the sacrament of admission into the covenant.*

It is at the same time necessary to understand how in the New Testament dispensation baptism has taken the place of circumcision. By making reference to what we have already said concerning circumcision and baptism, we in fact reach the conclusion that baptism corresponds exactly to circumcision taken in its spiritual sense.

Circumcision was the sign and seal of the remission of sins, of justification, of change of heart, of sanctification, of the objective work of the grace of God. It conveyed the promise of eternal life ; it was the sacrament of admission into the covenant of grace. Its basis was the promise of God's mercy, its content Jesus Christ. According to the New Testament all this applies equally to baptism.

When one compares these sacraments in the two dispensations of the covenant of grace it is established that, apart from the external sign, they correspond with each other in every point. The *promise* which is the basis of circumcision is equally the basis of baptism ; the *thing represented* is the same ; the *cause*, which is the love of God, is the same ; the *content*, Jesus Christ, is the same ; the *reason* and *motive* for the giving of the sign are the same. We shall soon see that their *usage* and *efficacy* are identical, as are also the *conditions of admission*. It is only the nature of the external sign that differs : after Christ's coming a sacrament could no longer be a bloody sacrifice. Let us not forget that the external sign is the least important part of a sacrament, " whereas the chief part consists in the promise and the thing signified."[1]

This "transition" from circumcision to baptism is corroborated by the New Testament, which insists strongly on the fact that circumcision, as such, could not continue. If the text of Genesis where God established circumcision and the commands of Christ (Mt. xxviii. 19 f. and Mk. xvi. 15 f.) are compared *within the perspective of the covenant*, it will be seen that baptism was substituted for circumcision with which there is no further concern.

The Synod of Jerusalem (Acts xv. 1 ff.) reached the conclusion that circumcision ought not to be administered to converted pagans. For them, *to begin with*, the practice was abolished. In the Epistle to the Galatians (ii. 3-5 ; v. 2, 6 ; vi. 12, 13, 15) Paul combats the Judaizing notion of circumcision when he declares : " If you are circumcized Christ will profit you nothing."

The text of Colossians ii. 11 f. plainly links circumcision to baptism and teaches that *the circumcision of Christ*, that is to say, the circumcision of the heart, signified by the circumcision in the flesh (cf. Rom. ii. 28 f.), is achieved by baptism, that is to say, by that which baptism signifies. The Colossians, proselytes won from paganism, are circum-

[1] Calvin : *Instt.* IV. xvi. 4.

cized as well as the Jews, not, however, with a carnal circumcision performed by human hands, but with a circumcision which consists in the putting off of the whole carnal and sinful nature. They are grafted into Christ by means and in virtue of the circumcision which Christ Himself endured in His death for sin, at the same moment as they are buried and resurrected with Christ by baptism. Through the death of Christ, which was a perfect burial of sin and a complete victory over sin, and which consequently fully realized the idea of circumcision, circumcision according to the flesh has lapsed into disuse and through baptism has reached its perfect accomplishment.

One may admit that during the Mosaic period circumcision acquired a certain typical significance. But originally it was a sign and seal of the covenant which was made with Abraham. In so far as it was a type, it naturally vanished with the appearance of the anti-type, and even in so far as it was the seal of the covenant it gave place to an unbloody sacrament expressly instituted by Jesus Christ for the Church, and recognized as such by the Apostles, for, thanks to His work of redemption, Christ put an end once for all to the shedding of blood.

" Circumcision," says Bannerman, " was independent either of the introduction or abolition of the law of Moses, and would have continued the standing ordinance for admission into the Church of God as the seal of the covenant of grace, had not baptism been expressly appointed as a substitute for it." [1] Baptism is thus more than circumcision, not in essence, but in degree, by reason of the greater riches of the new dispensation of the covenant of grace. Circumcision looked forward to the death of Christ, while baptism points back to it. With this death the one is concluded and the other commences. The fulfilment of baptism is the fulfilment of circumcision.

The Confession of the Netherlands alone, in its article on baptism (Art. 34), mentions this fact—the Churches of that country have had to face the violent opposition of anabaptists : " We believe and confess that Jesus Christ, who

---

[1] *The Church of Christ*, II, p. 98, quoted by Berkhof, *Reformed Dogmatics*, p. 636.

is the end of the Law, has by the shedding of His blood put an end to all other effusions of blood which might be made for the propitiation or satisfaction of sins and, having abolished circumcision which was performed with blood, has ordained the sacrament of baptism in its place."[1]

This New Testament fact, that the sacrament of baptism has taken the place of the sacrament of circumcision, can only be denied by those who, as we have seen, rob circumcision of its true nature by making it a carnal institution, and who by a consequence that is inevitable then expunge it from the list of the sacraments. It is obvious that, since a sacrament is by definition a sign of spiritual things, a carnal sign of a carnal reality can no longer be a sacrament. Viewed in this light, the opposition between baptism—a spiritual sacrament—and circumcision—a sign of a carnal reality—becomes such that it is no longer possible to maintain that baptism has taken the place of circumcision. Not only as regards the sign, but as regards the things signified, it becomes an essentially new sacrament, peculiar to the New Testament, and one which—it immediately follows—ought to be administered in accordance with entirely different rules. We have shown with the support of texts that such a conception cannot be maintained, precisely in accordance with the scheme of the New Testament, and that its partisans ought to revise their philosophical conceptions upon which this artificial *a priori* construction is founded.

It has been objected that circumcision concerns only males, whereas baptism concerns both sexes, and that there is consequently no correspondence between them. To this objection Calvin replies : " If they would consider well the proper character of circumcision, they would abandon this very frivolous argument (that women ought not to be baptized if baptism is to be made conformable to circumcision). For since by this sign the Lord demonstrated the sanctification of the seed of Israel, it is certain that it served for women equally with men ; but it was not applied to women because they are by nature not fitted for it. Thus the Lord, in ordaining that the male should be circumcized,

---

[1] Cf. also the Heidelberg Catechism, XXVII. 74 ; O. Cullmann, *op. cit.*, pp. 56 ff.—ch. 4 on " Baptism and Circumcision."

involved with him the female who, though unable to receive circumcision in her own body, yet shared in a certain sense in the circumcision of the male." [1] H. Bavinck says : " The sacrament of the old dispensation was administered only to persons of the male sex, while the sacrament of the new dispensation is administered equally to persons of the feminine sex. On this point even the opponents of infant baptism recognize the richer grace of baptism, . . . Christ has placed the woman in an independent relationship with Himself and has made her, together with the man, a partaker of His grace. In Him, there is no longer either male or female and it is for this reason that both together are buried with Christ in baptism and raised to newness of life. Finally, the greatest value of the grace of the sacrament of the new dispensation is apparent also in this, that circumcision could only be performed on the eighth day after birth because during that period the child participated in the impurity of the mother ; but now, under the New Testament economy, children have the right of baptism from the moment of their birth, because from the first moment of their existence they participate in the grace of Christ."[2]

3. *Baptism an act of God*

Baptism represents *in the first place* an act of the grace of God, an offering and a gift, accomplished in virtue of the promise. This objective basis of baptism should be resolutely emphasized : *adults are baptized because of the covenant which is offered to them and which they accept, not because of their faith or their repentance, which are fruits of the covenant.* The basis of baptism is not the faith and repentance of the believer who requests it, but the covenant in virtue of which this faith and this repentance have been rendered possible. Faith and repentance are already consequences. One is not baptized on the ground of one's faith and repentance ! In accordance with its foundation, baptism does not *in the first place* illustrate the subjective sentiments of man and his response to the grace of God, but the work of God's grace to which it has reference and the call of God to enter into the

---

[1] *Instt.* IV. xvi. 16.
[2] *Gereformeerde Dogmatiek*, IV, p. 285. Cf. O. Cullmann, *op. cit.*, p. 65.

covenant and to live in it according to His promise. *In the first place and above all* baptism is the sign and seal of the free grace of God, granted in virtue of the promise, and realized in him who believes.

Every attempt to base baptism on one of the consequences or fruits of the promise (knowledge of salvation, personal faith, change of heart, etc.) is bound to fail; it is entangled in insurmountable difficulties and insoluble contradictions, and—a fact decisive in our judgment—it does not take into account the united testimony of the biblical data which relate or are relevant to baptism as a sacrament of the covenant of grace.

It is not man who is the principal actor in the sacrament of baptism : it is God and Jesus Christ, acting through the Holy Spirit, in exactly the same manner as in the preaching of the Word. " It must be observed," affirms Calvin [1] and the Reformed theologians after him, " that the sacraments when rightly understood are not properly works of men, but of God. For both in baptism and the Lord's supper we do nothing except present ourselves to God in order to receive His grace. Baptism then, as it concerns us, is a passive work, for we bring nothing to it except faith, which seeks everything in Christ and relies entirely on Him." We may recall also a citation from Calvin which we have already given earlier : " In receiving the sacraments we do not deserve any commendation, and, because this action is passive as regards us, it is not even right to attribute anything at all to ourselves. I call this action passive because God does everything and we only receive." [2]

When he hears the Word man is active *only by his faith* in order that he may receive and accept the Gospel and the grace of the covenant ; and the same is the case when he partakes of the sacraments. The *action* is divine. It is essential to stress that this assertion is not a piece of *a priori* dogmatizing ; the exegetes of the New Testament hold to it because the texts compel them to do so. " It belongs to the essence of Christian baptism in the New Testament," says Cullmann, " that it is Christ that operates, while the person baptized is the passive object of His deed." [3] ; and Preiss writes that " the sacraments, like the miracles,

---

[1] *Comm.* on Gal. v. 3.   [2] *Instt.*, IV. xiv. 26.   [3] *Op. cit.*, p. 15.

are the work of Christ, acting through the Spirit, a testimony
to the power of the new world." [1]

In the New Testament texts referring to baptism the verbs
are constantly passive in form : " We have been baptized
into his death ; . . . being buried with Him by baptism ; . . .
we have been planted together in the likeness of His death ;
. . . . our old man is crucified with Him ; . . . you have been
washed, sanctified, justified ; . . . not by works of righteousness which we have done, but according to His mercy He
saved us, by the washing of regeneration and renewing of
the Holy Ghost." One *is baptized*, one *receives* baptism, just
as one receives circumcision (Col. ii. 11), just as one receives
the Word preached, just as the new-born babe is nourished
at his mother's breast.

It is likewise an act of God whereby one is incorporated
into Christ and into the visible Church : baptism is the
sacrament by which the Church is constituted. " What
happens in the act of baptism is clearly defined in the
decisive Pauline texts 1 Cor. xii. 13 and Gal. iii. 27 f. as a
setting within the body of Christ," says Cullmann. " God
sets a man within, *not merely informs him that he sets him
within*, the body of Christ ; and *at this moment* therefore
the reception of this act on the part of the person baptized
consists in nothing else than that he is *the passive object of
God's dealing*, that he *is really set within* the body of Christ by
God. He is 'added' (Acts ii. 41), an unambiguous passive." [2]

On the one hand, the love and mercy of God, and His will
and decree, are anterior to every procedure of man ; the
offer of the covenant, presented by the audible Word, is
antecedent. On the other hand, the events fulfilled by Christ
in conformity with the plan of the covenant, which render
possible its realization and to which baptism has reference,
are displayed in a perfectly objective and antecedent manner, independently of every human decision and will and of
all personal experience. The exegetes insist on this point. [3]

Thus from the point of view of the intentions and acts of

[1] *Op. cit.*, p. 119.   [2] *Op. cit.*, p. 31.
[3] On the activity of Christ in baptism and the interval between the
events and their effects, cf. F.-J. Leenhardt, *op. cit.*, pp. 46, 47, 63, 64,
65, and *Foi et Vie, op. cit.*, p. 78 ; Th. Preiss, *op. cit.* ; O. Cullmann, *op. cit.*,
pp. 32-35, etc.

God the divine activity has priority over human activity ; human activity, which is aroused by the preaching of the Word and by the sacrament, is a consequence of the preceding divine activity. From the point of view of man, on the other hand, passivity has priority over the activity which is produced by the Word or the sacraments. It is a mistake, fraught with serious consequences, either to invert the order of the terms or to wish to make them exist together in an immediate temporal simultaneousness.

B. BAPTISM AS A MEANS OF GRACE

1. Its Efficacy

The Bible teaches that God sanctifies and saves men by the Truth, that the Spirit with and by the Truth applies the benefits of redemption to man. The question as to *how* this truth penetrates man's spirit by being read or heard, or by the use of divinely instituted signs, is not one of importance. The fundamental truths which we have enumerated are clearly taught in a manner which is as penetrating in the sacrament of baptism as in the words of our beloved Saviour Himself. Consequently, it is just as easy (or, according to others, just as difficult) to understand *how* the Spirit makes the truth signified in baptism a means of sanctification, as to understand *how* He makes this same truth, read or heard, an effective means of salvation.

The Holy Spirit acts *together with the Word*, without His power and action being contained *in* the Word ; He acts likewise *together with* the water of baptism. In Ephesians v. 26 Paul clearly distinguishes the action of Christ by the Word from that by the water ; and this is equally the case in Hebrews x. 22 and I Peter iii. 21. It is not the minister, and it is not the water, *but Christ who sanctifies and gives the thing signified* (Mt. iii. 11 ; I Cor. vi. 11 ; Heb. ix. 14 ; I Jn. i. 7) [1] The water of baptism represents the blood of

[1] In Eph. v. 26 the phrase " by the word " is not, as some have wished it to be, a more precise definition of " the washing of water," for that would require a preceding article—τῷ or τοῦ before ἐν ῥήματι. The phrase should be associated with ἁγιάσῃ—" that He might sanctify." Christ sanctifies His Church by the Word of the Gospel at the same time as He purifies her by the washing of water. If it were the water of baptism that effected regeneration, Paul would not have been able to say in I Cor. i. 14 that Christ had not sent him to baptize, but to preach the Gospel.

Christ, which is our true and only purification ; it brings us in the first place confirmation and assurance of the grace acquired through Jesus Christ. " Saint Paul here shows the means by which we are assured of our membership in the body of our Lord Jesus Christ. I have already said that there is no need for us to look for any other cause than the pure bounty of God, for if we wander off elsewhere we are like men who are desperately thirsty and who yet turn their backs on the fountain of water. Let us learn, then, that it is God alone who, by His pure liberality, unites us to our Lord Jesus Christ, and does so by the secret operation of His Holy Spirit ; yet *He does not hesitate to work through baptism as through an inferior instrument*, just as we see that all light proceeds from Him, so that even before the sun and moon appeared there was light in the world. As it is today God has established the sun to give us light here below ; but the sun is not intended to derogate from the virtue which is in God alone." [1]

In consideration of the fact that, according to our Reformed conception, the baptism of adults and of proselytes presupposes regeneration, faith, conversion, and justification, it is quite certain that these things cannot be considered as being *effected* by baptism. No more does baptism produce a *special* sacramental grace by which the recipient is incorporated or grafted into the body of Jesus Christ. The incorporation of the believer into mystical union with Jesus Christ is equally presupposed : *he is already within the covenant of grace and that is why he receives baptism*. With the exception that the Word, as distinct from the sacraments, is also an instrumental cause in the generation of faith, both Word and sacraments convey and produce exactly the same sort of blessings. The sacrament of baptism strengthens faith and, because faith plays a vital part in all the other operations of divine grace, it is of real service to these operations.

Baptism is thus not only a sign and a seal, but also a means of grace : the blessings which are signified by it are also offered and applied to us by it ; the promises which are sealed by it are also assured and fulfilled for and in all those who are baptized, on condition that they believe.

[1] Calvin : *Sermon* on Gal. iii. 26-29, Opera, L, p. 562.

When a man receives the Gospel with a true faith he receives the benefits which the Gospel promises ; when he receives baptism with faith he receives the blessings of which baptism is the sign and seal. For him who receives it—unless he is insincere—baptism is an act of faith by which and in which he receives and appropriates the blessings of the redemption of Christ which are offered to him. This is the reason why everything which in the Scriptures is attributed to faith can also be properly attributed to baptism. Not only does baptism cleanse away our sins, justify and regenerate us, cause us to die with Christ, and unite us to Him and make us children of God ; not only is it the washing of regeneration and our incorporation into the Church ; *but it is for the believer a means of grace as real as the Word itself.* It causes the truth to penetrate to the spirit, it confirms the promise of God, it is a means used by the Holy Spirit for communicating to believers the blessings of redemption.   Baptism is not limited to signifying, sealing, and representing : to him who believes it *presents* afresh and offers the truths and blessings of the Gospel : *the reality is joined to the sign.* " We ought in the water of baptism to contemplate the blood of our Lord Jesus Christ and the redemption which He has acquired for us. It confronts us as it were with a living picture ; and not only that, *but with the portrait and image is conjoined the truth,* in such a way that the effect ought to be perceived in it. . . . Let us be certain that our Lord in no way amuses us with the toys and baubles of little children when He gives us the sacraments, but it is the truth for which we are looking that He gives us, so that we may be joined to Him and may perceive that His power is always close at hand." [1] " From the fact that the sign has been given to us we can infer that the reality is truly communicated to us. . . . Believers, in fact, ought always to hold fast to this rule, namely, that *on each occasion when they see the signs ordained by God they may be in the same way assured that the truth of the thing represented is linked to it, and of this they should be firmly convinced.*" [2]

As a visible Word, concretely confronting a particular

---

[1] Calvin : *Sermon* on Deut. xvi. 13-17, Opera, XXVI, p. 406.

[2] Calvin : *Instt.*, IV, xvii. 10.

man, baptism actualizes and individualizes the preaching of the Word for him who receives it. God designates *this particular man* and not another as the beneficiary of His promise; this particular man is concretely singled out, gripped, seized; this particular man is loved by God; this particular man has been loved by Christ; for him personally Christ gave Himself up to death (Gal. ii. 20), in order that this particular man should die to sin. For him personally Christ was raised, in order that this particular man might be raised to newness of life. His adoption, his election, his entry into the covenant are personally and concretely signified and sealed to him. In Question 69 of the Heidelberg Catechism the master inquires of the catechumen: " How is it signified and sealed unto *thee* in holy baptism that *thou* hast part in the one sacrifice of Christ on the Cross ? " and to this the pupil responds : " Thus: that Christ has appointed this outward washing with water, and has joined therewith His promise that *I* am washed with His blood and Spirit from the pollution of *my* soul, that is, from all *my* sins, as certainly as *I* am washed outwardly with water, whereby commonly the filthiness of the body is taken away."

These things being so, how ought we to receive or make use of baptism ? " Inasmuch as it has been appointed to elevate, nourish, and confirm our faith, we ought to receive it as from the hand of its own Author, being firmly persuaded that it is He Himself who speaks to us by means of the sign, that it is He Himself who washes and purifies us, and effaces the remembrance of our sins ; that it is He Himself who makes us the partakers of His death and destroys the kingdom of Satan and subdues the power of our concupiscence ; indeed, that He makes Himself one with us, so that by this union we may also be truly accounted children of God. We ought thus to believe and be assured that, just as we see our body externally washed, immersed, and surrounded by water, so also He truly and certainly performs all these things internally in our soul. For this analogy or similitude furnishes the surest rule of the sacraments, namely, that in corporeal things we are to view and contemplate spiritual things, just as though they were actually exhibited before our eyes, since it has pleased the Lord to represent them to us by such figures ; not that such blessings are bound to or included in the sacrament, or that they are conferred on us by its efficacy, but only that by this sign and badge the Lord declares to us that it is His will to bestow all these things upon us ; nor does He merely regale our eyes with a bare and empty spectacle, but leads us at once to the actual object and effectually performs that which it figures."[1] " When there is a melody and a mutual accord between God and us . . . when we accept this, then all that is figured in baptism is fulfilled." [2]

All this is said in setting out from the supposition that baptism is what it claims to be : *an act of faith.* We have nothing else in baptism than what we receive by faith. For those who do not believe, the Gospel of our salvation, whether it be the Word spoken or visible, is a savour of death which leads to death (2 Cor. ii. 15 f.).

The Word of God is declared to be the wisdom and the power of God for our salvation ; it is the means employed by the Holy Spirit for conferring on man the blessings of redemption. But it goes without saying that not all those who read or hear the Word are saved ; no more do all those who receive the baptism of water experience the baptism of the Holy Spirit. The Holy Spirit does not always co-operate with the truth which is heard so as to make it a means of grace to salvation, nor is He always present at the administration of baptism with His saving and sanctifying power. Baptism only produces its fruits in those who believe. But this does not invalidate the fact that the Word is the means of salvation and that baptism is the washing of regeneration. Our Lord affirms that we are sanctified by the truth, and, according to Paul, we have by baptism put on Christ (Gal. iii. 27).

The Reformed doctrine concerning the efficacy of baptism thus rejects and disavows the following affirmations :

(*a*) That baptism transmits grace *ex opere operato*, in the sense which Roman Catholics attach to this expression, through some sort of objective supernatural power belonging

[1] Calvin : *Instt.*, IV. xv. 14.
[2] Calvin : *Sermon* on Gal. iii. 26-29, Opera, L, p. 561.

to the ordinance itself, or in virtue of a divine efficiency inherent in the words or the promise of God joined to the sacrament ;

(*b*) that the co-operation of the Spirit, to which the efficacy of the ordinance is due, is always present and always accompanies its administration, in such a way that those who are baptized receive in every instance the remission of sins and the renewing of the Holy Spirit ;

(*c*) that baptism is prescribed as the ordinary means or channel for the transmission, in the first place, of the merits of the death of Christ and the saving action of the Spirit, in such a way that these blessings, except in extraordinary cases, cannot be obtained before or without baptism.

Reformed doctrine rejects equally everything which, in the administration of baptism, has been added to the sign of water.[1]

To sum up, the blessings which are bestowed on believers in baptism are all comprised in communion with God, Father, Son, and Holy Spirit. *The Father* attests in baptism that He establishes with us an eternal covenant and that He receives us as His own children and heirs. *The Son* seals us in the assurance that He washes us in His own blood and incorporates us into the communion of His death and resurrection. *The Holy Spirit* seals us in the assurance that He dwells in us and sanctifies us as members of Jesus Christ.

In consideration of all these facts revealed in Scripture, the Confession of faith of the Reformed Churches of France defines the efficacy of baptism with characteristic brevity : " Baptism is given to us as a testimony of our adoption, because by it we are grafted into the body of Christ so that we may be washed and cleansed by His blood, and then renewed in sanctity of life by His Holy Spirit " (para. 35). The Second Helvetic Confession and the Confession of the Netherlands are more explicit : " (In baptism) we are internally regenerated, purified, and renewed by God through the Holy Spirit, when we receive externally a seal and

[1] Cf. Helv. Conf., XX. 5.

testimony of His great gifts in the water of baptism, whereby the great benefits of our God are represented to us and as it were displayed before our gaze. It is for this reason that we are baptized, that is to say, sprinkled and washed with visible water. For water cleanses objects that are dirty, re-creates and invigorates things which wilt because of heat, and refreshes the body ; but the grace of God grants all these things to our souls in an invisible and spiritual manner. We believe that baptism in the Church has been sanctified by the original ordinance of God and consecrated through His Word, and that it retains even to the present time its efficacy and force because of the original blessing of God."[1]
" We have thus been commanded to baptize all those who are His, in the name of the Father and of the Son and of the Holy Spirit, with pure water, which signifies to us that as water washes the uncleanness of the body when it is poured over us, which is also seen when a person is baptized and sprinkled, so the blood of Christ effects the same internally in the soul by the Holy Spirit, sprinkling it and cleansing away its sins, and regenerating us from children of wrath into children of God ; not that the physical water effects this, but it is the sprinkling of the precious blood of God's Son, which is our Red Sea, through which He causes us to pass so that we may escape from the tyranny of Pharaoh, who is the devil, and to enter into the spiritual land of Canaan. Thus the ministers for their part give us the sacrament and that which is visible ; but the Lord gives that which is signified by the sacrament, namely, to know the invisible gifts and blessings, washing, purifying, and cleansing our souls from all uncleanness and iniquity, renewing our hearts and filling them with all consolation, giving us a true assurance of His paternal bounty, clothing us with the new man and stripping us of the old man with all his deeds." [2]

---

[1] 2nd Helv. Conf., para. 20, sections 3 and 4.
[2] Neth. Conf., para. 34 ; cf. Conf. of Geneva, XV ; Art. XXVII of the Church of England ; The Irish Articles, No. LXXXIX ; Westm. Conf., XXVIII. 1. Whoever wishes to make a thorough investigation of the question of the efficacy of the sacraments ought to study the *Consensus Tigurinus*, which is found *in extenso* in the *Opera Calvini*, and which is the fullest and most elaborate text of the time of the Reformation.

2. *The time of the efficacy of baptism*

(a) *When, at what moment*, is the baptism received efficacious ? If this question is put to a Protestant, one is —in the majority of cases—amazed at his response or at his ignorance which hinders him from responding. It is extremely distressing to see that in the Reformed Church the great majority of Christians never refer back to their baptism.

In Calvin's Catechism, para. 47, the master addresses the question : " *When* do the sacraments produce their effect ? " and the catechumen replies : " *When one receives them with faith*, seeking in them only Jesus Christ and His grace." But this reception by faith of the sacrament of baptism is not bound to a precise moment dependent on external circumstances ; it depends on the state of soul of the believer, for whom his baptism bears fruit *on each occasion on which he refers back to it with faith. The memory of the sacrament received is equivalent to a new reception by faith of this baptism.* This is not the consequence of a subjective mechanism, but of the promise of which the sacrament is the sign, and of the efficacy—which is not subject to temporal limits—of the death and resurrection of Jesus Christ. God's promise endures in time ; through the sign received, the memory of which we preserve, we refer back to this immutable promise and to the divine events which it continues to signify and seal. This is so with baptism and with the Lord's supper, as also with the Word which has been heard and which we remember.

When God promised to Noah that He would never again destroy the world by a deluge He placed the rainbow in the heavens as a pledge of the promise which He had just made with him. Today there is nobody who, believing in the Word of God and in the validity of the signs which He has instituted, can regard the rainbow without experiencing a strengthening of his faith in the promise that the earth will never again be submerged by a deluge.

When God promised to Abraham to be his God and the God of his posterity after him He established circumcision as a seal and pledge of this promise. Today no pious Jew can contemplate this sign in his own flesh or be present as a witness at a circumcision without experiencing a strengthening of his faith in the assurance that Jehovah is his God and that he is His child.

Similarly, when our God and Father promised to save man by the blood of Jesus Christ and to renew him by the Holy Spirit He established baptism to be not only a sign, but also the seal and pledge of these remarkable promises. Today no Christian, if he has been well instructed in the things of God, can recall his own baptism or witness another's baptism without experiencing a strengthening of his faith in the sublime promise of redemption, and without being confirmed in the assurance that he is indeed the adopted son of God, the brother of Jesus Christ, and a member of the covenant of grace. On each occasion he applies and appropriates to himself anew the promise : " The blood of Jesus Christ cleanses thee from all sin. . . . He has saved thee by the washing of regeneration and the renewing of the Holy Spirit."

Baptism is not simply given us for a time that is past in such a way that we have need of other remedies if we are to be cleansed from sins committed after we have received it. " The perfection of baptism, which extends even to death, is improperly restricted to one day or to one moment of time."[1] No matter when we were baptized, our baptism is the sign and seal that we have been justified by the blood of Jesus Christ and that this blood cleanses us for the whole length of our life. Once signified and sealed, the truth is not effaced by our subsequent sins. The divine events and acts of our salvation, accomplished in Jesus Christ, cannot be annulled by our sins. On the contrary, their efficacy remains so that we may be purified from every defilement. The memory of the sign received confers afresh on baptism the validity and efficacy which it had at the time of its institution and reception. Let us, therefore, constantly recall our baptism to mind !

In this efficacy of the sacrament which prevails throughout life we ascertain a mysterious reciprocal action. Just as light and the eye presuppose and are interrelated with each

---

[1] Calvin : *Instt.*, IV. xvi. 31.

other, so also faith, the stronger it is, the more it profits
from the sacraments and at the same time and in the same
way is by their means sealed and strengthened. It is for this
reason that the significance of the sacraments does not
gradually diminish for the believer as he grows older. For
him, on the contrary, their value is always increasing. They
display, in a manner which is ever more attractive and
glorious, the riches of the grace of God before the eyes of
faith.

" Let us esteem highly the testimony which has been
granted to us in baptism so that we may be able to oppose
every temptation and doubt with which Satan confronts
us in order to unsettle our faith. If we are so stupid that we
are not conscious of our vices, like people unaware of their
own bad breath, so much the worse for us ! But when we are
roused to the realization that an account has to be rendered
to God, that day and night He reminds us that He is the
Judge of the world, and that He cannot neglect this office,
after we have looked within ourselves to examine our sins,
we ought certainly to be overtaken by fear and misgiving ;
and if we have no remedy for our consolation, we can but
be plunged into the depths of despair. But let us take refuge
in our baptism, and in the fact that we know that it is not
in vain that God has called us to be partakers of the purity
of His only Son and that we have been made one with Him ;
and let us be assured that by this means the blood which He
shed will be effective in purging away every spot, so that we
shall be able to come boldly before God—not with arrogance
like the hypocrites and those who are self-sufficient, but
confiding in His inestimable bounty, since He has informed
us that everything which belongs to our Lord Jesus Christ
is communicated to us. And so, even if we have committed
so many offences that we feel the wrath of God to be burning
against us, Jesus Christ is there who has offered a sacrifice
by which we know that reconciliation has been made between
God and us, and thus that God has testified to us of the love
which He bears towards us in such a manner that we cannot
doubt that He always is at hand when we seek Him with a
true faith, that is to say, in a manner so plain that we may
by no means doubt that He has no wish to disappoint us

ing to

when He has shown Himself so generous towards us. This, then, is the way in which we ought to esteem our baptism : we should use it as a shield for repelling all the doubts which overtake us and which would hinder us from praying to God and having our whole refuge in Him, were it not that we had come to Him. Now, it is true that I have within myself so great a number of sins that I am rendered hateful before God : but it is not as though I come to Him in my own person ; I renounce myself and my nature in which only shame and confusion are to be found ; but I come to Him in the name of our Lord Jesus Christ, and it is even the case that He comes before me, He gives me as it were His own garment, He speaks for me, and it is in His name that I present myself, just as though I were He Himself, since it has pleased Him to be so gracious as to unite me to Himself. In this way, then, we ought to forget who we are when we come to God, and we ought to lay hold of the person of our Lord Jesus Christ, and forget ourselves : not that we are insensible of our faults and are not truly humiliated because of them and deplore them ; but it is necessary that we should grasp this persuasion and certitude that God accepts us as coming to Him in the person of His only Son. There are, however, all too few who give thought to this matter ! " [1]

The Christian, by his faith, ought to render the blessings which *are* and *remain* signified and offered by his baptism an ever-present reality in his daily life. He ought constantly to refer back to them so that he may be strengthened in the assurance that the sacrifice of Jesus Christ was consummated for his own benefit. " Just as it is true," he says, " that I was baptized and that the mark of this baptism cannot be effaced, so also it is true that God, who remains faithful to His promises, offers again today, to me personally, remission of my sins, justification, and eternal life. He wishes again today to be my Father and my Saviour." The Christian ought to refer back without ceasing to his baptism in order to gather progressively from it its fruits, *in accordance with his faith*. The moment I recall my baptism with faith, then in my heart and soul I receive and appropriate

[1] Calvin : *Sermon* on Gal. iii. 26-29, Opera, L, pp. 564 f.

to myself that which God represents and offers to me in it, just as was the case at the moment of the baptism itself.

The efficacy of baptism thus continues to display itself throughout the length of the Christian life. " The perfection of baptism extends even to death." [1]

(*b*) It is, therefore, neither necessary, nor indispensable, nor possible that all the blessings signified and sealed by baptism should precede it. Baptism is not the mark of a Christian life which is already completed ; it is the sacrament of the promise in accordance with which the Christian life will become more and more complete in the believer, in Jesus Christ, by the Holy Spirit, culminating in eternal life.

It is a significant fact that all the principal texts referring to baptism in the Epistles were not written with a view to informing us of the conditions necessary for admission to it, but with the purpose of describing the fruits which ought to follow *for those who have already received it,* and to define the ends to which it should conduct those who are careful to preserve the memory of the baptism they have received.

Romans vi. 3-11 must be placed in its context of vi. 1 f. and 15-23. Paul writes to those who have been baptized : " Do you not know that we who *were* baptized into Jesus Christ *were* baptized into His death ? Therefore we *were* buried with Him by baptism into death." Then, *by constantly linking to the present and the future the baptism which has been accomplished once for all,* he enumerates the fruits which ought to *follow* from baptism, today and tomorrow. It is essential to understand how the present and the future are implicated together with this past event in the experience of the believer. Paul continues : " If we *have been* planted together with Him in the likeness of His death, we *shall be* also in the likeness of His resurrection (ver. 5). . . . Our old man *was* crucified with Him *in order that* the body of sin might be destroyed and that *henceforth* we should not serve

[1] Calvin : *Instt.,* IV. xvi. 31. P.-Ch. Marcel, *A l'Ecole de Dieu,* p. 165. Cf. also, Conf. of French Reformed Churches, para. 35 ; 2nd Helv. Conf. 20. 2 ; Neth. Conf., para. 30 ; Westm. Conf., XXVIII. 6.

sin (ver. 6). . . . If we *died* with Christ, we believe that we *shall* also live with Him (ver. 8). . . . *Reckon yourselves* to be dead indeed unto sin (ver. 11). . . . *Let not* sin therefore reign in your mortal body, that you should *obey* its lusts (ver. 12). . . . *Do not yield* your members to sin, but *yield* yourselves to God (ver. 13). . . . For sin *shall not* have dominion over you (ver. 14). . . . So *now* yield your members servants to righteousness *unto holiness* (ver. 19). . . . *Now* you have your fruit unto holiness and the end everlasting life (ver. 22)." Death to sin has been achieved in principle : it remains for it to be put into practice, today and tomorrow, by a progressive sanctification, consecrating a new life with a view to eternal life.

Galatians iii. 27 ought likewise to be placed in its context of iii. 1-7, iv. 9-11 and 19 f., v. 1-12 and 13-26. These pages written to baptized persons ought to be read again. The sorrowful exclamations of the apostle are significant. It was needful that the Galatians, by faith, should turn their baptism to account.

Colossians ii. 11 f., placed in the context of ii. 8, 20-23, and iii. 1, which clearly has reference to baptism, leads to the exhortation of iii. 5 ff., " *Mortify therefore* your members which are on the earth. . . ." (cf. 9 f.). The death of the carnal man, achieved in principle and signified by baptism, also requires to be progressively realized. All the remainder of the Epistle develops the subject of what the fruits of this baptism ought to be.

According to the New Testament that which is represented in baptism does not necessarily precede it. In baptism one puts on Christ not because one has already *hitherto* lived in Christ, but in order that one may *henceforth* live in Him. One can only be profoundly impressed by the manner in which Paul constantly links the present and the future of the believer to his baptism which took place in the past and stresses the unceasingly dynamic character of baptism in the Christian life for every moment lived, in the " now " of our subjective consciousness, *on condition that* what it signifies is not ignored, but remembered and kept in mind.

In texts such as Matthew iii. 11a, Luke iii. 3, and Acts ii.

38, do we sufficiently notice to what extent baptism is presented as a point of departure and is orientated towards the future ? In Luke vii. 29 f., one of the rare texts in which Christ Himself speaks to us concerning baptism, those who were baptized by John " justified God," whereas the others " rejected God's plan for themselves." They continued in unbelief and, not having been baptized, their whole future is one which hypothetically involves them in rejection of God's plan. This *justification* of God by him who has laid hold of the Word is the first act of faith ; everything else in the Christian life depends on this justification of God, on this acquiescence, on this approbation by man of God's plans for him. According to John iii. 33 he who receives the witness of Christ sets to his seal that God is true. This " justification " of God, this " confirmation " by man of the divine truthfulness, is the point of departure of the Christian life, starting from which the plan of God is fulfilled, and it is signified and sealed by baptism.

Let us observe also that, according to Acts, the religious instruction of proselytes is carried out with disconcerting speed ! It scarcely lasts a few hours, after which at the first sign of faith indicating that the proselyte believes in his adoption, from the moment that he " justifies " God's plan for him, " sets to his seal " that God is true, and " welcomes" the message, he is himself " sealed " by baptism.

In Acts ii the instruction of proselytes commences at 9 a.m. and they are baptized before evening (verse 41). The Ethiopian eunuch is baptized after a brief conversation with Philip (viii. 26-39). By order of the glorified Christ Saul is immediately baptized (ix. 17-19). Cornelius and many others are baptized on the same day as they receive instruction (x. 30-48). The Philippian gaoler is baptized within the hour—" straightway " (xvi. 33) ; and so it goes on. It is impossible to assume that these proselytes had had time to live really and concretely in Christ or to display evidently all the fruits of faith before their baptism. The Apostles did not even think of judging concerning their sincerity and the depth of their convictions. Many were baptized who, as we have observed earlier, turned back from Christ.

At the first sign of faith and repentance, and following on their decision to be disciples and to live *thenceforward* a new life in view of the life eternal, they received baptism. We point to the Church's conviction that it was God who was acting, in His Son, by the Holy Spirit, and that the promise, once received, would in due course produce its fruits in the lives of those baptized. The idea of setting up a community of " proved " Christians, who would then be admitted to baptism, is not found in the Apostolic Church. *This breadth of the Church, this liberality of reception, despite its accompanying dangers, is most remarkable.*

In wiping out the sinner's past and signifying to him that he is a new creature in Christ, baptism thus points to the future. Its efficacy and perfection ought to develop and expand and be progressively realized right up till death.

3. *The Sphere of Efficacy of Baptism*

We have seen that the extension of the sacraments is less than that of the Word. The sacraments are administered only to those who are in the visible Church. Though they have no significance for people who are outside, yet for all those who are within their significance and efficacy are certain, not only for each member taken separately, but for the entire body which is the Church. " Christ loved the Church and gave Himself for it, in order that He might sanctify it after having cleansed it by the washing of water and by the Word, that He might present it to Himself a glorious Church, without spot or wrinkle or any such thing, but holy and without blemish " (Eph. v. 25-27). This text establishes a bond between baptism and the sanctification, purification, and glorification *of the Church*. Baptism does not only concern him who receives it. It is not just the means —as the individualist perspective would have it—of adding a believer to other believers. Like the family, the Church is much more than the sum of the believers of which it is composed : the Church is the body of Christ, a living organism. In the Church, each one does not live only for himself, but for the whole body (cf. 1 Cor. xii. 11-27 ; Eph. iv. 1-16 ; Rom. xii. 3-8, etc.). The effectiveness of the spiritual events which succeeded each other in the life of each member (regeneration, faith, conversion, repentance, sanctification, the baptism of the Holy Spirit, and so on) surpasses the narrow limits of the life of the individual ; it extends to the whole body, taken simultaneously in its totality *and* in each of its parts. Baptism not only sets apart a new believer, but edifies *the Church*, sanctifies *the Church*, cleanses and glorifies *the Church*, both as such and in each of its members. Because of this fact, and also because of what we have said concerning the memory of the sacrament, the efficacy of a baptism administered in the Church extends to all those who participate in it or are present at it, and thence to the whole Church. As Cullmann says, baptism " concerns not only the individual, as is usually said, but also the Church as a whole."[1]

In the spiritual solidarity which unites the family, the local community, and the whole body of the Church, the efficacy of baptism is essentially polyvalent and collective. It is absolutely impossible to restrict its efficacy to the single individual who receives it. On the strength of the text of Ephesians v. 25-27 we incline to the view that there is in every baptism something as real for the Church itself as for the individual baptized and for each believer who sees it administered to one of his brothers, with whom he knows that he personally—in virtue of the Church's unity and communion—is " bone of his bone and flesh of his flesh."

It is unthinkable to celebrate a baptism as a private ceremony, which borders on depriving the person baptized and his family of a portion of its benefits. Every baptism concerns the entire Church and ought to be celebrated before the Church and in the Church. The baptized person ought to be commended to God by the intercession of all. He ought to enter publicly into the covenant and into the Church and not secretly and unnoticed. The baptized person ought also to be publicly taken care of by the people of God. " Why is it that baptism takes place in the company of the faithful? . . . . We have in it a mirror of the good which has been already communicated to us, so that we may benefit from it right to the end. For we see that unbelievers forfeit and

---

[1] *Op. cit.*, p. 32.

exclude themselves from this adoption of God through their ingratitude. Thus, that we may be strengthened more and more, we ought to consider carefully when a baptism is celebrated that it makes contact with us and that God calls us to Himself in order to show us in the person of another that by nature we were lost and damned. But since He has united us to the body of our Lord Jesus Christ we are no longer regarded in our own nature, God does not consider who we are nor what we have merited, but He views us as if Jesus Christ were in us : as if, indeed, we ought never to be separated from Him." [1]

C. THE NECESSITY OF BAPTISM. BAPTISM IS A DUTY

Baptism is a condition of salvation. This is a consequence of Christ's command to the Apostles (Mt. xxviii. 19 ; Mk. xvi. 16). As we have seen when studying the sacraments in general, baptism has the necessity of precept, not the necessity of means. Our Lord has not said that he who has not been baptized will be condemned : that is the lot of those who will not believe.

In accordance with the customs of human society, when a man is appointed to an important office he ought to be solemnly installed in this office and to swear fidelity. It is not the uttering of an oath by the Prime Minister that makes him Prime Minister. It does not confer on him the right to assume this office, and no more does it give him the competence required for the adequate performance of his duties. Circumcision did not make a Jew of the man who received it ; as such, it gave him neither the knowledge nor the grace necessary for him to be one of the true children of Israel. It was the established means for declaring publicly that he was a Jew and the sign that he was numbered amongst those who worshipped the true God. It assured to him the privileges of the theocracy.

No more does baptism make a Christian of the man who receives it. Many are baptized who nullify the grace of God. Baptism is the established means whereby a man declares publicly that he is a Christian. It is the mark of his Christian

---

[1] Calvin : *Sermon* on Gal. iii., 26-29, Opera, L, p. 566.

profession before men ; it assures to him the privileges of membership in the visible Church and, if he is sincere and faithful, it is the pledge given by God that he will participate in all the blessings of redemption. It is in this sense alone that the Reformed Churches teach the necessity of baptism —the necessity of a divine precept. Even though it was not a means of salvation, the advantages of circumcision were immense (Rom. iii. 1) ; and it is the same with baptism, the blessings of which are still more excellent and the usefulness of which is great in every respect.

Perhaps we may be permitted a further quotation full of freshness and vitality : " It does not suffice that God exercises His power on our behalf and loves us, and even that He shows by the results that this is so, but we have need of some visible signs so that we may be all the more strengthened. And this is because of our immaturity. By His Word God teaches us sufficient concerning His love and infinite bounty, and this ought to be quite sufficient for us. We enjoy also the experience of the love which He bestows on us, since He does not allow us to lack anything. We see that we are sustained by His hand and that He has such pity towards us that we want for nothing. Ought not this to be sufficient to convince us of the mercy of God towards us so that we should trust in Him, call upon Him, and have all our refuge in Him ? Yes, indeed ! But we are so brutish and earthly that after God has spoken to us, after He has stretched out His hand to cause us to experience his bounty, we are even yet deaf and blind and as it were altogether stupid. It is for this reason that, from the beginning, God has wished to add sacraments, which should be like pledges to make men more certain of what would not commonly be sufficiently known to them. . . . This being so, it is impossible for men to dispense with sacraments and visible signs. . . . Let us carefully observe, then, when we wish to use the sacraments as God has ordained, that they should be like ladders for raising us on high : for we are heavy and cumbrous and held down by earthly things. Thus, because we are unable to fly high enough to draw near to God, He has ordained sacraments for us, like ladders. If a man wishes to leap on high he will break his neck in the attempt ;

but if he has steps he is able to proceed with confidence. So also, if we are to reach our God, we must use the means which He has instituted for us, since He knows what is suitable for us. . . . Thus let us carefully observe that it is God who holds out His hand to us, when we have the sacraments to lead us to Him."[1]

Consequently, baptism is a duty. If a man desires to be a disciple of Jesus Christ, and to be regarded as such, he is bound to be baptized, thus submitting himself to the commandment of Christ, as well as to the invariable practice of the Apostles and to the constant and universal usage of the Christian Churches in all ages and in all parts of the world.

D. THE SUBJECTIVE ASPECTS OF BAPTISM

Baptism is primarily an act of God's grace. But since the professing Christian ought to submit to it voluntarily, it can and should also be considered from man's point of view under its subjective aspect. The offer and the gift of God ought to be followed by acceptance on the part of man. Baptism thus also signifies that man accepts the covenant and its obligations. It is not the seal of a covenant which is simply offered, but of a covenant which is both offered and *accepted*, that is to say, of a covenant concluded. Viewed from this angle, baptism is the sign and seal of the believer's obligations towards God and His Church. Having in the first place been the object of God's action, the baptized person in his turn becomes active.

(*a*) *The baptized person is obliged to walk in newness of life and to keep the commandments of Christ.* The assurance that his sins are forgiven, or that sin will remain in him until death, cannot by any means be a motive for casting off restraint and a reason for him to live after the flesh. On the contrary ! The assurance of pardon is the gateway to sanctification and to good works performed after the Spirit.[2] " We must not hence assume a licence of sinning for the future, for this doctrine is intended only for those who, when they

---

[1] Calvin : *Sermon* on 1 Cor. x. 1-5, Opera, XLIX, pp. 585-587.
[2] Cf. Pierre.-Ch. Marcel, *A l'Ecole de Dieu*, pp. 106-108 ; *A l'Ecoute de Dieu*, pp. 87-92, 109-114.

have sinned, are distressed and blame themselves, being weary and cast down by the burden of their sins, so that they may have means of support and consolation and not fall away into confusion and despair. . . . (Christ) has been given for poor sinners who, wounded and seared in conscience, sigh for the physician." [1] We are baptized on the condition that we consecrate ourselves wholly to our God.

(b) *The baptized person is obliged at all times to confess the thrice holy name of God and to witness concerning his faith and his salvation.* " In so far as baptism is a sign and token of our confession," says Calvin, " we ought thereby to testify that our trust is in the mercy of God and that we are pure through the remission of sins which Jesus Christ has procured for us." [2]

(c) *The baptized person ought to maintain fellowship with his Church and to be constantly at its service* (1 Cor. xii. 13). " By baptism we ought to testify . . . that we have entered into the Church of God, so that with one consent of faith and love we may live in accord with all believers." [3] The Gospels and Epistles give emphatic expression to the obligations which are binding upon disciples of the Lord. It would be superfluous to produce texts here in justification of the three following affirmations, taken from the Second Helvetic Confession (20. 4) :

" When we are baptized we make profession of our faith, committing ourselves before God to true obedience, to mortification of our flesh, and to newness of life ;

" and we are at the same time enrolled in the holy army of Christ, in order throughout our lives to fight under His banner against the world, Satan, and our own flesh.

" We are likewise baptized into the one body of the Church, in order that we may experience true harmony and firm agreement with all the members of the Church in one and the same religion and in all mutual duties."

In order to be faithful to his commitments and obligations, the baptized person makes his own all the promises of the covenant of grace, which are precisely signified and sealed by his baptism. Not only ought he to respond affirmatively

---

[1] Calvin : *Instt.*, IV. xv. 3.   [2] *Instt.*, IV. xv. 15.   [3] *Ibid.*

at all times to God's offers of grace, but, in accordance with the promise, he can do so, so that God's glory may at all times be exalted and extolled.

Here again, as always, for the fulfilment of our obligations we possess no other power than that which we receive through faith. If we lack faith, the promises of the covenant of grace and the sacrament of baptism will be witnesses *against us* of our ingratitude and will accuse us before God of unbelief in the promises which were made to us.

For the sake of completeness, it should be observed that the obligations resulting from baptism have also an ecclesiastical subjective character, which relates to the faith of the Church in connection with the promises made to baptized persons, to the ministry which the Church is obliged to fulfil towards all that are hers, and to the faithfulness and perseverance of the Church. We shall return to this question.

Baptism, sacrament of the covenant of grace, is entirely, both objectively and subjectively, to the glory of God, who reveals Himself in the covenant, gives grace and the means of receiving it, and also the ability to remain in it and persevere in it. In the covenant God glorifies Himself, and we glorify Him : He is our glory and we become His glory. The covenant and the sacraments are the highest glorification of Father, Son, and Holy Spirit, the work of salvation which the Triune God has decreed, accomplished, and applied in time and for eternity. " In Him we have obtained an inheritance, being predestinated according to the purpose of Him who performs all things after the counsel of His own will, *so that we should be to the praise of His glory* " (Eph. i. 11 f.).

" Let us realize, then," says Calvin, " that we are baptized on this condition, namely, that we should devote ourselves fully to our God . . . so that we may glorify Him who has shown Himself so liberal towards us and who has exercised such pity. Every time that God's benefits are recalled to our memory, and especially the remembrance that it has pleased Him to call us to the knowledge of His truth, we should add this : that it is in order that our life should be dedicated completely to His honour and to His service." [1] And again

---

[1] *Sermon* on Deut. vi. 20-25, Opera, XXVI, p. 490.

he writes : " Baptism is our confession before men jnasmuch as it is a mark and token by which we openly declare that we wish to be numbered among the people of God, by which we testify that we agree and concur with all Christians in the service of one God and in one religion, by which, in short, we publicly assert and declare our faith, in order that God may be glorified not only in our hearts, but also that our tongues and all the members of our body may, to the utmost of their ability, sound forth His praises. For in this way all that is ours is employed, as is fitting, in promoting the glory of God, which ought everywhere to be displayed ; and others are stimulated by our example to the same course."[1]

E. ON WHAT CONDITIONS CAN BAPTISM BE ADMINISTERED TO ADULTS ?

Since baptism is a sacrament of the covenant of grace, its administration is identical with that of the covenant. The conditions of admission to baptism cannot be different from those required for participation in the Lord's supper and for being or continuing a member of the Church.

It is universally admitted in all the Christian Churches that the candidate for baptism ought to give evidence of repentance and of faith, and to declare his desire to obey Jesus Christ. He ought thus to be instructed in the knowledge of the fundamental doctrines of the Gospel, to make a sincere profession of faith, and to manifest conduct which is free from scandal. In every Reformed Church which still possesses a discipline these conditions apply to baptized persons and communicant members. The way in which one evaluates these facts always depends on one's conception

---

[1] *Instt.*, IV. xv. 13. On this subject Karl Barth expresses himself as follows (*op. cit.*, pp. 30 f.) : " It is a strange gap in the baptismal teaching of all Confessions—the Reformed included—that the meaning and work of baptism have never been understood in principle as a glorifying of God, that is, as a moment in His self-revelation." We lose ourselves in conjectures trying to discover how it was possible for Karl Barth to utter such a categorical affirmation. The whole *Reformed* doctrine of baptism, founded on the covenant of grace, is *from beginning to end*—objectively and subjectively—a glorification, which could not be more pronounced in the theology and life of believers, of the fact of God's self-revelation.

of the Church.   In Protestantism, we have two different
conceptions.

Firstly, there are those who, contending for a Church of
so-called " professing " Christians, maintain that the visible
Church ought to be composed only of regenerate individuals.
There is then a profound distinction between the Church
and the parish.   The former is composed of communicant
members, but the latter of those who, although not communicants, attend public worship and participate in the
Church's commitments.   " Entering the Church " consequently denotes joining the number of those who are
admitted to the Lord's supper. It is only the communicant
members who are in the Church.   Those who adhere to this
theory are of the opinion that it is the duty and prerogative
of the Church to decide whether the candidate for
baptism is truly born of God.   According to them, the
Church should be persuaded that the candidate is really
regenerate.

The Reformed Churches, however, hold that there is no
biblical foundation for such an attitude and for attributing
such prerogatives to the Church, and that vocation and
election ought not to be confused, nor disciples and regenerate.   These assumptions and these claims are contrary to the
laws of the administration of the covenant, and they are
impracticable. Christ has not given the Church the power to
probe men's hearts and to discern their innermost thoughts ;
and thus He could not have imposed on them this duty which
implies the possession of such a power.

Reformed doctrine willingly grants to " professing "
Christians that the true Church, the body of Christ, is
composed only of the elect, that on earth it is only true
believers who constitute the true Church, and that the
profession of faith made by those who are baptized or who
are communicants should be the profession of a true Christian
faith.   But the truth and purity of the Church are confessed
in faith and are not the object of subjective judgments.
In fact, where " professing " Christians reckon that the
adjectives " true " and " sincere " (applying to repentance,
regeneration, or faith professed) ought to supply the Church
with the proof of compelling evidence which carries con-

viction and permits the Church to estimate and affirm the reality of the candidate's regeneration and faith, Reformed Christians interpret the terms in the sense of " that which is credible," that which can be admitted as possible, that is to say, that against which nothing evident or tangible can be objected. Churches, pastors, parish councils cannot ever be sure of the reality of the regeneration, the repentance, the conversion, or the faith of the baptismal candidates, nor of those who partake of the Lord's supper. Nothing at any time authorizes us to refuse a man admission to the Church, except a serious fact which would justify his exclusion from the Church if he were already a member of it. If such a candidate gives clear evidence of being a heretic, or if his manner of life openly contradicts his profession of faith and obedience to Jesus Christ, he cannot be received for baptism, just as also a member of the Church who is guilty of scandalous behaviour ought to be debarred from the Lord's supper, no matter what his profession of faith or the nature of his experiences may otherwise have been.

The Church baptizes adults and administers the Lord's supper without ever having ultimate proof that the recipients are true believers. A co-efficient of uncertainty will always be present. In accordance with the judgment of charity enjoined by Christ, the Church has no right to suspect the sincerity of those who desire her sacraments, and she cannot deprive them of the ministry of grace and impose her censure so long as she is unable to lay her finger on scandalous behaviour such as should exclude the guilty person from the Church. No matter how cautious she may be, she can be and has often been inexpert in her attempts to dismiss unworthy people from her sacraments, nor is this really her fault for she is not omniscient, and the scriptural conditions for admission to the sacraments are such that hypocrites and unregenerate persons are able to satisfy them in their externals. We have already stressed the fact that there were numerous unregenerate persons in the Apostolic Church, and that none the less she continued to welcome with large-hearted charity and without suspecting their good faith those who desired baptism. No Church, if it wishes to avoid infringing the Lord's commandments, and if it is not to

make arrogant claims to exorbitant powers and to be
swamped by Pharisaism, can pretend to a greater efficiency
and to be more circumspect or more exacting than was the
Apostolic Church.

It has been important to emphasize that, in the administration of the sacraments *to adults*, the Church is never
sure that this is being done with good reason and that these
are being distributed only to those who are truly the children
of God and who receive them in faith.

II

THE BAPTISM OF CHILDREN [1]

A. THE SILENCE OF THE NEW TESTAMENT

As we commence this last section of our study we find ourselves immediately confronted with one of the most serious of the objections urged by the adversaries of infant baptism, namely, that in Scripture there is no explicit commandment requiring the baptism of the little children of believers. This is quite true. But we at once make the rejoinder that the adversaries of infant baptism have no right to draw the conclusion that the baptism of children is therefore forbidden.

1. In a question that is related, for it directly concerns the administration of the sacraments, those who in the name of Scripture oppose the baptism of children fail themselves to take into account a silence of Scripture that is complete. We refer to the fact that the New Testament nowhere makes mention of women having received the Holy Communion at the time of the Apostles ; it neither enjoins nor forbids that they should partake of the Lord's supper. Why do those who exclude every possibility of the baptism of children, on the ground that the New Testament does not explicitly enjoin it and establish its practice, interpose no difficulty when it comes to receiving women at Communion ? Does not the problem present itself in exactly the same terms ? Certainly ; yet those who differ from us do not experience the least difficulty in utilizing here the principle of *the analogy of faith* : they refer first of all to the institution of the Lord's supper, to its meaning and import, and to the intentions of our Lord ; they study the New Testament dispensation of grace, gladly produce texts such as Galatians iii. 28, and conclude that, in accordance with its institution,

[1] We would point out that if this section of our study is to be adequately assessed it is essential first of all to have read the chapters which precede.

the Lord's supper is suitable for women as well as for men.
Here indeed is most sane theology ! But it must be admitted
that the proof of the communion of women is not *direct*,
but *indirect*, and based upon a theological argument which is
irreproachably conducted in accordance with the analogy
of faith.

When we likewise take the analogy of faith as our point
of departure and show that by institution, nature, and
content baptism is suitable for children as well as for adults,
in what way does our procedure differ from that of those
Baptists who prove that women can and ought to be
communicants ? Why is one procedure acceptable if the
other is not ? Why forbid to others that which one permits
for oneself ? [1]

2. It is, however, affirmed by those who leave the above
facts out of account that baptism ought not to be administered to children in the absence of a scriptural command to
do so. We are obliged to demand where is the scriptural
foundation according to which baptism ought to be administered to *the children of Christians* only when they have
reached the age of discretion and desire it ? In the New
Testament we do not find the slightest allusion to such a
practice ! " I should like," says O. Cullmann, " with all
force to emphasize at the outset that there are in the New
Testament decidedly *fewer traces, indeed none at all, of the
Baptism of adults born of parents already Christian and
brought up by them. . . .* Those who dispute the Biblical
character of infant Baptism have therefore to reckon with
the fact *that adult Baptism for sons and daughters born of
Christian parents, which they recommend, is even worse
attested by the New Testament than infant Baptism* (for which
certain possible traces are discoverable) *and indeed lacks
any kind of proof.*"[2]

To be true to the theory which they wish to impose on us
those who oppose infant baptism ought to consent only to
the baptism of proselytes, since in their eyes the baptism
of proselytes is alone attested in the New Testament. It is

[1] Cf. Calvin : *Instt.* IV. xvi. 8 ; *Against the Anabaptists*, Opera, VII.
p. 64.
[2] *Op. cit.*, p. 26.

going a bit far to classify proselytes together with the children of believers when they come to faith. The whole of Scripture teaches that *the children of believers are not the same as proselytes.* To affirm the contrary in spite of Scripture is a quite gratuitous begging of the question. The *a priori* premisses upon which the Baptist system is reared do not survive being confronted with Scripture on this point. Unless they consent to be taken in the very act of blatant contradiction, the opponents of infant baptism are unable to reproach our method in any respect.

3. The legitimacy of infant baptism depends entirely on the question of the manner in which Scripture regards the children of believers and wishes us, consequently, to regard them. If Scripture speaks of these children in the same way as of adult believers, and if the promises which are made to them and the benefits of the grace received by them are the same, then the legitimacy and, still more, the duty of infant baptism are securely established ; we cannot withhold from children that which is granted to adults.

Just as circumcision was to begin with given to Abraham and then later administered to his son Isaac, we admit that the *original* baptism was the baptism of adults and that the baptism of the children of believers *succeeded* it. There was an interval between the circumcision given to Abraham and that given to his son ; but for the whole of his posterity according to the flesh, this interval was unique, because Abraham was the unique *father*, for all his descendants relate back to him. The same interval recurred on every occasion when a proselyte was incorporated into the people of Israel and when, because of his faith, his minor children were circumcised. When the Christian Church is built up by the incorporation of proselytes we observe once more this interval between the baptism of the parents and that of their minor children. Thus it is not the baptism of adults which ought to be made to conform to the baptism of children, but the latter which ought to be in accord with the former, just as the circumcision of Isaac was made to conform to that of his father. Here a legitimate deduction is involved, analogous to that of the admission of women to the Lord's supper. In theology, that which follows by legitimate deductions from scriptural norms is as exact as that which is explicitly stated. Theologians and the Church constantly put this principle into practice in the ministry of the Word, in the regulation of the Christian life, and in the elaboration of doctrine : the Church never confines herself merely to the letter, but, working from the data of Scripture and under the control of the Holy Spirit, she affirms normative principles and elaborates the consequences and applications which make her life and development possible and effective. Were it not so, the exercise of the pastoral ministry, the cure of souls, preaching, discipline, and so on, would be absolutely impossible ! It is thus that the Church operates when she passes from adult to infant baptism. Scripture affords general instruction on baptism, its meaning and value, and the Church applies it concretely in life. If Scripture assigns to the children of believers the enjoyment of the same privileges as are experienced by those who are of an age to confess their faith, and since it nowhere makes mention of a baptismal ministry which should have been applied to adults *born of Christian parents*, it has said sufficient on this point, without needing to have prescribed literally the baptism of infants. So much for our method, applied exactly by those who disagree with us, but in matters other than the baptism of children.

4. In the absence of any prohibition of Christ, and realizing the supreme importance throughout the whole of Scripture of the doctrine of the covenant of grace, the harmony with which its different parts accord with each other, and the confirmation which the New Testament affords to the entire theology of the covenant, the principle of the analogy of faith forbids us, in the New Testament administration of the covenant, to suppress arbitrarily one of its elements on the score that there is no reference to it in the texts.

5. From Abraham onwards, for a period of twenty centuries, children were expressly received into the Church *from the time of their birth* if they were born of Jewish parents, or *as minors* if they belonged to families of which the father had been converted to Judaism. Through twenty centuries not only tradition and ritual, but religious and theological

thought fashioned by the promises and prescriptions of the covenant of grace, which is the foundation doctrine of the Old Testament, confirmed *in all points* in the New, owed their organic character to this covenant. Has the force and vigour of this conception according to which children ought to receive the sacrament of the covenant been truly represented ? In reality, the silence of the New Testament regarding the baptism of children militates in favour of rather than against this practice. To overthrow completely notions so vital, impressed for more than two thousand years on the soul of the people, to withdraw from children the sacrament of admission into the covenant, the Apostolic Church ought to have received from the Lord *an explicit prohibition*, so revolutionary in itself that a record of it would have been preserved in the New Testament. Not only, however, does the eternal covenant remain intact in the New Testament, but in Jesus Christ it reaches its supreme fulfilment. Had our Lord wished the reception of children into this ever valid covenant to be discontinued He would have said so in order that no one might be in any doubt.

B. THE CHILDREN OF BELIEVERS ARE BORN WITHIN THE COVENANT OF GRACE

Let us recall some of our previous conclusions.

By a sovereign decree, independently of any human point of view, God decides that the children of believers shall be included in His covenant. In His sovereignty He imposes this relationship upon them. It pleases God to make this covenant with them. He chooses these children as the heirs of the promise. God's decision and the offer of the blessings of the covenant precede the faith of the child. The character of this covenant is sovereignly objective.

The children of believers are the heirs of all the promises of the covenant. In the same way as the baptized proselyte they are separate from the profane world and are placed neither under God's judgment nor under Satan's power. God regards them as members of His kingdom. He promises to circumcize their hearts in order that they may love Him and live. He wishes to be their Father, to cause them to enjoy the benefits of His grace, and to lead them to salvation. The children of believers are considered by God as being involved in the faith of their parents ; the family, as such, forms a concrete whole. They are members of the Church.

Since the children of believers are " set apart," separate from the profane world, " holy "—to use the biblical expression—from the moment of their birth ; since God includes them in the covenant and they belong to Christ's body the Church ; in short, since they participate in all the promises and all the spiritual realities signified and sealed in baptism, we say that they are fit to receive it ; *there is no other reason for administering baptism to them.* The grace of their adoption precedes baptism which is the sign and seal of it. This basis of the baptism of children is fundamentally *objective* and *rigorously established upon the New Testament.*

The covenant of grace, in fact, remains one and the same in the New Testament, the Church remains the same, and the children of believers are a part of it. Christ confirms the spiritual solidarity of the family. In the New Testament we encounter the same *effects* of the covenant of grace relating to the children of believers. If the effects are the same, so also are the principles.

1. Christ regards children as members of the covenant, members of His kingdom, and of the Church ; this is proved beyond contradiction by all that He says about them and by the manner in which He treats them. Commenting on Matthew xix. 13 f. and the parallel passages, Calvin says : " This narrative is highly useful, for it shows that Christ receives not only those who, moved by holy desire and faith, voluntarily approach Him, but also those who are not yet of age to realize how much they need His grace. These little children have not yet any understanding nor rational faculty that should lead them to desire His blessing ; but when they are presented to Him He receives them gently and with great sweetness, and dedicates them to God His Father by a solemn act of blessing. . . .

" That He should be interrupted by little children seems to (His disciples) something unworthy of His character.

And, indeed, their error was not without plausibility: for what has the sovereign Prophet and Son of God to do with children ? But this shows us that those who judge of Christ according to their carnal perception judge of Him incorrectly ; for at every turn it results that they deprive Him of His peculiar excellencies, and, while thinking that they are doing Him honour, they actually attribute things to Him that are quite out of harmony with His character. . . . . Therefore let us learn not to think of Him otherwise than as He Himself teaches us, and not to assign to Him any quality or office other than the Father has bestowed upon Him. . . .

" He declares that He wishes to receive children to Himself ; and at length, when He has taken them in His arms, He not only embraces them, but blesses them also by placing His hands upon them. Hence we gather that His grace is extended even to those who are of this age. And no wonder : for since the whole posterity of Adam is shut up under the sentence of death, all must necessarily perish except those whom the only Redeemer delivers. To exclude from the grace of God those who are of such an age would be something too cruel. It is therefore not without reason that we employ this passage as a defence against the Anabaptists. . . . Certainly, the laying on of His hands was not a trifling or whimsical sign, and when Christ here offered up prayer it is perfectly certain that He was not vainly beating the air. But He could not have offered these children to God without giving them purity. And what other prayer did He utter for them than that they should be received into the number of the children of God ? It follows, then, that they were regenerated by the Spirit in the hope of salvation. In short, even His embracing of them was a testimony that Jesus acknowledged them to belong to His flock. Now, if they were partakers of the spiritual gifts which are represented by baptism, it is unreasonable to refuse them the outward sign. It is, indeed, an audacity and presumption full of sacrilege to drive far from the fold of Christ those whom He lovingly holds to His bosom, and to exclude as strangers those whom He does not wish to be forbidden to come to Him."

N

2. Peter and Paul uphold the vitality of the covenant in its New Testament dispensation and confirm that its benefits are extended to the children of believers : Acts ii. 39 and xvi. 31. The former reference, it is true, is valid primarily for the Jews ; pagans are brought in only in the words, " and to all that are afar off." But this did not hinder the Jews who were converted to Christ from receiving the promise of the covenant not only for themselves, but also for their children ; and the pagans who believed participated in the same privileges. According to the whole New Testament, in no respect did they fall behind the believers who had come to Jerusalem.[1] In Acts xvi. 31, Paul and Silas say to the gaoler, " Believe on the Lord Jesus Christ and thou shalt be saved, *thou and thy household,*" thus emphatically confirming the fundamental organic principle of the covenant of grace.

3. When one considers the texts which relate the baptism of entire " houses," keeping in mind the scriptural doctrine of the covenant of grace, such texts have more to say about the baptism of children than those who oppose it are willing to admit. Is it not surprising, to begin with, that *all* the members of a family hearing the Good News believe forthwith ? Does this astonish nobody ? How does it come to pass ? Most certainly it is the result of the Holy Spirit's action in *all* the members of the family. But this willingness of the Spirit to bestow salvation on *all* the members of the family *without exception*—parents and children, whatever their age—is precisely the clearest demonstration that *the Spirit is acting in the organic line of the covenant of grace.* These household baptisms confirm in a decisive manner all that we have said concerning the covenant. The Spirit acts within the covenant and promotes it, and the Apostles act in their turn in accordance with the principle which had always been in force under the old economy : they baptize the whole family, even when frequently, according to the texts, only a single member of the family makes confession of faith. In no instance does the New Testament give us to understand that such " family " baptisms were out of the

---

[1] One must not confuse the " called " and the " elect," as some do by making everyone " called " also " elect."

ordinary or that in these cases the Spirit was acting in an exceptional manner : on the contrary it speaks of them as something entirely natural. " From these passages," says O. Cullmann, " we can at all events draw this conclusion concerning the doctrine of Baptism, that here also the solidarity of the family in Baptism is the decisive considera- tion, and not the individual decision of the single member. A baptismal grace valid for a whole community as such, namely, the people of Israel which passes through the Red Sea, is presupposed also in 1 Cor. 10. 1 ff., a passage which ought to be much more carefully observed in the discussion of child Baptism. It is here quite plain that the act of grace, which is regarded as the type of Baptism, concerns the covenant which God made with the whole people."[1]

How is it that the opponents of the baptism of children are not impressed by these facts ? On the basis of their individualism they cannot account for it otherwise than by invoking the complete liberty of the Spirit ! They speak to us of the sequence : proclamation of the Word, faith, baptism. We inquire what is the significance of this sequence in face of the accounts which testify to the baptism of *entire families* ? Is it not surprising that those who differ from us are here compelled by their logic to explain the baptism of these " families " as the individual baptisms of adults each separately confessing their faith and each separately requesting the sacrament ? It is only the covenant of grace that can account for the fact that the family, a " collective personality," is baptized *as such* in the totality of its members.[2]

[1] *Op. cit.*, p. 45.

[2] These passages are, indeed, quite disastrous for those who oppose the baptism of children. For proof of this, it will suffice us to refer to the translation given by Norcott (*Le baptême scripturaire*, pp. 27 f.) of Acts xvi. 34 : " He rejoiced in that he had believed in God *with all his house* " (the italics are his). Again, on p. 13 he says : " We see from verse 34 that he afterwards rejoiced because ' with *all* his house he had *believed* in God '." The order of the words in Greek, however, is as follows and cannot support being inverted here : " Believe in the Lord Jesus Christ and *thou* shalt be saved, *thou and thy family.* . . . He was baptized, *he and all his*, and *he* rejoiced, with all his family, in that *he* had believed in God." We can judge that recourse to such arguments for maintaining a position displays strikingly its weaknesses in the exegetical field. We could indicate other shifts of the same character.

It is naturally possible, though not very probable, that none of these " houses " contained little children. If there were little children in them, it is *morally* certain that they were baptized at the same time as their parents, or that they had the right to be. That whole households believed and were baptized does not thus afford *proof* that infant baptism was already being practised by the Apostles, but, granting the silence of the texts, still less can the contrary be deduced. We state here with all desirable precision that these passages have never served and still do not serve, in *good* Reformed theology, as a *basis* or *justification* of infant baptism. These texts are not, as Karl Barth would like them to be, the only " thin thread to which one may perhaps hold (and then hardly !) for a proof of infant-baptism from the New Testament."[1] These texts simply confirm, and once more within the scheme of the New Testament, the doctrine of the covenant of grace.

4. In 1 Corinthians vii. 14 Paul affirms that the children of believers are " holy." Like the rest, this text ought not to be considered as a *direct* proof of the baptism of children, but as a confirmation of the covenant. It shows, in fact, that all the advantages of the covenant formerly accorded to the believing Jewish family are now made available to the Christian family. In order to prove that a Christian husband or wife ought not to leave the unbelieving partner, Paul uses an argument which ought, in the Church, to be unquestioned and accepted by all : " *Your children are holy and not unclean,*" he says. This being so, the believing partner sanctifies the unbelieving partner. By the faith of one only the entire conjugal union is sanctified. The main point of the argument is that the children of a family in which the father or the mother is a believer *are reckoned to the believing partner, even if it is the wife.* The confession of Christ gives the tone to such a house ; it is the criterion in accordance with which the whole house is judged ; here, *it is faith which dominates everything.* The holiness of which Paul is speaking ought not to be regarded as subjective or internal, but as an objective theocratic holiness, unless the children are holy

or sanctified, not from the fact of the faith of father or mother, but in themselves. The children of believers, however, are not holy *by nature* (Job xiv. 4 ; Ps. li. 7 ; Jn. iii. 6 ; Eph. ii. 3), but *by the privilege of the covenant*. They are neither pagans nor children of Satan, nor have they need, as some teach, of being exorcized by baptism. They are the children of the covenant to whom the promise belongs just as much as it does to adults.

" This passage," says Calvin, commenting on 1 Corinthians vii. 14, " is a remarkable one, and drawn from the depths of theology ; for it teaches that the children of believers are set apart from others by a sort of exclusive privilege, so as to be reckoned holy in the Church. But how will this statement correspond with what Paul says elsewhere—that we are all by nature the children of wrath (Eph. ii. 3), and with David's statement—' Behold, I was conceived in sin ' (Ps. li. 7) ? I reply that there is a universal distribution of sin and damnation throughout the posterity of Adam, and that there is therefore no one who is not included in this curse, whether he is a child, of believers or of unbelievers. For it is not as regenerated by the Spirit that believers beget children after the flesh. Thus the natural condition of all is alike, so that all are liable equally to sin and to eternal death. And as for the Apostle's attribution here of a special privilege to the children of believers, this flows from the blessing of the covenant, by the intervention of which the curse of nature is removed, in such a way that those who were unholy by nature are consecrated to God by grace. Hence Saint Paul argues, in Romans xi. 16, that the whole race of Abraham is holy because God contracted the covenant of life with him—'If the root be holy,' he says, ' then the branches are holy also ' ; and all those who are descended from Israel God calls His children. Now, since the wall of partition is broken down, this same covenant of salvation which was made with Abraham and his posterity is communicated to us."

It is seen with what pointedness and precision Calvin has already answered certain of our contemporaries who, in speaking of spiritual solidarity or " collective sanctity," make the serious error of confusing and identifying a community constituted by covenant with a biological consanguinary group.[1]

All that Paul seeks to do in this passage is to show that Christian faith does not break the natural laws of life, but strengthens and sanctifies them. This text is not a *direct* proof of infant baptism, but, yet again, a notable confirmation of the covenant of grace, which is the basis of infant baptism. In the covenant the whole family is reckoned to the believing parent. The believer's vocation is to serve the Lord not only by himself, but with all that is his and with all his family. " If the children of believers are exempted from the common lot of mankind so as to be set apart to the Lord," says Calvin, " why should we deny them the sign ? If the Lord receives them into His Church by His Word, why should we refuse them the sign ? "[2] Again, he says elsewhere : " Since the Holy Spirit, the Author and Source of all sanctification, testifies that the children of Christians are holy, is it for us to exclude them from such a benefit ? Now, if the truth of baptism is in them, how is it that we dare to deprive them of the sign, which is something less and inferior ? "[3]

C. THE COVENANT IS THE SOLE BASIS OF INFANT BAPTISM

The children of believing parents are baptized by reason of the fact that they are the children of the covenant and, as such, heirs of *all* the promises made by God at the institution of this covenant, included in which are the promises of the remission of sins and of the Holy Spirit for their regeneration and sanctification. In the covenant God endows children with certain gifts in a definite and objective manner; He requires that in due course they should accept these gifts by faith, and He promises that through the operation of the Holy Spirit these gifts will become a living reality in their life.

The covenant, together with its promises, constitutes the objective and legal basis of infant baptism. Infant baptism is the sign, seal, and pledge of all that these promises imply. As Calvin says in his work on *The true method of reforming the*

---

[1] Cf. e.g., F.-J. Leenhardt, *Foi et Vie, op. cit.*, pp. 83-85.
[2] *Comm.* on I Cor. vii. 14.
[3] *Against the Anabaptists*, Opera, VII, p. 62.

Church, " The children of believers are holy from the time of their birth, because before coming into the world they are adopted into the covenant of eternal life ; and *there is absolutely no other reason for receiving them into the Church except that already beforehand they belong to the body of Christ. . . . It is necessary that the grace of adoption should precede baptism."

H. Bavinck, the celebrated dogmatician, expresses himself as follows : " This covenant was the solid, biblical, and objective foundation upon which *all the Reformers unanimously and without exception* rested the legitimacy of infant baptism. They had no other deeper and more solid foundation."[1] What Barth calls motives foreign to the exegesis and to the heart of the problem [2] are *never*, either in Calvin or in the Reformed dogmaticians, invoked as the " motive " or " basis " of baptism ; they are simply *consequences* of baptism or, better still, *consequences* of the covenant of which baptism is the sacrament, studied and systematized in a theological consideration which is *a posteriori* and not *a priori*. From the beginning of the Reformation Reformed theologians abandoned the position of Augustine : *credit in altero, qui peccavit in altero*, which made the faith of parents and of the Church, that is, *fides aliena*, the basis of infant baptism. For them, *fides aliena*—the faith of another—could not in any instance be the basis of baptism. It is obvious that those who, like Karl Barth, reject the Reformed doctrine of the covenant of grace are compelled to search for and to find in the writings of our theologians other foundations for infant baptism, and in consequence to regard as the basis and foundation of baptism that which, for our dogmaticians, has no place except amongst the consequences. That the opponents of infant baptism should be led to reject all these supposed foundations of baptism does not surprise us in the least, and in this connection we can but approve their perspicacity, for we are in full agreement with them. The *consequences* of infant baptism can never become its foundation. With the rejection of the covenant of grace every possible foundation of infant baptism disappears. The advocates of infant baptism ought to be fully persuaded

[1] *Gereformeerde Dogmatiek*, IV. 282.   [2] *Op. cit.*, pp. 49 f.

of this and, consequently, to render themselves completely conversant with the doctrine of the covenant.

While recognizing that the children of believers are baptized because they are in the covenant and are, as such, heirs of the promises implying a right to justification and to the regenerating and sanctifying influence of the Holy Spirit, a certain number of Reformed theologians have attempted to add one of the *effects* of the covenant of grace to the foundation of infant baptism, namely, presumptive regeneration. They have considered that presumptive regeneration could be the *ultimate* ground of baptism, more so even than the covenant. It must be acknowledged that this attempt has failed. Presumptive regeneration cannot be regarded naturally as the legal ground of infant baptism, for this cannot be anything other than the promises of God contained in the covenant. The ground of baptism must be something objective. One cannot baptize *on the basis* of a presumption. To the question : " Why can you presume the regeneration of the children of believers ? " one can only reply : " Because they are born of believing parents " ; or, in other words, *because they are born into the covenant.* Besides, Scripture and experience afford proof that not all the children born into the covenant are regenerated to salvation.[1]

It is obvious that to refuse to consider this presumptive regeneration as the *foundation* of baptism is not at all the same as saying that it is impossible or unjustifiable to assume that the little children of believers are regenerate : we shall return to this point. But, in accordance with the indications of the Word of God, we do not wish in any way to restrict the divine liberty which acts in sovereign independence when and as it wills, and which is never confined to means. The *promise* of the regeneration of the children of the covenant is sufficient for us. It is not for us to define whether this regeneration in view of salvation is found in the elect children before or at the moment of baptism, or sometimes even years afterwards.[2]

---

[1] Cf. Berkhof : *Reformed Dogmatics*, pp. 639 f. ; H. Bavinck : *Gereformeerde Dogmatiek*, IV, pp. 266, 268.

[2] This was the opinion of Calvin, Beza, Zanchius, Bucanus, Walaeus, Amesius, Heidegger, Turretin, etc. It is the opinion of practically all present Calvinist theologians.

The ground of infant baptism is that " the Lord receives amongst His people the children of those to whom He has shown Himself as Saviour, and that for the sake of the fathers he accepts their offspring. . . . The present truth which we must consider at baptism, when it is granted to little children, is that it testifies to their salvation by sealing and confirming the covenant of God upon them." [1]

The ground of baptism is thus *identical both for adults and for children*. It is erroneous to object that if children are baptized because of the fact that they are born into the covenant and that they are consequently heirs of the promise, the ground of their baptism is different from that of adults who were baptized because of their faith or their profession of faith. Calvin and his successors, together with practically all the modern Reformed dogmaticians, affirm very clearly that it is the covenant that is the ground of the baptism of both adults and children. " He who is an unbeliever, and the child of unbelievers, is a stranger to the covenant until he comes to the knowledge of God. For this reason it is in no way remarkable that he does not partake of the sign, for were it administered it would be on false grounds. Thus St. Paul says that the Gentiles, while they continued in their idolatry, were strangers to the covenant (Eph. ii. 12). The matter seems to me plain enough : those of adult years who wish to yield themselves to our Lord ought not to be received for baptism without faith and repentance, since this is the sole entry which they have into the covenant whose mark is that of baptism. However, the children of Christian parents to whom the inheritance belongs by virtue of the promise are for this reason alone fit to be admitted to baptism."[2] The objection urged by some that, in Reformed theology, the baptism of adults and the baptism of children do not have the same foundation and that, in consequence, it is as regards their essence a question of two different sacraments, cannot for a moment survive an examination of the texts and concepts.[3]

The affirmations of our symbols are entirely in harmony with the position held by our theologians, namely, that the children of believing parents, or those who have only one

[1] Calvin : *Instt.*, IV. xvi. 15, 21.   [2] Calvin : *Instt.* IV. xvi. 24.
[3] Cf. F.-J. Leenhardt, *op. cit.*, p. 70.

believing parent, are baptized because they belong to the covenant.

Confession of the French Reformed Churches, para. 35 :

" Now, although baptism is a sacrament of faith and repentance, none the less because God receives little children into His Church together with their fathers we say that on the authority of Jesus Christ little children born of believers ought to be baptized."

Confession of the Netherlands, para. 34 :

" We believe that the little children of believers ought to be baptized and sealed with the sign of the covenant, as the little children were circumcized in Israel on the strength of the same promises which are made to our children. Also, in truth, Christ shed His blood no less for washing the little children of believers than for adults. That is why they ought to receive the sign and the sacrament of that which Christ has done for them ; as in the law the Lord commanded that they should participate in the sacrament of the death and passion of Christ by offering for them, when they were newly born, a lamb which was the sacrament of Jesus Christ.   And, further, what circumcision did for the Jewish people, baptism does the same for our children : it is for this reason that Saint Paul calls baptism the circumcision of Christ."

The Second Helvetic Confession, 20, 6 :

" We condemn the Anabaptists who deny that newly born children ought to be baptized by believers.   For, following the evangelical doctrine, little children belong to the kingdom of God and are included in the covenant of God : why then should the sign of this covenant be refused to them ? And why should they not be consecrated to God by holy baptism, in view of the fact that they are in the Church of God as His own property and treasure ? "

Confession of Geneva, para. 15 :

" Now, since our children belong to such a covenant of our Lord, we are certain that the external sign is administered to them with good reason."

Heidelberg Catechism, Q. 74 :

" Ought little children also to be baptized ?—Yes : for since they, as well as their parents, belong to God's covenant and Church, and since redemption from sin and the Holy Spirit, who produces faith, are promised to them no less than to adults, they ought to be incorporated into the Christian Church by baptism, which is the sign of the covenant, and to be distinguished from the children of unbelievers, as was done in the Old Testament by circumcision, in place of which baptism has been instituted in the New Testament."

D. THE OBJECTIVITY OF INFANT BAPTISM

It is necessary to emphasize strongly the essential *objectivity* of the basis of infant baptism, which is identical on this point with the objectivity which we have studied on the subject of adult baptism. The basis of infant baptism is the promise of the covenant and of all the blessings which it conveys. God is sovereign in His choice. He makes decisions and it is not for us to discuss the methods of His grace. The sequence, *God's action – man's response,* is determinative on the subject of the baptism of adults baptized by reason of their incorporation into the covenant by God's free grace, offered prior to every procedure of man, and the sign and seal of which they receive by baptism. This sequence, *God's action – man's response,* prevails also in connection with God's decree to regard the children of believers as being in the covenant and to set them within the sphere of His grace. *In both cases faith is the response of man to the initiative of God.*

The child cannot protest against this treatment of himself by God any more than against the fact that his parents give him their name, or that he receives their nationality. As far as these facts are concerned, the child is at first entirely passive ; and this is also the case when God, in a manner sovereign and beyond all debate, places him in the covenant. To receive the sign of the covenant, the child has no more need of understanding the position in which he is set than he has of giving his personal permission for his inclusion in his own family.

The taking hold of a child by God does not depend

initially, any more than does that of an adult whom He calls
to faith, on the knowledge which the subject can have of
this decision. *It is because he is taken hold of by God that the
child is able to believe.* As a member of God's people, by a
divine decree, he has the right to bear the seal of it, and we
have the obligation to give it to him. Once again, membership of the Church is not bound to a faith which has been
confessed beforehand.

It is not simply a question of knowing who *wants* to receive
baptism and to take its responsibility, that is, of knowing
who *wants* to be a Christian ! It is also a question of knowing
whom Christ requires to take a responsibility, *with whom*
amongst men God wishes to meet in the freedom of His love
and sovereignty, *from whom* He awaits the profession of
Christian faith. Scripture reveals to us that such persons
are not only those to whom the Word is proclaimed *beforehand*
and who are capable of understanding it, but others with
them, the children of the covenant, so that the Word may
be proclaimed to them and they may believe. With its
promise that God's Word will not be without effect in those
to whom He swears that He will circumcize their heart so
that they may hear His voice, and love Him, and perform
His commandments, the covenant is the seed-bed of election.
the place of Christian vocation. God has decided that He
will act primarily and above all in the posterity of believers
whom He claims as His personal possession : *the human faith
which follows is thus a consequence of the divine decision.*

It is objected that this does violence to the child's liberty
and that he ought to have the right to determine his choice
for himself : he ought to " demand " baptism, that is to
say, he ought to demand to be made a member of God's
people. It is for the child to determine his spiritual setting !

We reply that such a requirement, which at first sight
manifests such a concern for the child's heart and his liberty
and personal decision, is stamped with the mark of philosophical idealism, of the individualism and subjectivism
which we have already so often unmasked ; and that it does
not sufficiently take into account what the Bible teaches us
concerning our personal corruption from birth, nor its
manner of regarding children and Christian education.

Is the child required to make a decision concerning his membership of the race of Adam or the sin which he inherits from birth ? Can he make a choice ? Is not his solidarity with all humanity one of the first objective facts of his life ? The New Testament teaches us that *to begin with* we are all by nature children of wrath, born in bondage, and of ourselves incapable of any good thing. Are these things matters for reflection which can be set before a child when he is growing so that he may make a personal decision and advise us of his opinion ? Obviously not, unless we make of sin a notion entirely different from that which is revealed to us in Scripture and sink into Pelagianism. The solidarity of parents and children in sin and wretchedness is real ; it is an *objective* fact regarding which nobody, small or great, is consulted and which is imposed on all as an inexorable law. By the divine will, however, another law and ordinance of God is revealed to us, namely, the solidarity within the covenant of children and parents in grace and blessing. *In Scripture children are always counted with their parents and reckoned in solidarity with them.* Notable blessings are accorded to them in virtue of the faith and obedience *of their parents.*[1]

This is a new and perfectly objective fact, resting on a divine decree, the complete *justice* of which God reveals to us in the perspective of the covenant. God *acts justly* to the child of the covenant who shares in the sin of his forbears, without his having been consulted or having been able to " demand " participation in it, when He *also*, by His grace, causes him to share in the faith and obedience of his parents and assures him that he will not be a slave of Satan. God wishes to justify this child although he belongs to a sinful race. Who will dispute His right to do so ? It is for this reason that in the covenant the grace and blessings of God are transmitted from child to child and from generation to generation.[2] It is for this reason that in Scripture little children share in the *worship* which their parents render to

---

[1] Ex. xx. 6 ; Dt. i. 36 f. ; iv. 40 ; v. 29 ; xii. 25, 28 ; Ezek. xxxvii. 25 ; Zech. x. 9 ; etc. The texts which we have cited in our section on the solidarity of the family should be added.

[2] Gen. ix. 12 ; xvii. 7, 9 ; Ex. iii. 15 ; xii. 17 ; xvi. 32 ; Dt. vii. 9 ; Ps. cv. 8 ff. ; etc.

God. They are *under the obligation* of serving God *in the same way* as their parents.[1] By them they ought to be taught the works and commandments of God in virtue of the just demands of the covenant.[2] · It is as *Christian* posterity that little children are exhorted in the Lord by the Apostles [3] and that they know Him and stand before the throne of the Lamb.[4]

Scripture knows absolutely nothing of a neutral education which permits children to choose in a free and autonomous manner whom they wish to serve when they have grown up. On the contrary, *their definite participation in the covenant is the sole means by which they can ultimately make a free, voluntary, and conscious choice.* If God had not placed His hand upon them in advance so that they might believe, if they were not in certain respects " chosen," " set apart," liberated from the lost world which is delivered over to Satan, if they were not " holy " through the privilege bestowed by the covenant, how could they ever make any other choice than to remain in that bondage which would lead them to revolt and to ruin ? To pose the problem of the personal liberty of children in abstract terms and to make it a matter of theoretical reflection, is to do violence to the children and to be guilty of an injustice towards them. The sole liberty of the man left to his own abilities, whether he be child or adult, is to sin, freely, voluntarily, consciously, and even with pleasure, and to run to destruction. According to the scriptural view, there is no choice between good and evil apart from the special grace of God ; apart from the efficacious and irresistible grace of God there is no salvation.

According to God, in order that the child may be able in due course truly to choose it is necessary for him to know that, through the divine good pleasure, he is reckoned in

---

[1] Dt. vi. 2 ; xxx. 2 ; xxxi. 12 f. ; Josh. xxiv. 15 ; Jer. xxxii. 39-41.

[2] Ex. x. 2 ; xii. 24-27 ; Dt. iv. 9 f. ; vii. 5-7 ; xi. 18-21 ; xxix. 29 ; Josh. iv. 6 f., 21-23 ; xxii. 24-27.

[3] Eph. vi. 1-3 ; Col. iii. 20 ; 2 Tim. iii. 15 ; 1 Jn. ii. 13.

[4] Jer. xxxi. 33 f., quoted in Heb. viii. 11 f. ; Rev. xi. 18 ; xix. 5 ; xx. 12. These three last texts are taken here as referring to little children and not to the " little people " or the " humble " of the earth as opposed to the rich and powerful.

the number of the members of the covenant, and it is necessary for him to understand its promises and requirements as well as its blessings which God in His faithfulness bestows upon him. His choice, his option, his liberty then involve either the rejection of God's grace, the decision not to enter into the covenant, or the acceptance of this grace, the confirmation of the covenant. Otherwise there is no liberty, but only enslavement. *Within the covenant, every other attitude does violence to the inalienable rights of the child.*

" It (baptism) declares, as being on its part real action upon man and power of disposal over him, that he stands, prior to all his experiences and decisions, within the sphere of Christ's lordship. Long before he can adopt an attitude to God, God has adopted an attitude to him. Whatever attitude he may take it will take place within and on the ground of the attitude taken towards him by God. If he comes to faith, that will be but the confirmation of the fact that he does possess God's promise, that he is claimed, judged, and blessed by God. If he does not come to faith, neither will that be a possibility he was free to choose. He will sin against God's Word. He will display himself, certainly not as a free man, but as an unfree. He will not choose, he will be rejected. It is not a possibility but the impossibility that he will grasp. In a word, he will, even in his very unbelief, be measured by the Word of God, touched by its power. It is just God's previous attitude towards him that will constitute his unbelief unbelief, his sin sin. Only in the realm of grace, and there for the first time, is there faith and unbelief, righteousness and sin. Only through the power of the Word of God and through it for the first time are found the two categories, those that are saved and those that are lost." These are the words of Karl Barth,[1] and, taking the peculiarities of his vocabulary into account, we can subscribe to this statement almost word for word.

Karl Barth says again : " The baptized man differs from the unbaptized in all circumstances as one who has been placed under the sign of the death and resurrection of Jesus

---

[1] *Church Dogmatics*, Vol. I, Part I, *The Doctrine of the Word of God*, p. 175 ; English translation by G. T. Thomson.

Christ, under the sign of His hope, His destiny, His advent, because of the divine decree accepted and expressed over him. He differs from the unbaptized in all circumstances ; whether he reflects upon it or not, whether he takes notice of it or not, whether he does it honour or not, he is by that sign a designated man, by that representation a man who has been thereby conditioned. This is not of his own making ; nor can he cease to be such of his own accord. He can put an end to the life given him by God. He cannot divest himself of his baptism, just as no one else can take it from him. He may become a Mohammedan, æsthete or atheist, a National Socialist or a Bolshevik, or—worst of all—a heretic, or a bad or a merely nominal Christian. He may become a Catholic. He does not however cease to stand under the sign."[1] All this is remarkably true, not only of believers baptized as adults, but of children placed in the covenant and baptized in virtue of the promise.

No one will dispute the redoubtable character of such a liberty whereby a person may reject the covenant, when one is conscious of the voluntary character of this revolt. *It is just here that the true choice lies.* The children of believers who refuse to confirm the covenant are marked throughout all their life by the consciousness of their revolt. It is important to consider carefully, in accordance with Scripture, this aspect of the question. In all this the baptism of children is entirely to the praise and glory of God who makes His self-revelation to the posterity of believers.

If the question is asked : Why not accept all this without, however, administering the sign of baptism ? Quite simply the answer is (we shall return to this point), because according to Scripture we ought to take notice of the blessings which God offers us, not only in connection with the assurances which He grants us through His audible Word, but also through His sacraments, the visible Word, which act for us as signs, seals, and pledges. *Word and sacraments cannot ever be dissociated in the Church.*

[1] *The Teaching of the Church regarding Baptism*, pp. 59 f. All that Barth adds concerning the manner of considering other baptized persons we ourselves hold regarding all those who are born within the covenant.

E. CHILDREN ARE LEGITIMATELY BAPTIZED, WITHOUT FAITH
OR REPENTANCE, BECAUSE THEY BELONG TO THE COVENANT

" According to the accounts of baptism in Scripture,"
we are told, " we see that all those who receive baptism
manifest an active faith and repentance, and profess their
faith. Faith and repentance are thus a condition of baptism :
children are incapable of faith and repentance, and thus they
cannot be baptized."

1. We shall observe, to begin with, that those who put
forward this objection are well aware that, according to the
New Testament texts, faith and repentance are not *in every
instance* manifested before baptism by those who are
baptized, and that Acts viii. 37 is not found in the better
of the more ancient manuscripts. O. Cullmann has brought
this point out very clearly. According to the texts, it is
completely illegitimate to draw from them an *absolute*
conclusion that *in every instance* faith and repentance were
demanded of the persons baptized, and that this condition
is linked to the doctrine or to the essence of baptism.

2. We put another question : In the texts which relate
the baptisms of adults and proselytes, or the baptisms of
" houses," where it appears that it is *only* the head of the
family who manifests repentance and confesses his faith,
how can one expect to find anything else than the requirements *habitually* demanded for the baptism of *adults* ?
Doubtless we shall be reproached with not having interested
ourselves in what the texts say about baptism and with
deriving from elsewhere our ideas of the sacrament. On the
contrary, however, we are vitally interested in all these texts,
but *we do not consider that the ecclesiastical methods of its
administration determine the fundamental doctrine and essence
of baptism.* Our ideas are derived quite simply from the very
nature of baptism as a sacrament of the covenant of grace,
to which it is indispensable to make reference. *It is the
doctrine which determines the methods of administration of
baptism, not the methods which control the doctrine.* This plan
is followed by the opponents of infant baptism when they
study the Lord's supper, without their imagining for a single

O

instant that it cannot in that case be perfectly legitimate. Why—once more !—should what they regard as legitimate in a related problem be illegitimate in the study of baptism.[1]

The opponents of infant baptism wish to establish a unique and absolute rule of the *administration* of baptism which is binding without any exception. They refuse to recognize the least distinction between adults and children. But we consider that we have the most legitimate grounds for making such a distinction since, according to Scripture, it is made *by God Himself* in the administration of circumcision.

Let us recall some of our conclusions : circumcision is a spiritual sacrament, a sign and seal of justification by faith and of cleansing from sins, implying for adults repentance, faith in the promise of pardon, and the obligation of living in conformity to the commandments of God. The New Testament establishes no *essential* difference between circumcision and baptism ; such differences as there are are only formal. Baptism has taken the place of circumcision.

It is a fact of great importance that, despite all that circumcision implied for adults, God ordained that it should be administered to the infants of the covenant. He thus decreed that a sacrament that for adults implied faith and repentance, of which infants are incapable, should none the less be administered to infants ; they received this sign although for them it was linked to no preceding faith. Why was it necessary for Abraham to believe in order to receive the sign of circumcision, or why was the sign administered to him only *after* he had believed, whereas his son Isaac received it *before* it was even possible for him to believe and repent ? It is because the adult who is not a member of the covenant must *first of all* know what it is in order to enter into it and receive its sign and seal : *this is the first rule.* But the child whom he begets, being *an heir of the covenant according to the promise* made by God to his father, is fitted to receive its sign and seal *before* it is possible for him to understand what it is : *this is the second rule.* Through the goodwill and the promise of God the believer's child, who

---

[1] F.-J. Leenhardt in particular reproaches us for using this plan, *op. cit.*, p. 70, and yet he himself employs it in all good conscience in his book *Le sacrement de la Sainte-Cène.*

participates in the covenant *without having the slightest subjective consciousness of it* and who participates, *without understanding it*, in the thing itself, can and ought, without understanding and without previous knowledge, to receive the sign and the seal which assures him that God declares Himself to be his Father. The children of believers are begotten *for God*.

Circumcision was administered by God's command in accordance with two distinct rules : (i) Adults could not receive it unless they had faith and repentance, for it was on this condition alone that they could be admitted into the covenant ; (ii) for children to receive it, it was sufficient that they should be born in the covenant. *In both cases the ground of circumcision is the same : it is the sign and seal of entry into the covenant.* Adults enter into it by faith ; children, although unconscious, are set in it by a sovereign decision of God. To remain in it, these latter have in their turn to close with the promises of the covenant and to exercise faith, repentance, and obedience. *From the subjective point of view there is thus for the children of the covenant an interval, of divine institution, between the moment when they receive the sign and the moment when they close with the truth.*

Had it been incompatible or contradictory for circumcision—a spiritual sacrament—to be administered to infants, God would never have commanded its administration. In making this ordinance for little children God shows us clearly enough that, so far as its subjective significance is concerned, circumcision was given to them for the time to come. Nobody can deny that this was an explicit divine command or that God is sovereignly wise, just, and reasonable in all that He commands.

If the command to circumcize infants is reasonable and just, and if the two sacraments of baptism and circumcision are identical as regards the promise and the thing represented, and as regards content, reason, motive, usage, and efficacy, then we demand to know what decisive arguments can be invoked in order to assert that that which was good and reasonable in the administration of circumcision to infants is bad and unreasonable where baptism is concerned. Just one clear prohibition, explicitly formulated in the New

Testament (analogous to that which sanctions the abolition of the typical ceremonies of the law), would be enough to restrain believers from according baptism to their children today.

Before receiving adults for baptism and giving them the sign and seal of their admission into the Christian Church, it is indispensable that they should be instructed concerning the covenant of grace and that they should manifest evidences of repentance and faith. This is the first rule of the administration of baptism, but it is not related to its *essence*; the baptismal ordinance is a consequence of the ground of baptism, and it does not interfere with its fundamental significance.[1] As for children, they receive baptism because of the promise of the covenant attested by God to their parents : this is the second rule.

Neither for adults nor for children are faith and repentance the ground of baptism, but the promise of the covenant of which, in both cases, baptism is the sign and the seal.[2] We must always distinguish—as we have carefully endeavoured to do— between the sovereign act of God, who incorporates persons into the covenant and the Church, and the external consequences of this act for the entire life of the individual. The subjective aspect of baptism cannot take precedence over its objective aspect. In the interrelation between faith and baptism the subjective pole cannot be exaggerated to such a point that the objective pole is obliterated or occupies only a secondary place. Such manipulation is impossible. In taking our stand upon the covenant of grace, which remains one and unchanged throughout all Scripture, and in affirming the manner in which circumcision was administered, " we thus have God for the author of this distinction upon which all the difficulty of the question hangs."[3]

" For this reason," says Calvin, " to allege that it is a contravention of reason for a sacrament which is a witness

---

[1] Cf. O. Cullmann, *op. cit.*, pp. 51 f., who in the course of his study verifies these points exegetically within the scheme of the New Testament.

[2] F.-J. Leenhardt, *op. cit.*, affirms to begin with (p. 62) that " baptism never precedes faith," but he goes on to show (pp. 70 f.) that regeneration and conversion are not a condition of baptism. Can one believe without being regenerated and converted ?

[3] Calvin : *Against the Anabaptists*, Opera, VII, p. 59.

of repentance and salvation to be administered to infants, is
to argue against God. What, then does this imply? Just
this, that if we accept all that God does as being good we
have a doctrine which teaches that it is not necessary for the
truth signified in a sacrament always to precede, but that it
is sufficient for it sometimes to follow, at least in part. For
the renewing of life was well signified by circumcision and
likewise the justification that we obtain by faith. In an
infant there is neither repentance nor faith. Yet this does
not incapacitate him for receiving the sacrament. Here, then,
we see how the sign precedes its truth. If formerly this was
legitimate and agreeable to reason, why should it now be
repugnant? ... *To wish the truth always to go before the sign
is to argue against God."* [1]

Baptism given to little children is the witness and attestation of their salvation, the seal and confirmation of the
covenant of grace which God contracts with them. Although
the children of the covenant had no understanding of the
significance of the circumcision which they received, they
were none the less circumcized for the regeneration of their
corrupt nature and for repentance and faith, in order that
they might be instructed in these matters as soon as possible.
Similarly, the children of believers are baptized for repentance and faith which ought to follow later, although we are
unable to discern them in the infants at the time of their
baptism. " The New Testament relation between faith and
Baptism does not so unambiguously and indisputably affirm
that faith leads to Baptism. This is, of course, true of the
cases recounted in the New Testament of adult heathen
and Jews. But for those other Baptisms mentioned, this
sequence of events does not hold good. On the contrary,
in them Baptism leads to faith, and this contrary order
applies to *all*. Baptism is the starting point of faith. What
applies to all must be regarded as fundamental." [2]

That in Scripture there are two distinct rules for the
administration of the sacrament, one for adults and one for
children, is something beyond dispute, provided that
nothing fundamental or essential is modified in the

[1] *Against the Anabaptists*, Opera, VII, pp. 60 f.
[2] O. Cullmann, *op. cit.*, pp. 53 f.

sacrament which remains essentially the same in both cases. There is no more a question here of " half-baptism " than there was formerly of " half-circumcision." [1] The principle is identical, the method of application alone differs. It is sufficient to observe that the sacrament is not simply a sign and seal of a promise concerning only the individual who receives it, but that it is the sign and seal of a promise of God relating *to him and to his posterity*. In the scope of the organic administration of the covenant, and of the divinely instituted spiritual solidarity of family and Church, he who closes with the promise receives it not for himself alone, but also for his descendants.

Since the objections urged against the baptism of infants are exactly the same as those that ought to be urged against the administration of circumcision to infants, we refer those who disagree with us to the command of God and leave them the task of appreciating its wisdom. In order to deny us the right of using this argument, the opponents of infant baptism are obliged—consciously or unconsciously, implicitly or explicitly—to transform circumcision into a carnal sign of a carnal reality and, in fact, to remove it from the list of sacraments. Exegetically this is a device of despair ! Being given the parallelism established by the New Testament between baptism and circumcision, to attack circumcision is to attack baptism. For us, the example of circumcision is vital and explicit.

3. One must also inquire of the opponents of infant baptism whether they regard the blessings of the New Testament dispensation as being less than those of the Old. Were not believers of the Old Testament ceaselessly exhorted to look towards Jesus Christ who would bring in the fulness of grace ? Is the promise that God wishes to be the Father of all who believe in Him and of their posterity no longer valid ? If Jewish children were called a holy posterity because they were heirs of the covenant and separate from the children of unbelievers, is the condition of the children of Christians inferior ? Under the New Testament the grace of God cannot be less generous and less certain than it was under the " shadows " of the law. Jewish children had

---

[1] K. Barth, *op. cit.*, p. 48.

circumcision as a confirmation of grace, of which baptism is today the sign and seal.

4. Despite all this the opponents of infant baptism wish to maintain an absolute rule : he who is incapable of faith and repentance cannot be baptized. But we inquire of them why their intransigeance is so pronounced on this point when on a far more important question, that of salvation by faith alone, they *unanimously* agree in recognising that the Lord, in His goodness, regards adults as capable of reflection and decision in a manner quite different from children, who are incapable of this.

It is explicitly said in Scripture that only he who believes is saved and has eternal life ; apart from faith there is no salvation. The logic of those who differ from us consequently imposes the following syllogism : faith is the necessary condition of salvation ; children are incapable of faith ; therefore all children dying in early years are condemned because they do not have faith. Or again : one can only be reconciled to God by faith ; children are incapable of faith ; therefore all children, even those of believers, are placed under the condemnation of sin and are in no way reconciled to the Lord. *But who accepts these conclusions ?* If one rejects them, why ?—unless, with good reason, one deems it necessary to introduce here other passages of Scripture and to establish that God acts in accordance with *two* distinct rules : the ordinary rule concerning those who have reached the age of discretion and are responsible for their thoughts and actions, and the ordinary rule concerning little children, here the children of believers. The rule of active faith and repentance is imperative for all adults in order that they may be saved ; but it is not so for little children.

When the opponents of infant baptism refer us to the text of the institution of baptism (Mark xvi. 15 f.) and affirm that Christ gives us an absolute rule, valid for all baptisms, and when they wish to impose the syllogism : active faith is the preliminary condition of baptism ; infants are not susceptible of faith ; therefore infants ought not to be baptized ; we reply : " According to your reasoning, it is necessary to say *also* and at the same time, by the same command of Christ and the same text : faith is the condition *sine qua non* of salvation ; infants cannot exhibit faith ; therefore they cannot be saved. Did Christ wish to say this ? Do you believe that children who are incapable of faith are condemned ? If not, why do you wish to impose on us the conclusion of your syllogism concerning the condition of baptism ? The consequences of your principles are unacceptable, even for yourselves : why do you wish to impose them on us ? If you yourselves reject them on the crucial question of salvation by faith, precisely by appealing to the same texts of which we make use for proving that children are in the covenant and thus that they have a right to baptism, why do you adhere to them on the secondary question of the administration of baptism, which is the sign and seal of the promise ? Not one of the texts which you point to affords the slightest argument against infant baptism."

5. Both advocates and adversaries of infant baptism agree in deeming that, according to Scripture, the little children of believers who die in early years are saved and inherit eternal life. They are beneficiaries of a promise which they are incapable of voluntarily and consciously rejecting. Consequently, if they die before the time when it becomes possible for them to make a choice, pious parents and the Church ought not to doubt concerning their election and salvation. The Synod of Dordrecht, whose conclusions were adopted and confirmed by the national Synod of the French Reformed Churches, pronounces on this subject as follows (I, Art. 17) : " Since we have to judge of the will of God in accordance with His Word, which testifies that the children of believers are holy, not by nature, but in virtue of the covenant of grace in which they are included together with their parents, pious parents ought not to doubt concerning the election and salvation of their children, should it please God to call them to Himself at a tender age."

The opponents of infant baptism agree in saying that little children who have died early are in the Kingdom. But *how* do they come to be there ? Is it possible to be a member of the Kingdom without first having been sanctified and regenerated by the Holy Spirit ? Can they enter into the Kingdom or into life eternal while remaining the children of Adam ? But Scripture teaches that in Adam we all die and that it is only through Christ that we have eternal life : to be heirs of eternal life, then, it is necessary for infants to be members of Christ. Scripture attests that we are by nature under the condemnation of sin : it is necessary, then, that they should leave their nature in order to have a part in the Kingdom of God. Scripture declares that flesh and blood cannot inherit the Kingdom : it is necessary, then, that their fallen state should be nullified so that they may become heirs of God. Christ affirms that He alone is the resurrection and the life : it is necessary, then, for them to be in Him in order to escape from bondage and death. Children must thus pass from Adam to Christ, from nature to grace, from the covenant of works to the covenant of grace.

The opponents of infant baptism affirm also that the little children of believers are, while yet living, in the Kingdom. Once again, how do they come to be there ? Is it because they are children of Adam ? Or is it rather as children of Christ, because He causes them to participate in His life ? If, then, according even to those who oppose infant baptism, the infant children of believers, whether they are living or dead, have a share not only in the promises, but in the Kingdom, if they are saved and redeemed by the blood of Christ, why should they not receive the sign of this membership and of this salvation, which is less than the event which it seals and confirms ? " God declares that He adopts our children for His own before they are born, when He says that He will be the God of our posterity after us (Gen. xvii. 7). It is on this word that their salvation rests, and it would be to offer a grave insult to God to deny that He is able to give effect to the substance of His promise. . . . Now, as we have said, one does great injury and despite to the truth of God if one does not confide in it alone as having by itself full and complete power to save. The sacrament is added afterwards as a seal, not to give effectiveness to the promise as though it were weak in itself, but simply to ratify it to us, so that we may grasp it with all the more certainty. *From this it*

*follows that the little children born to Christians are not baptized
in order that they may begin to be children of God, as though
they had previously not in any way belonged to Him and had
been aliens from the Church, but rather in order that it might
be declared by this formal sign that they are received into the
Church as being already members of Christ's body."* [1]

F. HOW DO DOCTRINE AND FAITH PRECEDE BAPTISM ?

1. In the Reformed doctrine of infant baptism, how is it
that the Word precedes the sign ? The opponents of infant
baptism maintain that, since the child is passive and
unconscious, the Word is not proclaimed to him, and that
consequently he is unfitted to receive the sign which seals it.
Such an exclusive view is only conceivable and possible
when the sacraments are seen distortedly in an individualistic
and subjective light, which regards the child in its individual
capacity as the sole and only recipient of the sacrament.
According to Scripture, this is not the correct conception
of the beneficiaries of the sacraments.

Ought the Word to precede the sacrament ? We are
firmly persuaded of it ! But it is needful to know how, and
not to neglect a consideration of the means by which, in
infant baptism, the Word precedes and the sacrament
follows. When a proselyte is introduced by baptism into
the communion of the Church it is necessary that he *himself*
should have heard the Word exhorting him to conversion,
to faith, and to repentance. But what is the promise that is
given to him and sealed by his baptism ? " I will be your
God *and the God of your children after you."* The promise
of salvation is not given to him for himself alone, *but also
for his children.* In virtue of the covenant which God has
made with their father, in their name and for their benefit,
*his children will be baptized on the basis of the doctrine which
their father has received*, the doctrine, namely, which declares
that God will be his Saviour not only for himself, but the
Saviour of his children also. " When a man has been a
stranger to the company of believers and is converted to our
Lord, the doctrine on which he is baptized is addressed to

[1] Calvin : *Instt.*, IV. xv. 20, 22 ; cf. IV. xvi. 17, 18, 21, 26.

him. That is why it is necessary for him to have heard and understood it before he is received for baptism. The doctrine on which the children of Christians are baptized is not addressed to them, but to their parents and to the whole Church. Thus it is not required that they should have heard the Word before receiving the sign." [1]

The doctrine certainly precedes the administration of the sacrament : the whole question is one of considering carefully how and by what means it does so. Once again, they alone can protest energetically against this way in which the Word precedes the administration of baptism to a little child, who have their vision clouded by an individualistic and subjective conception of the sacrament and are unable to rid themselves of the *a priori* notion that it is the baptized person *alone* who benefits from the sacrament.

And faith also precedes baptism ! We know that in every case the sacrament demands a faith already aroused and evoked by the Word and needing to be strengthened. However feeble one may imagine this faith to be, one cannot conceive of it as a mere virtuality ; one must envisage it as an active faith, a faith in action.

It is, once more, quite simply a matter of answering a single question : who is the true *beneficiary* of the sacrament ? The child alone ? Certainly not ! It is he who receives the sign of baptism, but in such a manner that he is incorporated " by covenant " into the body which comprises his parents, the witnesses, and even the entire community : in short, the Church. The child receives the sign and seal of the covenant, and we shall soon see in what way baptism is for him a " means of grace " ; but the parents, the witnesses, the community, and the Church receive, although differently, the same confirmation and the same seal of grace. The child is as yet only passive and unconscious. The parents, the witnesses, and the community have faith and confess it, and by this baptism they are confirmed and sealed in this faith ; this baptism is a means of grace for them also. Besides, in conformity with the covenant's obligations received in faith and confirmed by this baptism, they all unitedly pledge themselves to instruct the child in the works and command-

[1] Calvin : *Against the Anabaptists*, Opera, VII, p. 58.

ments of God and to teach him to walk in the way of the covenant, *by continuing in it themselves with perseverance.*

To regard the child alone, the child " himself," as the sole true beneficiary of the sacrament is a fundamental error, committed by all those who raise objections against infant baptism.

Let us be careful ! It is not a matter of faith " by substitution." Children are not baptized *by reason of* the confession of faith of the Church or of their parents or of their sponsors. It is the covenant that is the sole basis of baptism. " The faith of the congregation," says O. Cullmann, " though not to be represented as vicarious faith, does yet at the moment of the baptismal event belong to the act of baptism. Attention must here be drawn to the Church that *prays* for the person being baptized (Acts viii. 15). It prays that God may complete the miracle of baptism in the baptized person, whether adult or infant. *This* faith which has the person baptized as its object is in fact an indispensable element in the baptismal act." [1] It is a faith which bursts into action. All those who present a child at the baptismal font participate, by faith, in the action which the true beneficiary of the sacrament ought to perform. The baptism of children is a sacrament as fruitful for the parents and the Church as for the children themselves. The promise of God is signified and sealed in a manner as certain for the parents as for the children, and still more it becomes real for the whole Church, which includes the children of the community. The children who receive baptism cannot and ought not to be considered as the sole beneficiaries of the sacrament because —and for us this is a scriptural and objective fact—they are not.

G. BAPTISM AND REGENERATION

We are asked a further question : Since baptism is the sign of regeneration produced in us by the preaching of faith, how then can it be administered to infants who are incapable of understanding the Word and consequently of being regenerated ? All that we have already said in this study affords a reply to this question : we shall add a few remarks.

[1] *Op. cit.*, p. 54.

1. It is quite true that, according to Scripture, faith *ordinarily* results from hearing. The preaching of the Word is the *ordinary* means employed by God so that those who are capable of hearing may come to faith. No Reformed theologian, however, will affirm that regeneration is the fruit *only* of the Word heard. Even where adults are concerned, regeneration is the result of a distinct and particular action of the Holy Spirit, which He can evidently effect on the occasion of the preaching of the Word, but which is not dependent on it. In speaking of the effects of the Word (in Romans x. 17 ff., for example) Paul tells us only of the ordinary manner in which the Lord works for giving faith to His own in the Church.[1] He *can* work differently, even with adults, for reaching their heart and bringing them to a knowledge of His Name without first causing them to hear the Word. True, we have absolutely no right to speculate on this possibility! But who will dare to assert that in the world's history, beyond those who have heard the Word and received it with faith, nobody has ever been saved by God? The ordinary rule which has been given us by Scripture is not an absolute rule which admits of no exception. Cannot God do for the children of the covenant what He does for adults who are not in the covenant?

2. Although God's working is incomprehensible and hidden from us, we affirm, taking our stand on the covenant which contains the promise of regeneration, that God does not forbear to act in the little children of believers. God declares that our children are acceptable to Him and that He loves thém. Since they are born in sin, that they may be acceptable to God it is necessary that they should be justified before Him. We have seen how He receives into His Kingdom those who die in infancy. We believe with Calvin that "children are renewed by the Spirit of God, according to the measure and capacity of their age, so that this divine virtue hidden within them gradually grows and in due course manifests itself plainly."[2] The regeneration of infants by the power of God is "wonderful and incomprehensible to us, but possible and easy for Him."[3]

---

[1] Cf. P.-Ch. Marcel, *A l'Ecole de Dieu*, pp. 132-148.

[2] *Comm.* on Mt. xix. 13 f.

[3] *Instt.*, IV. xvi. 18 ; cf. O. Cullmann, *op. cit.*, pp. 41 ff

When we said that presumptive regeneration could not be the basis of infant baptism there was no question of dissociating regeneration from baptism and of considering it *only* as a sacrament of the Church and a token for the posterity of believers taken in the mass, or as a simple confirmation of the objective but conditional promises of the Gospel, or as a simple attestation of external membership of the covenant of grace, or as a guarantee of a regeneration which could be lost since it was not indissolubly bound to salvation and required to be confirmed by a personal faith, or merely as a means of education whereby baptized persons would be stimulated to a true conversion later on in life.

In the covenant regeneration and baptism cannot be dissociated from each other. " We do not wish to affirm that children have faith since we do not know in what way God works in them ; but our intention is to show the rashness and presumption of those people who, according to their wild fancy, assert and deny whatever suits them, without showing regard for any reason that may be produced. . . . It is most uncertain and insecure to assert that the Lord cannot manifest Himself to them in any way He pleases. . . . I inquire of them why they wish to restrict the power of God so that He cannot now perform in children in part that which He performs in them in full measure a little later ? . . . We only desire to show the injustice of those who wish to restrict the power of God towards little children." [1]

Do not the examples of Jeremiah (Jer. i. 5), John the Baptist (Lk. i. 15), and others afford proof that the Lord sanctifies infants when it pleases Him to do so ? Now, He solemnly promises that He will sanctify the children of the covenant. Shall it be said that this is not consonant with His power ? It is not a question here of our being confronted with a theoretical problem which must be resolved by appealing to scientific analysis and the investigations of reason : it is a question of *a reality of faith. God performs what He promises.* Do we wish to plumb the mystery and to know *how* God acts in the hearts of little children when we are and remain incapable of analysing or saying *how* He acts in the hearts of adults and even in our own heart ? When our

[1] Calvin : *Instt.*, IV. xvi. 19, 18, 19, 17.

curiosity is too fully aroused let us read again chapters xxxviii to xlii of the book of Job, and we shall perhaps abandon the way of reason and return to that of faith in the Word of our God. He who believes is not accustomed to probe the " how " of the divine actions when God has not revealed it to him. We refuse to impose on God the time or the means or the circumstances of His action in the heart of our children and to confine it within the categories of our reason. *He has promised: He acts: the thing is sure since we believe in Him!* God promises and, quite simply, we believe and affirm that children as well as adults have a share in the benefits of His grace, that they are or will be regenerated by the Holy Spirit, and that baptism is also given to them as a sign, seal, and pledge of this regeneration. It is, in this respect, similar to circumcision. We are perfectly right to *believe* that the Holy Spirit has the power to communicate Himself to little children, not that he does it just because of our faith, but because God Himself has, on many, occasions, solemnly promised it. It is not a matter of proving that He does so, nor that it is *reasonable* to believe it, but simply of *believing*.[1]

H. BAPTISM A MEANS OF GRACE FOR THE CHILD

How can infant baptism be considered a means of grace ? Since they are incapable of *actual* faith how, we are asked, can little children be strengthened and established ?

[1] Cf. F.-J. Leenhardt, *Le Baptême chrétien*, pp. 23 f. : " We cannot say anything precise regarding the nature of God's dealings with our inner being, regarding His action within us. Faith affirms the existence of this interior life and the reality of the activity of God, but what do we know of the moments *when* it appears ? When does man, in his development from the fœtus to the adult state, pass from the state of living organic matter to the condition of being responsible before God ? . . . Let us have the simplicity to recognize our incompetence in that which concerns the origin and formation of the spiritual being." All this is remarkably accurate. But why does Leenhardt, in his article in *Foi et Vie*, return to this affirmation and yet wish to impose limits, within time, to the action of God's grace on the score of the complexity of the question of the " relationships of God's grace and will " and of the application to man of " the objective work " ?

We consider it unnecessary to reply to the question posed anew by Karl Barth (*op. cit.*, p. 52) : Why cannot and indeed ought not infants to participate also in the Lord's supper ? The elements of the reply will be found in O. Cullmann, *op. cit.*, pp. 29-32, Calvin, *Instt.*, IV. xvi. 30, and especially a remarkable and very clear passage in *Ref. Errorum Mich. Serveti*, Opera, VIII, pp. 482-484.

1. To begin with, we must observe that it is an error to regard the child only from the angle of his own subjective consciousness. A whole assemblage of facts does and can react, from the time of his birth, for his good or ill without his having the slightest consciousness of it in the sense in which the opponents of infant baptism require that the child should be "conscious." Air, light, milk, cleanliness, love, and a peaceful atmosphere are, for every child, *blessings* which contribute to his development, strengthen him, and play a decisive and vital part in his growth to manhood. The child does not remain indifferent to his mother's affection and the sweet and peaceful atmosphere of the home, nor to the reproaches and chidings which he receives. There is not a word or a gesture which is not for or against him, to his advantage or to his detriment, to his favour or disfavour, and which from the earliest days of his life has not had a profound influence on what he will be tomorrow, not only in his physical being, but also in his psychical, moral, and spiritual being. Those who are familiar with little children know to what degree they react to everything that takes place and is done and said around them and in their homes.

And yet the little child has no subjective consciousness of the blessings of which he is the object in the covenant ; he is ignorant of that of which his baptism is the sign and seal ; he, however, benefits directly, for already, thanks to the promise sealed by his baptism, a whole beneficent and *redemptive* spiritual reality surrounds him, of which the craftsmen are respectively God, his parents, eventually his brothers and sisters, his friends, and the Church. How is this ?

The child is presented for baptism by adults and the Church. For all those who participate in it as conscious individuals his baptism signifies, attests, and seals that he is a member of the covenant, that all the promises are for him, and that he is a child of the Kingdom and of the Church. In the covenant which his baptism seals his parents, his brothers and sisters who understand what is taking place, and the Church regard this child quite otherwise than they would if he were outside the covenant and the Church. They all, in faith, form an opinion of this child and his relationship to God. All this is of the utmost importance.

In *this* baptism God tells us many things concerning *this child*. The manner of considering *him*, infant though he is, is not indifferent to the constitution of his personality and to his entire being as a child of God. He is, it is true, still unconscious, but what he will be later depends already on the manner in which people treat him, think about him, speak about him, regard him, and love him, in short, on the attitude of others towards him. Now, because of the promises of the covenant sealed by this baptism the parents and the Church are strengthened in the faith which causes them to consider this infant as a child of God and a lamb in Christ's fold. They know that he no longer belongs to the race of Adam, that he is placed under the direct protection of the Lord, and that God loves him and regards him with affection. They know that this child is the heir presumptive of salvation and that it is henceforth necessary to instruct him in such a manner that he may be able to walk in the way of the covenant, since he is under obligation to follow it, and so that he may become receptive to the influences of the Spirit. Conscious of these blessings, they all pray the Lord to grant them to him according to His promise, fervently commending him to His goodness, and surrounding him with the solicitude of faith.

The baptism accorded to the child strengthens these thoughts in his parents and in the Church and determines the standards of his Christian education in accordance with the pedagogy of the covenant. Around the child, still totally dependent on others and on the setting in which he lives, a climate of grace and love is created of which he is the immediate beneficiary. It is for this reason that we feel able to affirm that in a *direct* manner his baptism is *immediately* for him a means of grace. Little by little the child will assume independence and will reflect ; it will require much time for him to become conscious of the blessings he has received, to acknowledge it, and to realize how he has been marked and enriched, from the earliest days of his life, by the solicitude of those who have instructed him to trust in the promises of the covenant, signified and sealed by his own baptism. Provided we take the promise and its seal *seriously*,

P

ought not this method of viewing some of the benefits directly conferred on the child by his baptism to be more familiar to us ?

2. From the judicial point of view, baptism also signifies to adults and to the Church the spiritual rights of the child in the covenant. The child has a *right* to the fulfilment of the promises ; he has a *right* to fellowship with Christ ; he has a *right* to citizenship in the Church with the people of God ; he has a *right* to eternal life ; he has a *right* to pardon ; he has a *right* to be instructed in the works and commandments of God ; he has a *right* to the obedience of his parents to the commands which God gives and shall give them for his education, and also to their prayers ; he has a *right* to the faithful and persevering ministry of the Church which is his mother. The covenant enables us to know *the child's declaration of spiritual rights*, judicially acknowledged by the " vows " of his parents and godparents. We ought to respect and honour these rights ; we cannot infringe them without offending God Himself and doing the child an injury. Baptism seals their inviolable character and is a means of grace for the child, unconscious though he still is of all these rights. Who will dare to say that the rights of the child recorded in our Civil Code and the legislations concerning him are of no avail to him because he is incapable of having any knowledge of them ? On the contrary, they are inscribed in the Law for his immediate good and advantage. To despise them is to attack the child directly and to injure his human status. The same is true of the spiritual rights which baptism expresses and seals, as a sign of the obligations of the covenant regarding this infant which God has imposed on parents and believers and the Church, and of the promises uttered by his heavenly Father on his behalf. It would be a good thing if in the course of the baptismal ceremony these rights, which involve obligations for the Church herself, were acknowledged in an ecclesiastical manner, pledging the entire congregation on behalf of the child. This is another of the immediate and permanent blessings of baptism, no matter how the child may come to regard them in later years.

3. The child of the covenant is not aroused to consciousness without being guided and instructed by his parents who ought not to delay to teach him and to bring the promises of the covenant progressively to his notice. Provided it is explained to him how, his baptism will strengthen his faith. Nor will it be for him merely the confirmation of the promises which God makes to him at present ; he will be assured that he is indeed the heir designate of the promised blessings ; he will be more inclined to serve the Lord who declared Himself to be his Father even before he could understand it and who has received him as a member of His people right from his birth. Little by little the child will come to a clear comprehension of the significance of his baptism, which will become for him the instrumental cause of the growth of his faith. The blessings of redemption are promised to him on the same conditions as to his parents, for baptism effectively signifies, seals, and communicates its blessings to all, whether children or adults, who close with the covenant of which it is the seal. Just as a believer by recalling one or other promise of Scripture, which he has read or heard, receives to the full the promised blessings, so a child who has reached maturity receives all the blessings of baptism, if he believes in the promises signified and sealed for him in the sacrament administered. Consequently, baptism benefits children in exactly the same manner as adults and on the same conditions.

4. There is still more. We believe that children, just as they are at the moment of their baptism, *can be* (we do not say *are*) placed personally and directly under the benefit of the blessings of baptism. Here prudence and discretion are essential. The souls of children do not give up their secrets under the scalpel of rational analysis which seeks to dissect them. We do not assert that infants are already in possession of the promised benefits ; we think it possible and even probable : they certainly participate in them in some manner hidden from us. " Because our Lord of old ordained circumcision for infants, He clearly shows that He causes them to participate in all that is represented by it. Otherwise it would mean that this institution was nothing

but a delusion and imposture and a showy vanity, something which could have been neither heard nor endured among the faithful." [1] In our opinion, it is certain that the blessings of baptism which our children receive today are greater than those which formerly flowed from circumcision (Rom. iii. 1 f. ; Eph. ii. 11 f. ; etc.).[2]

5. The baptism of children has a *collective* efficacy, that is to say, all who participate in it are equally its beneficiaries. It is a personal means of grace for the parents who, independently of all that they may have grasped concerning their child, are themselves strengthened anew in the grace of their own baptism. It strengthens in them the realization of their responsibility to give their child a Christian education. The parents are encouraged to serve God more wholeheartedly when they realize that their God and Father cares not only for them, but also for the children which He in His love has given them. " When our heavenly Father visibly testifies to us by the sign of baptism that because of His love to us He wishes to interest Himself in our posterity and to be the God of our children, have we not good cause for rejoicing, like David, considering that God acts towards us as the good Father of a family by extending His providence not only to us, but to our children after our death ? In such rejoicing God is singularly glorified." [3]

The sum total of believers, which includes the minister,

---

[1] Calvin : *Instt.*, IV. xvi. 5. A little further on (IV. xvi. 18) Calvin introduces an argument based on the participation which little children have in the incarnation of Christ : " Christ was sanctified from His infancy in order that all, at any age, might be sanctified in Him." This question seems to us complex, and since we have not studied it so as to be able to give our own judgment on it, we prefer to pass it over.

[2] Th. Preiss has offered some valuable thoughts in dealing with a remarkable text, namely, John vii. 23 : " If a man receive circumcision on the sabbath day," said Jesus, " in order that the law of Moses should not be broken, are you angry with Me *because I have made an entire man whole on the sabbath day ?* " ὅτι ὅλον ἄνθρωπον ὑγιῆ ἐποίησα ἐν σαββάτῳ It seems possible to interpret Christ's words as follows : Since you yourselves, through respect for the law of Moses, do not hesitate to circumcise a child on the sabbath day (that is to say, *to make him whole at least in part*, or *in a part of his body*), why are you angry with Me because I have made a man whole *in his entire body* ? If such was the objective potency of circumcision as a means of grace for the new-born child who received it, it would be difficult to accord to baptism an inferior potency.

[3] Calvin : *Instt.*, IV. xvi. 32.

participates in the same blessings. The whole Church is purified and sanctified by this baptism ; as such, she is reminded of the duties of her vocation concerning the faithfulness of her preaching and ministry, and of the obligations which she assumes regarding every aspect of the Christian education of the children which she receives into her bosom.

For every individual believer and for the entire Church this baptism is a proof of grace received, a sign of God's faithfulness, an incentive to prayer, a support to faith, and an exhortation to fresh thankfulness and fresh obedience. In all this God is supremely glorified, His faithfulness confessed, and the magnificence of His Name exalted.

I. RESPONSIBILITY OF CHURCH, PARENTS, AND CHILDREN

It remains for us to examine the responsibility which follows for the Church, for the parents, and for the children themselves from the administration of baptism to the little children of the covenant.

1. There are some who declare that the Church's responsibility is gravely compromised by the fact that when baptizing infants she exposes herself to the charge of baptizing those who are unregenerate. " Alas ! " exclaims F. Lovsky, " is it not true that it is impossible today to point to the efficacy of baptism as a reply to those who criticize the use which is made of it ? Is it not true that for the last couple of hundred years the Church's enemies have been baptized in their infancy ? [1] " In the *practical* sphere," says F.-J. Leenhardt, " one may state that pedobaptism has not proved itself, for the Church today is quite definitely multitudinist."[2]

Today large numbers of Protestants accept these reproaches which, such as are formulated, bring numerous questions on to the scene. Despite an appearance of good logic, indeed precisely because the observations or arguments appear to be logical, we say that their setting is outside of faith and revelation.

[1] *Notes d'Histoire pour contribuer a l'étude du problème baptismal,* Foi et Vie, 1950, I, p. 139.
[2] *Op. cit.,* p. 72, note.

Is it only for the last couple of hundred years, and in the Protestant Churches alone, that the " enemies " of the Church have been baptized in their infancy ? To speak only of the New Testament Church, were not certain enemies of the Apostolic Church baptized as adults ? We know of no revelation or divine commandment which has since been interposed in order to render this state of affairs *impossible*.

Those who feel humiliated by these reproaches infer forthwith that the Church would do better to surround herself with adequate safeguards and to revise the regulations for the administration of baptism by refusing it to children. It is not, however, for the Church to decide by herself, in the pursuit of the *effectiveness of her ministry*, what ought to be the regulations and principles of this ministry ; for they have been given to her in Scripture. The Christian Church is the Church of the covenant ; her whole ministry is that of the covenant ; her ministers are the " ministers of the covenant " (2 Cor. iii. 6). There is only one thing she can do, namely, promote, realize, accomplish the covenant of grace in its fulness for the greatest number, by the preaching of the Gospel and *in faith*. The Church ought thus to submit to the regulations of the administration of the covenant as they have been revealed to her. In no case has she the right or the competence or the power to establish by herself, and in accordance with her desire to be more " effective," different norms of action.

As the servant of the God of the covenant, the Church cannot in any instance be judge of the fruits of the liberty of the Spirit. " It is never her objective to make an inventory of results and a balance-sheet of the effects which the grace of God has permitted her to glimpse ; most of the Spirit's activity is unobserved and will remain hidden to the end. Evidences of the Spirit confirm that He is active, but they do not determine His activity. What determines it is the Church's obedience to God and her faith in His promise alone : nothing can exempt the Church from proceeding only by faith. Thus it is not the Church's business to reform water baptism by adding to it signs which she cannot control ; she would exceed her rights and fetter her charity, and she would circumscribe that which God alone can circumscribe, by wielding without misgivings the reaping-hook which the angels alone know how to handle." [1]

When one wishes to place the finger on the fruits of the Spirit and His effectiveness, to mould the Church's demeanour according to what one hopes to see, and to make pronouncements concerning this effectiveness, one is sinking right down into materialism, and that too—curiously enough! —in the name of the Spirit. Since they are not based on faith in God's promises, the Spirit's power, and the divine faithfulness, nor on complete obedience to the requirements of God, who defines the standards of the Church's task and dictates the content of her preaching, all possible theories of the " effectiveness of the Church " are first cousins to the theories of effectiveness propounded by the instructors of various political and economic schools. He who is observant of the signs of the times can only be astonished to remark in our religious press, and under the greatest diversity of authorship, the unhappy evidences of this theological (if one can call it that!) or ecclesiastical materialism in the mentality of some of our scholars and pastors for whom the effectiveness of the Church is the problem of first priority—a materialism that is fostered by the political ideologies and " programmes " in vogue.

To yield here is to leave the path of faith for that of statistics and demonstrations ; it is to transform the Church into a propaganda society, anxious for its own power and effectiveness ; it is to quench the Spirit, who effects His ends through the preaching of the Word ; it is to cease from the prophetic function and to become a substantial *bourgeois* association, enamoured of its reputation and desiring only that activity which involves the least possible risk. No, the attitude of the Church can only be that of faith, in obedience and humility, which are the sole vouchers of her faithfulness.

The covenant and its administration show that, because of the manner in which God calls, it is impossible that there should not be unregenerate persons in the Church, in the first place because it pleases God to call some who will refuse to respond to Him, and also because it is an essential part of the Church's ministry to preach repentance, conversion,

[1] J. Deransart : *Le Baptême et l'Eglise*, Matin Vient, July 1937, p. 138.

and regeneration to all, whether they are in the covenant or not.

It is a fact beyond dispute that, in the covenant of grace, the Church may be called upon to baptize adults or children who are not yet or who will never be regenerate. No matter how great the Church's vigilance, she has, according to Scripture, neither the gifts nor the discernment which would preserve her from such a risk. When she baptizes adults and distributes the holy communion the Church can never have the assurance that none who receive the sacrament will do so hypocritically or illegitimately. The faith and repentance to which adults testify never convey the *certitude* that they truly possess them : they indicate that it is probable. The Church has not the ability to judge hearts : *de intimis non judicat ecclesia.* Since she is dependent on external appearances, she can only, in accordance with Christ's commandment, express a charitable judgment by which she regards as believers those who, on the conditions we have stated, confess their faith. She administers the sacrament to them only in virtue of the present *probability* of their faith or in virtue of its *subsequent* probability.

In the baptism of children the Church can demand no more and no less than she does from adults. The question brings us to this point : Is the certainty that we have to do with believers, or, where the children of the covenant are concerned, with future believers, the same as the certainty which we have regarding those who as adults confess their faith and demand baptism ? If the children of believers are considered, as Scripture teaches us to consider them, as being within the perspective of the covenant, they have —according to the divine institution of baptism—a right to this sacrament in the same way and even more so than adults who profess faith : the promises of God respecting the children of believers are more sure for us and more objective than the subjective declarations of adults who demand baptism can ever be. It is more likely that God will perform what He promises than that adults will remain faithful to the disposition of heart which they experience and to the testimony which they give of it. In accordance with the assurance which God vouchsafes to us regarding His faithfulness, and according to the charitable judgment which He demands for the children of the covenant, we reckon the children of believers in the number of the believers themselves because it is God who associates them with their parents in the covenant of grace. For us, the likelihood that those baptized are or will be true believers is greater with children than with adults.[1]

Neither for adults nor for children is there any infallible decision which makes it possible to establish the salvation of each person baptized ; there is only a rule which Scripture requires us to observe in the practice of ecclesiastical life. He who desires absolute certitude will never be able to administer baptism, either to adults or to infants, nor to distribute the holy communion. Despite all that he says elsewhere, Karl Barth is conscious of this fact. " Without any legalism," he says,[2] " it would easily be possible so to shape baptismal practice that the baptizing Church assured herself—not with regard to the faith, regeneration, conversion, endowment with the Spirit of those she baptizes, but of their free resolve and confession." Despite his exegetical conclusions, then, preliminary faith is not for Karl Barth the condition *sine qua non* of baptism.

The foundation of baptism is not the supposition that each one is regenerated, nor even regeneration itself, but simply the covenant of God. No more is it a question of proving that the elect are always regenerated by the Holy Spirit in their infancy, before baptism or even before birth. God is free in the distribution of His blessings and can cause the fruit of baptism, as a sign and seal of the promises of the covenant, to be received also at a very advanced age, whether baptism has been administered in adulthood or in infancy. It is for this reason that there is still place in the Christian Church for the preaching of the Gospel, for regeneration, faith and repentance, and the miracles of the Spirit. For this reason the prophets, John the Baptist, and Jesus Christ appeared *in the midst of their people* who none the less were *the Lord's*

---

[1] This is said on the understanding that the covenant is correctly and faithfully administered. We shall see below how, in our estimation, it can and ought to be so administered.

[2] *Op. cit.*, p. 51.

possession. So also the Apostles were ministers of the Word not only to reveal the life hidden with Christ in God, but they proclaimed it also as a seed of regeneration and a means for producing faith in the covenant.

The essence of baptism, therefore, must not be made to depend on its effects in life. True faith remains what it is, although it may be subject to all sorts of deviations and distortions ; similarly, baptism is and cannot be anything other than what Scripture tells us concerning it. Just like the Word, it remains objective. He who receives the Word, and equally he who receives baptism in faith, participates really in the promises which God communicates through Word and sacrament. God remains true to Himself and gives salvation to all who believe.

2. This is not to make the Church a couch of slothfulness. Could that possibly be so, if she is aware of the obligations which lie upon her in the covenant of grace, of which she is the administratrix ?

(a) In the administration of baptism to children *the Church ought to be able to recognize whether the child is in fact in the covenant.* She can only grant baptism if at least one of the child's parents avows belief in the Lord's promise. In the perspective of the covenant the baptism of the child is truly what it claims to be only if faith is present in the family that demands it. The faith of the Church cannot make up for the absence of faith in the parents. It is in the first place the family that receives the promise of the covenant. It is also necessary that the Church should be reasonably assured that a Christian education, or at least Christian religious instruction, will be given to the child. In many cases the Church can reasonably have one or other of these assurances, and the baptism which she administers, since it is a *complete* baptism, is perfectly legitimate.

When the faith of those who present a child for baptism is manifestly non-existent, when families give evidence by their works of an unmistakable impiety, when there is no probability that the children will receive a Christian upbringing, when it is obvious that the presentation of the child for baptism is only a superstitious or mundane formality, it is quite clear from the Church's point of view that such families—even though they still come under the ministry of the covenant—are not living in the covenant, and that the baptism of their children would, according to the standards of its legitimacy within the covenant, be a mutilated baptism, and thus an impossible and unacceptable baptism. It is incontestable that this sort of baptism has been tolerated and is still practised in our churches, and because of it they bear a heavy responsibility.

The distress and pain of baptizing the children of those who are indifferent, namely, of our Lord's enemies, which every faithful pastor has felt when he has been obliged, in the absence of an ecclesiastical discipline, to baptize certain children, and which some have pointed to as an argument against infant baptism, has absolutely nothing to do with baptism itself, but is immediately connected with the *indiscipline* of the Church. A Church lacking baptismal discipline can no longer be a *Christian* Church. It is not a matter of setting up age categories, but of disciplining the administration of baptism in every category, for adults as well as for children.

If, according to certain opponents of infant baptism,[1] the true notion of baptism is not entirely contrary to the baptism of certain children *when there exists a discipline*, we perceive that it is not infant baptism, as such, that ought to be suppressed, *but the indiscipline of baptism. What is needed is not a suppression of infant baptism, but a restoration of baptismal discipline.* Once one is convinced of the legitimacy of the baptism of certain children—those of believers— the true question confronting the Church is primarily one of discipline. One thing is certain, namely, that the Church ought to do what is necessary in order that the administration of baptism to children (as also to adults) may be performed in faithfulness and submission to the terms of the covenant. She knows that the efficacy of God's promises, in so far as God acts through secondary causes, depends on her obedience and her faith. But in her submission to her Lord the Church will never allow her judgment to be swayed by the " results " of her faithfulness.

[1] E.g. F.-J. Leenhardt, *op. cit.*, p. 72.

(b) *The Church ought to preach the covenant of grace.* She ought to instruct and remind and make its promises and requirements a living reality for her whole flock, both parents and children.

When we are told that it is " impossible today to point to the effectiveness of baptism as a reply to those who criticize the use which is made of it," we have the impression that such a statement betrays a really bad theology. We put the question : What can the " effectiveness of baptism " be without the Word which it signifies and of which it is the seal ? It is most surprising that anyone should wish to make baptism efficacious by itself ! What is the use of the sign if the Word does not accompany it, since it is its concrete portrayal as the visible Word ? If there is no place for preaching which conforms to the message of the Gospel, what will be the effectiveness of the Lord's supper ? If no place is found for preaching, and precisely *this* preaching on which the legitimacy of infant baptism is founded, what can baptism be except a rite deprived of its content and meaning, incapable of signifying and sealing the Word spoken and of strengthening one's assurance of its truth ? If faith in the only legitimate foundation of baptism exists neither in the Church nor in the parents, how can this sign or any other strengthen it ? Yet again, the consequences of baptism have been taken for its foundation : the one seems to be bad and therefore (it is said) the other must be suppressed. Once more, it is wrong to infer that this baptism is for this reason illegitimate, for *it is sufficient to return to the preaching of the covenant—which is the Gospel—so that the conditions of its effectiveness, as laid down by God, may exist.* In itself the thing is excellent ; it is only the use that one makes of it that is defective. It is a serious error to attack the consequences without going back to the cause. To change the method of the administration of baptism by withholding it from children will not render baptism " effective." To assail the consequences of an evil does not do away with that evil, but only diminishes the signs of it. Independently of her lack of discipline, the cause of the ineffectiveness of infant baptism is attributable to the unfaithfulness of the Church who has too often renounced her vocation to preach the Word *according to the Scriptures.* May she repent and fulfil her vocation, and God will act as He intends in accordance with His promise!

Since baptism has been given to the Church for her to administer it to adults and to children, her preaching ought to spring forth from baptism, or rather baptism, administered fully and without mutilation, ought to spring forth from her preaching. "Baptism is nothing," says J. Deransart, "if the Church does not preach to its recipient this humble and dutiful message : ' It is He who will baptize you with the Spirit '."[1] If the Church is to administer baptism faithfully, her preaching must be faithful. She must preach the covenant of grace, salvation by the outpoured blood of Christ, the necessity of the new birth, regeneration by the Holy Spirit. In the Epistles the Apostles insist on the meaning of baptism and are careful that nothing should rob it of its grace. *Each member of the covenant ought to become what his baptism signifies.* Assured of God's faithfulness to His promises, the Church preaches : " I will circumcize thy heart. . . . Ye shall be baptized with the Holy Spirit. . . . I will be thy God and thou shalt be My son, etc. . . ." This charitable ministry of the Church must not be exercised carelessly.

It is not baptism which needs to be reformed, but preaching, which must be grounded in the covenant whose sign and seal is baptism. The covenant is the very blossoming of the preaching of baptism.[2]

Karl Barth declares that we ought " to give opportunity once more for the free movement and control of the Holy Spirit in the calling and assembling of the Church, to which the present-day baptismal practice tries to do grievous violence."[3] To decide to give the Holy Spirit opportunity for free movement is to decide to submit oneself to the standards of the Word which tell us how the Spirit in His freedom wishes to act. His freedom to " call and assemble the Church " is, as we know, that of the covenant. It is not so much the " present-day baptismal practice " which does

---

[1] *Op. cit.*, p. 127.

[2] Cf. the fine passage in J. Deransart, *op. cit.*, pp. 134-139.

[3] *Op. cit.*, p. 51.

violence to the Holy Spirit, but more often the sickly-sweet preaching of the Church which, for reasons that must always be contested, drastically pares down the Word and refuses to take into account fundamental doctrines of God's revelation. In our eyes, this is being done by all those who assert that the covenant of grace, as such, has no further place in the Christian Church, or who affirm that it is an outmoded doctrine, when it is and remains the secret of God which He reveals to those whom He loves (Psalm xxv. 14). For us, the Holy Spirit moves above all through the preaching of the Word, the preaching of the covenant of redemption and grace. Baptism is but the sign and seal of this preaching. Of itself it in no way hinders or does violence to the Holy Spirit. The real wound caused by the Church is that of incorrect preaching, and we estimate its incorrectness in accordance with the discrepancy, arbitrarily created, between this preaching and its objective signs. Where preaching is sane and biblical, there the Church is sane also and the administration of the sacraments is sane.

When F.-J. Leenhardt, despite all that he says elsewhere, declares : " Infant baptism cannot be tolerated . . . except in the setting of a community of faithful, conscious, adult believers,"[1] he is, in fact, explicitly recognizing the legitimacy of administering baptism to the children of believers, as it is prescribed in the covenant of grace. Where there is no Church—in the proper sense of the word—what place is there for its sacraments ? What significance could they have then ? When it is asserted that infant baptism is " tolerable " where there is a living Church, the limits of the real and only problem are accurately defined, namely, to make our Churches living Churches once more ; and this can only be achieved by the preaching of the Word *according to the Scriptures*. The problem of infant baptism is exactly that of knowing whether the Church is the Church in the New Testament sense of the word, or merely a society for entertaining and gratifying religious sentiment, whether her doctrine is that of heresy or of the Gospel. Baptism is not a problem in itself ; the true and only problem is that of the Church's faithfulness to the standards and conditions of her

[1] *Op. cit.*, p. 72.

existence which are given and *imposed* in Scripture. We entirely agree that baptism can only be correctly administered in a Church that is ceaselessly preoccupied with her own reform—*a reform, however, always undertaken according to the standard of God's Word.* Now, the Word preaches the covenant of grace to us. By wishing to replace this standard by others one relapses into slackness and indiscipline in the name of liberty.

(c) *The Church ought to preach the covenant to parents.* She ought to convince them that their children have not been begotten for themselves, but for God, and that their baptism is only the first step in the Lord's working and requires that the child should be led by the Spirit to the point of communion with the crucified Saviour. She ought to apprise them of the spiritual ministry which is theirs, in accordance with which they ought, on the one hand, to remove every obstacle in the way of their children that would deprive them of the testimony of the Word, and, on the other hand, to apply themselves to the injunctions which the Lord has given them for the education of their children in the works and commandments of God. Parents are the true pastors of their own hearth and ought to close with the promises of the covenant not only for themselves, but also for their posterity. They ought to believe and be converted and sanctified for their children's sake. Woe to the parent who is a cause of stumbling to his child !

Parents ought to comply with the Church's discipline in the matter of the religious instruction of their children, and should entrust them to the ministry of their spiritual Mother. But, so that they may be faithful to their vocation, the Church should never seek to relieve the parents of their responsibility. It is F.-J. Leenhardt again who affirms : " There is a way of understanding pedobaptism which is not absolutely contrary to the true notion of baptism, namely, that those who have taken the responsibility of administering the sacrament to this child, who today is unconscious of what has been done to him, ought to make good this lack. They have the duty of rendering this child conscious of what has been done to him, in order that his faith may respond to the act of God in Christ which baptism has indicated sacramentally. . . . The practice of infant baptism can be understood in a strict sense when Christian education is guaranteed." [1]

Such, despite his previous exegetical conclusions, are the remarks of an opponent of infant baptism. Who will not recognize the importance of this " concession " ? We have shown, however, that it is not a matter of a concession, but of a command of God. That Christian education ought to be guaranteed is an integral part of our case, and it is guaranteed whenever the child's parents or his family are " believers," that is to say, living members of the covenant of grace. It is not so much they who take the " responsibility " ; it is God who takes the responsibility for what He ordains, by adding to it the promises and then instructing the parents, by the Holy Spirit and Scripture and with the assistance of the Church, concerning their true responsibility in the administration of the covenant of grace to their children. All this can only be achieved in faith, and that is why believing parents *ought* to have their children baptized. " It should not be said that the promise alone ought to be sufficient to assure us of the salvation of our children," remarks Calvin ; " for God has considered otherwise, who, knowing the infirmity of our faith, has wished to give it support at this point. This is why it is the duty of all who trust firmly in the promise that God wishes to show mercy to their offspring to present their children so that they may receive the sign of this mercy, and that they themselves may be consoled by it and fortified when with their own eyes they see the covenant of the Lord signified in the bodies of their children."[2]

" But someone may say that it does not detract from the grace of God towards us if children are not received for baptism, provided it is not denied that God is merciful to them just as He was to the children of the Jews," writes Calvin in another place.[3] " I reply that it does," he continues : " for we must estimate the grace of God principally by what He has declared to us, *by His sacraments as well as by His Word*. Since, then, baptism is now ordained

[1] *Op. cit.*, p. 72.   [2] *Instt.*, IV. xvi. 9.
[3] *Against the Anabaptists*, Opera, VII, p. 61.

for us in order that the promise of salvation may be sealed in our bodies, just as circumcision served formerly for the Jewish people, it would deprive Christians of a very special consolation if their children were denied this confirmation, which believers have always enjoyed, namely, the possession of a visible sign by which our Lord makes it plain to them that He welcomes their children into the communion of His Church."

Given the nature of our faith and that of the sacraments, he who refuses the sign is in danger also of refusing the thing signified. By refusing the sign of the covenant for our children we are not far from believing that they are not in the covenant. And in view of the fact that, according to the dispensation of the covenant, the salvation of our children depends partly on the manner in which the promise is grasped by their parents and administered by the Church, the refusal of baptism—a sign of the refusal of faith—will in many cases hinder the salvation of the children who have been deprived of it. It is a great evil for our children to be strangers to the people of God, strangers to the covenant. Believing parents sin gravely against the souls of their own children when they neglect to consecrate them to God by the institution of baptism, even if these children should ultimately choose to be blotted out of the book of life. " The reason why Satan does his utmost to deprive our children of the ceremony of baptism is that he may efface from our gaze this attestation that the Lord has ordained for confirming to us the blessings which He desires them to enjoy, and *that thus at the same time we may forget, little by little, the promise which He has given us for them.* From this there must follow not only ingratitude and contempt for God's mercy towards us, but failure to instruct our children in the fear and discipline of His law and in the knowledge of His Gospel. For it is no small incentive to us to nurture them in true piety and obedience to God when we understand that from their birth the Lord has received them amongst His people and as members of His Church. Therefore let us not turn our backs on the great kindness of our Lord, but boldly present our children to Him, to whom He has promised admission into the company of those whom He

Q

acknowledges as His own friends and family, that is, the Christian Church." To oppose the baptism of children is " to minimize the singular fruit of confidence and consolation which the Lord wishes to give us by His promise, and to this extent to obscure the glory of His Name, which is so much the more exalted as the bounties of His mercy are liberally bestowed upon men."[1]

(*d*) *The Church ought to preach the covenant to children.* It is part of the Church's task to preach and appeal to children, and necessarily more so than their parents. She ought to reveal to them the grace of the covenant and of their baptism, and to teach them to walk in the way of the covenant and to ratify it. " It were better that the Church should not baptize them," says J. Deransart, " than that she should baptize them and then cause them to stumble by the unfaithfulness of her preaching."[2] Baptized persons who do not inquire about the significance of their baptism are culpable, but the Church that neglects to reveal to them, in accordance with her vocation, its meaning and comeliness is still more culpable. " It is a fact," says Calvin, " that however much we make profession of the Gospel, we shall find many who are ignorant of the use and value of baptism and also of the purpose for which it was ordained. Now, it will cost such people very dear to have received such a pledge from God, and it will show that it is a thing too precious to be abused, when they are told that it is the means by which we are united to our Lord Jesus Christ and grafted into His death and resurrection. Thus when many receive baptism in infancy and shall afterwards live forty or fifty years in this world without knowing why they were baptized, it would have been better for their mothers to have miscarried and for them to have been buried a hundred times in the earth, than thus to have profaned a thing so sacred. And so let us consider how much it will be to our advantage to learn that as often as just a little water is poured on the head it is not a vain ceremony, for God speaks from heaven and Jesus Christ is the witness to us of the use and value of this sacrament ; but above all let us learn that His death and resurrection are ratified to us by it. Let us consider these

---

[1] Calvin : *Instt.* IV. xvi. 32.   [2] *Op. cit.*, pp. 134 f.

things carefully so that we may know why we are baptized, and how it benefits us, and thus that it may take firm root in our hearts." [1]

The Church must not neglect to exercise faithfully the ministry of the covenant for children who, if baptized, are within the sphere of its benefits, or to whom, if not yet baptized, it is offered. Everything should be done to incorporate them into the covenant and to cause them to remain in it. We have said that when the children of believers reach the age of discretion they can refuse to confirm the covenant and separate themselves from God by renouncing the truth of their baptism as it affects them. But God in His goodness will none the less have " chosen and separated them from others so that His salvation may be offered to them," [2] and the Church will not cease to exercise on their behalf the cure of souls of the covenant. " It is infinitely worse," says O. Cullmann, " for those who are baptized than for those who are not, if they fall from the participation in Christ's death and resurrection bestowed upon them at their reception into the Church, that is, in faith, the response which ought unconditionally to follow does not occur." [3]

" In the last four years," wrote Pastor Conord in 1949, " the number of baptisms has annually exceeded by more than a thousand the number of funerals. . . . It remains to be seen whether . . . all the children baptized will become catechumens and then living members of the Church." [4] Independently of the fact that the number of births has, during these last years, been greater than the number of deaths, and that some children counted in our statistics have been illegitimately baptized, the question of knowing whether all the children baptized will become catechumens, and then living members of the Church, is precisely the whole question of the covenant and its administration. From its *numerical* aspect the problem cannot in any case be a cause of concern or reflection for the Church. Do all who are baptized as adults continue as living members of the Church

[1] *Sermon* on Gal. iii. 26-29, Opera, L, p. 565.
[2] Calvin : *Against the Anabaptists*, Opera, VII, p. 62.
[3] *Op. cit.*, p. 36.
[4] *Le Christianisme au XXe siècle*, August 11th, 1949.

and inherit eternal life ? The question is that of knowing whether the Church will or will not be the administratrix of the covenant, whether her preaching will or will not be that of the Gospel, and whether her members, parents and children, will on hearing this preaching continue as members of the covenant or be incorporated into it. If the Church is unfaithful those who have been baptized will not remain in her, or if they do they will not, apart from exceptional instances, be more faithful than their unfaithful Mother. If the Church is faithful and preaches the covenant, promises, and requirements of God, she will have fulfilled her task as servant. The rest is not her concern. It is a matter of the liberty and power of the Holy Spirit, who will elect to salvation whom He wills.

When the preaching of the covenant and of baptism which seals it is given its due place, we, in our personal ministry, have discerned a twofold reaction amongst parents : (i) Indifferent parents who would not have had their children baptized, or believing parents who have not had their children baptized, believe the promise and request baptism for their children ; (ii) indifferent parents who would have requested baptism for their children reflect and often renounce baptism ; but they entrust their children to the Church, and in due course these children, if they request it, will be baptized at the conclusion of their religious instruction.

We also discern a double reaction amongst children : (i) Children who have been baptized in their infancy, although they belong to Christian families, when they realize that they lack faith after having received a course of religious instruction, request either a supplementary course of instruction before deciding to confirm the covenant of the Lord, or that they may not be confirmed, while retaining the liberty to be so at a later date ; (ii) some children who have commenced their religious instruction, when confronted with the promises and requirements of the covenant, feel such antagonism within themselves, generally the result of definite actions and known misbehaviour, that they freely, voluntarily, and consciously decide to break off their religious instruction. In effect, they deny the covenant and its promises. Other children, again, who have not been baptized, request baptism at the conclusion of their religious instruction.

All these facts are of the greatest importance and their significance is supreme, because they indicate the vitality of the covenant. The Church ought to do everything possible to see that each individual is able to make his decision freely and in a manner clear of every mark of dishonour, both within the community of believers and within the family.

When the covenant of grace is administered in conformity with the Word it shows that baptisms of infants, baptisms of adolescent catechumens, and baptisms of adults *ought to coexist*. Both usages have every right to be practised in the Church. Any systematization of the one practice to the exclusion of the other is indefensible and should be avoided.

CONCLUSION

" I WANT readers to give their attention firstly and exclusively to the *theological* question—undisturbed by considerations of ecclesiastical politics—and to measure my statement by *theological* standards," says Karl Barth.[1] This undoubtedly has been the desire of every theologian who has given himself the trouble of writing on baptism. We think that we have acceded to the wish of this eminent master and· have given our attention firstly and exclusively to this problem in accordance with the laws of theology. We are grateful to the opponents of infant baptism who have constrained us to undertake this work and we thank them for their critical studies.

Their criticisms, however, have not caught us unprepared. Since it is founded on Scripture and has been thoroughly elaborated according to Scripture by its Churches and doctors, Reformed theology does not permit of being caught out so easily. The whole question is to know with what philosophical or religious *a priori* ideas the problem of infant baptism is approached. We are convinced that the objections offered by antipedobaptists do not spring in fact from Scripture, which on this subject gives us the most ample guidance on condition that we start from the doctrine that underlies the sacrament, but from human concepts, of which in other respects the opponents of infant baptism speak quite openly, and which, for us, are foreign to the Word of God. In any and every work against infant baptism, or, what comes to the same thing, in favour of the baptism of adults only, it is easy to put one's finger immediately on the subjective individualistic *a priori* premisses that constitute the backcloth against which parade the arguments that one could wish were simply " objective " and " biblical."

On the subject of the position adopted by those who disagree with us, and despite all the differences which

[1] *Op. cit.*, p. 54.

characterize them, we have in the course of this study put a number of questions to which they ought to reply if they wish to remain loyal to their thesis.

From the *methodological* point of view, we have shown that amongst the opponents of infant baptism there are contradictory attitudes, reversals of methods and of standards depending on the subjects of which they are treating, so that in the matter of infant baptism they proscribe the very method which they themselves employ without the least hesitation in other connected and often more important theological questions. Such inconsistencies are unacceptable in so far as theology and dogmatics are sciences which make appeal to the scientific methods that are proper to them and that are, at the same time, no less binding on them. In theology it is not possible to change the method when changing the subject, and to condemn in one place what one approves elsewhere.

As to the *foundation*, infant baptism cannot be brushed aside by declaring that many doctrines explicitly revealed in Holy Scripture are outmoded, or by refusing to take notice of them. It is not sufficient to say that they are scarcely applicable to " modern " man and that they fail to satisfy the " contemporary spirit." The modernism of man, who upholds the sovereignty of his own thought and emotion, is shattered little by little under the regenerating influence of the Holy Spirit in the case of those who are given the ability which permits them, and consequently *obliges* them, to undertake a critical re-examination of their presuppositions.

In the antipedobaptist perspective there is a *basic* opposition between Old and New Testaments, the Church of Israel and the Christian Church, and between their respective sacraments. *It is a fact of extreme seriousness that the whole doctrine of the covenant of grace disappears*, nor does this take place without " injury " and without " violence." " It is disturbing," says Theo Preiss, " that in the history of the Church every attack against pedobaptism has involved either implicit or explicit alterations of the biblical notion of grace."[1] Nor is it merely a question of a devaluation of

[1] *Op. cit.*, p. 116.

what is called " prevenient " grace, but an active mutilation of the whole doctrine of grace as it is revealed to us in the Old and New Testaments, and, together with it, of the doctrine of sin—for the two doctrines are intertwined.

We pass, in fact, into another theological world ! In this new world—to cite only a few facts, without wishing to paint too black a picture—the children of believers are no longer heirs of the promises, indeed, they are not in the covenant, since it no longer exists ; they are no longer in the Church which cannot embrace them because of their unconscious state ; the family is spiritually and organically disintegrated and disrupted ; the man-in-himself, removed from his setting and from the collectivities, albeit divinely instituted, of which he forms a part, and separated from his own, is placed alone in the presence of his God who acts only towards him and for him. It is desired to bestow upon the children of believers a dangerous and imaginary liberty which they will misuse. The Church becomes a society of adults to which our children are admitted as proselytes at the time when each on his own believes and is converted and sanctified. The ministry and discipline of the Church are not the same as previously ; the concepts of the responsibility of individuals, of parents, of children, and of the Church are quite different, because the methods of divine action are no longer the same and God no longer addresses Himself to man and to the Church in the same manner. The cure of souls is deprived of powerful means. For some, the sacraments are no longer seals ; they no longer remain for any the sacraments of the covenant of grace as revealed to us in Scripture.

When we examine the theology, whether subjacent or explicitly formulated, of the opponents of infant baptism and all that it finds itself obliged to sacrifice or ignore, we discover that we are in a dismantled building and we experience the most desperate impoverishment. Of what have we been despoiled ? Of doctrines invented by men, of rudiments of the law, done away by the infinite riches of the Gospel of Jesus Christ ? By no means ! It is of a good part of this Gospel that we are despoiled together with the blessings it affords for each of us, for our families, for the

Church. Our very faith is maimed, and the repose of heart and conscience is menaced for us and for our children. Is it really on such ruins that it is desired to base the prohibition to baptize the children of believers ? And why is it that it can be based only on these ruins ? On this debris the attempt is made to establish the baptism of believers' children who have reached adult age, which cannot be supported by the vestige of a text or justification from the New Testament, and the institution of a ceremony called " dedication " or " blessing " of which again there is not the least trace in the New Testament ! The impulse of the *a priori* notions which lie behind these devices seems, indeed, to be irresistible !

It should not be thought that the acceptance or rejection of infant baptism is independent of the cast of one's theology and its premises. The doctrine of the sacraments, in which infant baptism has a share, is the touchstone of all theology. A Reformed Christian cannot be *theologically* opposed to infant baptism and at the same time preserve the principles of Reformed theology any more than a Barthian or a Baptist can accept infant baptism and remain true to the premises of his own theology. While visiting Holland in 1933—if our memory serves us right—when there was as yet no question in his mind of attacking infant baptism, Karl Barth was warned by Dr. G. C. Berkouwer (now Professor of Dogmatics in the Faculty of Theology of the Free University of Amsterdam) that, given the premises of his dogmatics, ten years would not pass before he would find himself in opposition to infant baptism. Had Barth not written in his monograph, *Die Lehre von den Sakramenten* (Zwischen den Zeit, 1929) : " He who accepts infant baptism will at all events be unable to maintain the contrary—*Wer die Kindertaufe bejaht, wird jedenfalls das Gegenteil nicht behaupten können*" ?[1] We have also seen what he wrote in his *Church Dogmatics*, published in 1932.[2] Even sooner than Professor Berkouwer predicted, Karl Barth discovered, despite what he himself had originally thought, that the principles of his theology distinctly implied the rejection of infant baptism. The

[1] P. 437, quoted by G. C. Berkouwer, *Karl Barth en de kinderdoop*, p. 16.
[2] See p. 207 above.

internal cohesion of his system is here more imperious than
the actual teaching of the biblical texts, for fifteen years ago [1]
Karl Barth read *the very same texts* otherwise than he does
today, that is to say, he read them in the same way, or
nearly so, as we Reformed theologians do. This *volte-face*
shows the decisive importance of *a priori* notions and of
points of departure in the understanding and comprehension
of scriptural texts. It is very remarkable that Karl Barth
makes no allusion in his pamphlet to his previous attitude,
which was so energetically pedobaptist. In terms which are
often quite ungracious he ridicules the attitude of Luther
and Calvin and of their " successors," but he does not explain
how he himself was able for so long a time to take his place
at their side. On this point Barth's pamphlet is inadequate
and too hasty.

To the questions which we put early on in this study [2]
the reply must simply be that this pamphlet of Karl Barth's
does not seem at all like a writing destined to cause the
Church to reflect, nor like a " foreign body " unconnected
with the rest of his thought and theology. We could show
to what point his doctrine of baptism is bound up with the
rest of his theology and forms an inseparable piece of the
whole.[3] His disciples are under obligation to follow their
master : they cannot reject his conclusions on baptism and
at the same time accept his theology.

The same holds good for Reformed Christians : they
cannot remain faithful to their theology while ceasing to
regard infant baptism as legitimate and scriptural. When
we are desired to believe the contrary, and when it is asserted
that " some thousands of Baptist Churches lay claim to
Calvinist doctrine, like the Reformed Churches in the
United States," [4] we at once demand that they should read
the texts and study closely the confessions of faith, and they
will then see whether these Churches have remained " Calvinist " and whether their doctrine differs from " Calvinist

[1] P.-Ch. Marcel wrote this in 1950.—P.E.H.
[2] On p. 16.
[3] Cf. G. C. Berkouwer, *Karl Barth en de kinderdoop*, ch. IX : *De Achter-
grond van Barth's kritiek*, pp. 105-135.
[4] F. Lovsky, *op. cit.*, p. 133.

doctrine " only on the question of baptism. Such assertions are not confirmed by the facts. We are sufficiently well placed to know the gulf which separates the doctrines of those who "lay claim to Calvinist doctrine" and this "Calvinist doctrine" taken in its real and precise scientific sense. It is one thing to lay claim to a doctrine, and quite another to profess it !

Those who differ from us would like people to think that we have a bad conscience in upholding the legitimacy of infant baptism, and consequently also—something that is extremely serious in the exercise of the pastoral ministry— *a bad conscience in administering it.* Thus F.-J. Leenhardt writes : " Calvin wished to show by direct proofs that infant baptism was taught in Scripture. His modern commentators find themselves constrained to recognize that his reasoning is not very compelling, *that he himself felt that his ground was not sure,* that his exegetical versatility was employed in a manner more clever than convincing, that, in brief, his writings hardly carry the conviction that infant baptism was of divine institution."[1] And Karl Barth writes : " The statement may be hazarded that the confusion, with which Luther and Calvin and their followers on both sides have thrown themselves in this matter, is hopeless. . . . It still has to be said that the actual information which one gets from them on the decisive point is, in fact, as incredible as its exegetical grounds are unsatisfactory. One may read the fifteenth and sixteenth chapters in Book IV of the *Institutio* one after the other and convince oneself where the great Calvin was sure of his subject *and where he obviously was not sure, but visibly nervous, in a hopelessly confused train of thought, abusing where he ought to inform and when he wants to convince, seeking a way in the fog, which can lead him to no goal, because he has none.* From the standpoint of a doctrine of baptism, infant baptism can hardly be preserved without exegetical and practical *artifices and sophisms*— the proof to the contrary has yet to be supplied ! One wants to preserve it only if one wants to do so on *grounds which lie outside the biblical passages on baptism and outside the thing itself.* The determination to defend it on extraneous grounds

[1] *Op. cit.,* pp. 66 f.

has certainly found expression from century to century." [1]

We, in turn, inquire through what spectacles Calvin's modern commentators or contradictors read what he wrote ? Calvin is unintelligible to a " modern " who has not discerned the formidable sway of " modern " ideas over his mind and heart which will cause him to talk all kinds of nonsense. A historic example, unhappily too often imitated, is seen in *La philosophie de Calvin*, by H. Bois.

According to Karl Barth, the theological consideration of infant baptism has not been taken up afresh since the sixteenth century.[2] We must observe that in the writings against infant baptism we have not discovered a single bibliographical note, nor even the briefest citation from works written by authentic Reformed theologians belonging to the Reformed Churches of the present day ! These critics have not even given themselves the trouble of reading what the Reformed Churches and their theologians are saying *today*, nor of taking notice of the result of the activity of Reformed thought through the course of the centuries and, indeed, the repudiating of certain errors which have been committed. Consequently they affirm that no serious consideration of infant baptism has been undertaken since the sixteenth century. We could reply that no more has Karl Barth undertaken any consideration which is more recent than the sixteenth century, since some of the fundamental themes which are at the basis of his criticism of infant baptism are found in the writings of the Anabaptists of the sixteenth century which our Reformers strove to combat.[3] But we do not desire to make that wood into an arrow ! Only, as they neglect all the modern sources that are typically Reformed, so they return to Calvin, as though he were the infallible inspiration of all Reformed theology, and spurn the theological and dogmatic meditation and reflection of the various Reformed Churches, independent of each other, and consider—somewhat naïvely, in our opinion— that an argument which holds good against Calvin holds good

---

[1] *Op. cit.*, pp. 48 f.   [2] *Op. cit.*, p. 54.
[3] Cf. G. C. Berkouwer, *op. cit.*, ch. VIII : *Reformatie en Anabaptisme*, pp. 76-105.

simultaneously against Reformed theology ! But they ought
to read Calvin again, free from prejudice, and without
interpreting him in the light of *a priori* notions which
certainly were not his own ! We have demonstrated that,
on the question of baptism, Karl Barth has not understood
Calvin, even though he may have summarized him admirably
on other questions. It is important to notice this cleavage,
both in space and in time, effected by some in the world of
theological thought, so that we may recognize its relation
to the manner in which they have drawn up their works
against infant baptism.

The National Synod of the Reformed Church of the
Netherlands, replying to the Reformed Church of France,
terminated its report by evaluating Karl Barth's attitude
as follows : " The battle that Barth wages against infant
baptism is very dangerous for the Churches which belong
to Reformed Protestantism. Barth couples a method which
emphasizes the rôle of the individual, when faith makes a
decision, with another authentically Calvinist method which
places God at the centre, exalts His sovereignty in revelation,
and seems to cut away all subjectivism and pietism and
every notion of a ' free Church.' Now, it is just the baptism
of infants which illustrates for us, and in a particularly
lively manner, the fundamental scriptural truth that the
grace of God is free and prevenient, as in 1 John iv. 10, for
example. Nevertheless, the accent which Barth's religious
thought places on the free prevenient grace of God towards
all has not been able to keep him from going the length of
rejecting infant baptism. By doing this he opens the gates
afresh and at one bound to the invasion of all sorts of errors
which are nourished by subjectivism, pietism, and spiritual-
ism, and which are agreeable to the partisans of a ' free
Church '."

That Christians should think and write reproaches such
as we have alluded to concerning " bad conscience," and
should suspect the good faith of their brothers in Christ,
is for us extremely distressing and causes us acute pain.
Irony, insinuation, and accusation are employed against
us, but without adducing the least definite proof, search
though one may in the train of such statements. We regard

such behaviour as contrary to our Lord's command of charity which enjoins us not to pass judgment regarding the *intentions* of our brethren. We will simply request every reader who knows Calvin well, even if he does not hold with his theology, to read the famous fifteenth and sixteenth chapters of Book IV of the *Christian Institutes* and to point out the passages where he is " visibly nervous," or where there is " a hopelessly confused train of thought," or where " he abuses where he ought to inform." For those who know Calvin this section is one of the most moderate in tone, one which, considering the importance of the controversy, he conducts with the greatest calm of thought, of form, and of vocabulary. Leaving aside Calvin, who is not our pope, we will inquire again where, in a study such as this which we offer, are our " exegetical and practical artifices and sophisms." Which are the " grounds which lie outside the biblical passages on baptism and outside the thing itself " ? We have not written a single line which is not directly related to baptism and its consequences. Where, finally, is the " confusion " in the doctrine which, founded on Holy Scripture, we have just expounded ? Here the discussion must be precise : every judgment of condemnation uncorroborated by the facts and by the biblical texts examined according to the analogy of faith is absolutely valueless.

Our critics do not hesitate to repeat today that " the true territory of pedobaptism is paganism on the one hand and Judaism on the other." [1]

Karl Barth has offered the uncomplimentary qualification of " theological Judaism," and F.-J. Leenhardt considers that we are obliged to " scrape together rags of texts in order to equip ourselves with weapons." [2]

We observe that such judgments are formulated simply because we refuse to adopt the philosophical *a priori* notions of those who criticize us, since we are persuaded that they are incompatible with Holy Scripture, and we are led to the conclusion that our critics, in passing such strictures, are lacking in courtesy and moderation. Does our attitude

[1] Lenoir, *Essai*, 1856, p. 213, quoted by Lovsky, *op. cit.*, p. 136.
[2] *Op. cit.*, p. 67.

really demand that we should be treated as pagans and judaizers ? Could our critics perhaps also be—since they approve of such expressions—" scrapers together " of Scripture and of the mysteries of God ? Are they able to offer a doctrine of baptism which respects with equal scrupulousness the general content of the Scriptures and is not elaborated at the expense of costly amputations performed not only on the text of God's Word, but on its noblest concepts ?

The doctrine of baptism, however, as it is elaborated by Reformed theologians, displays the degree to which it is bound to Scripture. Amongst the theological systems which, commencing from the biblical data, bring into play the *faculties* of believing man, and which consequently *never* achieve the last degree of perfection and are *always* open to revision, the Reformed doctrine is the only one which does justice to the entirety of the elements revealed in Scripture and integrates them harmoniously into a co-ordinated whole. Every other system of doctrine rejects, explicitly or implicitly, consciously or unconsciously, important elements of the revelation and renders only a partial account of the entirety of the Scriptures. In their theology of baptism Reformed theologians have been able and are still able to avoid all sectarianism ; they preserve a breadth of heart and a conception of the administration of the covenant that are authentically Christian. It is worth while to know this and to be assured of it, and then to be proud of it.

To my colleagues in the ministry of the covenant I would say : It is in all good conscience, as men, as Christians, and as theologians, that, taking our stand upon Holy Scripture, we not only can, but must baptize the children of believers, since they are born in the covenant, in conformity with the administration of the covenant of which we are all the servants. We exercise this sacred charge before God, for His glory, praising Him for the infinite liberality of His promises and gifts and for the free bestowal of His mercy from generation to generation, in the assurance that by preaching the covenant of God our Saviour and Comforter, and that by sealing those who are His with the sacred seal

with which He Himself has marked us and our children,
we labour faithfully in the vineyard of His Kingdom, in
order that the greatest number may, in accordance with His
purposes, take their place for eternity at the heavenly
banquet. Ours is the conviction, sealed in our hearts by the
Holy Spirit, that the baptism of the children of believers
" has certain and assured foundation in Holy Scripture." [1]
But let us never forget that for this the price must be paid,
namely, a restored preaching of the Gospel, a firm theology,
and a relentless self-criticism so that we may not cease to
eradicate those *a priori* notions which, under the tremendous
pressure of world conditions and habits of thought, seek
to make us read the Scriptures through distorting spectacles ;
a price that entails, further, the constant desire to be
reformed according to the Word of God and by it ; living
Churches of consecrated members ; a ministry of prayer and
intercession in the indestructible spiritual solidarity which
unites all into one body ; and the constant demand of the
Holy Spirit that we should be humble and faithful servants
of our crucified and glorified Lord. By faith and in faith we
ought to devote ourselves wholly to the eternal glory,
manifested in time, of the Only God, Father, Son and Holy
Spirit, who has honoured us and glorified us beyond all
measure by making us His children and by promising that
He will also be glorified by and in our posterity, in accordance
with the promises of His eternal covenant.

[1] Calvin : *Instt.*, IV. xvi. 32.

Lightning Source UK Ltd.
Milton Keynes UK
UKOW021223210112

185806UK00001B/20/A